TWISTING
THREADS

TWISTING
THREADS

A Skein of Life
on the
Ocean Wave

Best wishes

Jess

JESS
SANDEMAN

Printed and published by Famedram Publishers Ltd, AB41 9EA
ISBN: 0 905489 72 1

Contents

CHAPTER

1	Early rumblings of war	9
2	Secret work in a submarine depot ship	20
3	Wrens swarming everywhere	38
4	Damp squib at D-Day	48
5	Peace and the party pooper	62
6	Behind the scenes at Kyles Hydro	69
7	Escape to sea	78
8	'Only' to Singapore	88
9	India via Africa	99
10	Three Arab kings	110
11	Sailing down 'The Coast'	125
12	Strike of the African crew	138
13	Coping with 100 children	148
14	Trouble in Nigeria	167
15	At home – mother's terminal illness	180
16	Off to Paris	191
17	Salt in my veins	197
18	Back on Aureol	209
19	A not so diplomatic scuffle	216
20	Slinging my hammock – Kames Castle	227

Chapter One

Early rumblings of war

The day of the funeral was bright and sunny, like so many of the days that long hot summer. It wasn't a sad day but one of remembrance and of tribute to the ninety-one year old. Always conscious of his Highland heritage, he would have been pleased and proud that a dozen kilted men stood amongst family and friends in the cemetery, and prouder still that his son and grandson played the bagpipes at the graveside. It was a day that won't easily be forgotten.

Deep in thought, we stood on the hillside at Croc-an-Raar as the last haunting notes of the pipes faded away. The memory of my own grandfather's funeral flashed back. A key figure in my early days, his sudden death when I was six, brought the first real sadness into my life. Lying sleepless in the hot sticky night that followed, my thoughts drifted back to the days before World War Two. I was born before plastic bags, penicillin, the Pill, potato crisps, cello tape, convenience foods, package holidays and before the computer age and man landed on the moon.

Many things in the world have changed since then and many things have changed in my life. I decided that I would write my story. I realise how uncertain life is and I must get it all down on paper before my time runs out.

It happened long ago and wanders into strange places, half across the world ......

Lost in the mists of time is the date on which the natives of Bute were first called Brandanes. I can't claim to be one as I was six months old when my mother took me to live with her parents on the Island of Bute. Grandfather had been appointed Head Postmaster the previous year and Grandmother and he had settled happily in Rothesay. After the untimely death of my father, my grandparents took charge, with my mother being like an older sister to me. What fun we had! Eventually to my surprise I discovered that other mothers didn't climb trees or walk on garden walls!

Ours was a happy loving home but not conventional. Books set us apart. There were books galore – books in every room including the bathroom. The neighbours regarded with awe and suspicion the glass-fronted bookcase reaching almost to the study ceiling. Grandfather, a gentle scholarly man, an avid reader and writer of short stories, was very wise and managed to answer my queries. He wasn't stumped by tough questions like "why is the sea so blue and sparkly one minute and grey and angry the next?

Ill health forced him to take early retirement. Three months later a great chance came his way, when a friend, Director in a small shipping company, arranged for him to "sign on" as Supernumerary Purser on a cargo vessel trading round South America across to the U.S.A. He was paid the nominal sum of one shilling per month. In those days few ordinary people went abroad and we didn't know anyone who had ever gone to an exotic part of the world like South America. Grandpa's letters and the stories he told on returning home, fired my imagination. Sugar Loaf Mountain sounded much more interesting that Barone Hill. I planned to be a nurse in Rio de Janeiro, a teacher in Valparaiso or a missionary in Montevideo when I left school.

After only being home for six weeks Grandpa had a massive cerebral haemorrhage and within a few hours was dead. I was told he had gone to Heaven but could never come back. It is impossible for a small child to understand the finality of "never". I'd heard that Heaven was a nice place, but was greatly puzzled that he was going to be buried in a hole at Croc-an-Raar. Watching red-eyed grownups rushing round, answering the door to neighbours and endlessly drinking tea, it never seemed to be the right moment to ask for a detailed explanation. The first little cloud crept across the sunny skies of my childhood.

When my great friend Irene came to play, Ardbeg burn was the perfect place for adventure. Pretending to explore the Amazon we traced the source through the Gortans fields. At a lovely spot, thick with marsh marigolds, we set up a laundry. Washing socks was easy enough, but when we washed our dresses the Oldies weren't too pleased, - Irene's Mum was scandalised.

A group of us (too innocent to be called a gang) dammed the burn, and dared to trespass on the far bank, knowing it was Mount

Clare property. Willie, the gardener, lurked behind a tree and would come roaring out at the sound of our voices. Squealing and splashing we rushed back to the safety of the field. Despite never catching us, he seemed to enjoy the game as much as we did.

The seashore with rocks to climb, shells to collect, sand pies and seaweed cakes to make, was an ideal playground, but best of all was the den in the owl tree. There we could hide from Irene's young brother and the grownups. Irene's Dad, passing discreetly with the hen's food ignored the giggles from the branches above.

My Granny, an active, bustling little lady, made us green uniforms from an old dress. She always wore a long black skirt, and although I knew she must have legs like everyone else, I never saw them. With equal ease she could bake a batch of scones or rebalance the cistern ballcock. Her great passion was the radio, "In Town Tonight" being her favourite programme. Helping with her stamp collection I soon learned the capitals and currencies of other countries. "Africa, Egypt, India" I mused and vowed "I'll go there one day". Strangely enough I later did.

At the Girl Guides we were taught all manner of things – First Aid, the Morse Code, Knot Tying, Country Dancing, recognition of wild flowers and birds. A great culinary feat was cooking sausages inside banana skins held by long sticks over the campfire. They tasted smoky but delicious.

The highlight of the summer camp at Otterferry was being invited to afternoon tea by the local lairds, the Macrae-Gilstraps. Their house at the end of a long rhododendron lined avenue reminded me of Manderley in "Rebecca", one of my favourite books. Although I don't recall eating cucumber sandwiches, it was that type of party with the particular thrill of being served by a butler. A butler! I never thought I'd meet one in the flesh!

My cousin Margaret was frequently in hospital and came to Rothesay to recuperate, but was unable to join in our adventures. We sometimes went to stay with relations in Glasgow but city life held little appeal for me. Despite enjoying visiting the Kelvingrove Art Galleries, the hot steamy greenhouse of the Botanic Gardens, the annual pantomime or plays like Peter Pan, I was always impatient to be back on Bute.

Usually spending July with Aunt Janie and Uncle Will in Dumfries, I found their daughter Grizel was a kindred spirit – a bookworm like me, devouring everything from Little Women to Ivanhoe. Spending our precious pocket money on little red notebooks, every evening we solemnly recorded the day's events. Sprawled on our beds we entered trivialities like "saw a field of bright yellow sheep", or tried to describe the romantic tale of Devorgilla in Sweetheart Abbey.

Most of my school friends had a Granny or Grandpa living with them. Grizel's grandfather a sunburnt little man, once a market gardener, still pottered contentedly amongst the plants. Irene boasted that her grandfather, Captain of a Clyde steamer, had once sailed "deep sea", while I was fiercely proud that my grandfather had sailed round Cape Horn. Dead for many years Ian's grandfather, as Master of a sailing ship trading to and from Australia had voyaged further than the others. I should explain about Ian. His mother Jenny although several years older was Mum's best friend and Ian was like my big brother. He must have often regarded me as a little pest, but would be the first to help if I was in trouble. Ian had only been a young baby when his father was lost at sea in 1918.

Granny Campbell, as the Captain's wife had sailed out to Australia several times, leaving Jenny, a teenager, in the care of her aunt and uncle in Innellan farm. When she was widowed, old and frail she had come to make her home in Rothesay with Jenny and Ian. In my eyes she wasn't just old but positively ancient. Wrapped in a big tartan plaid she sat by the fireside sleeping the hours away and dreaming a lot too. Sometimes she'd tell us about the terrible heat in the Red Sea or of an encounter with pirates off the coast of China. Frequently her voice faded away at a vital part of the story and she'd drift back to sleep. We made up the story endings ourselves and soon couldn't remember what was true or what we'd invented.

It was all very thrilling and we longed to go to sea too. Ian told me dismissively "You are only a girl. No one will let you go unless you marry a Captain." Little did we imagine what lay ahead. When Ian was about 15 he changed his mind and then wanted to become an Air Force Pilot. Jenny raised all kinds of objections as she felt it would be a dangerous occupation. They reached a compromise. He agreed to work in a local bank when he left school on condition that when he was 21 if he still hankered after the R.A.F. Jenny would give her blessing. Alas, it was not to be.

One day in January 1936 when I came home from school it was to discover that Ian had been kept in bed with swollen glands and a high temperature. Suspecting it was more serious than mumps or glandular fever the Dr. had taken a blood test. When the results came his worst fears were confirmed – it was leukaemia, at that time a terminal illness with rapid progression. Next morning Mum and Jenny left with Ian by ambulance for Glasgow Western Infirmary where a research unit offered a faint strand of hope.

Troubles never come singly. My grandmother had suffered a mild heart attack and I was kept off school to look after her. That day the radio bulletins told the nation of King George V's grave illness. Sitting by Granny's bed, alarmed by her unnatural breathing and worried sick about Ian I only vaguely heard solemn music being interrupted by the announcer saying "The King's life is slowly drawing to a close." Early next morning when the Minister arrived I sensed he was the bearer of bad news. Ian had died just ten hours after admission to hospital. Dead? How could someone so full of fun and laughter be dead? Apart from having chickenpox and the odd snuffly cold he had never been ill. It didn't make sense.

The whole town was shocked by the sudden death of this popular nineteen year old – a keen athlete and a particularly good swimmer. Blaming herself for preventing him from joining the R.A.F. Jenny was devastated. "It was selfish of me", she said, very selfish". I was pleased he had a good permanent job, but what school leaver wants to be trapped in a good steady job?" She feared his last year had been boring not joyous. When her husband died she had had a tiny baby and her ailing mother to look after, but now she was alone. All alone. It took her a long time to get over her tragic loss – if ever.

Ian was buried in Dunoon beside his seafaring grandparents. I cried "It isn't fair – he had neither been in an aeroplane nor sailed any further than Campbeltown."

Our own troubles diminished the death of the King and these two events in 1936 forever fuse together in my mind. The new King (as Duke of Rothesay, his premier Scottish title) had already visited the town. I dismissed all the rumours of his affair with Mrs Wallis Simpson as a silly fuss. Ever the romantic, I thought "The King can't marry the lady he loves because she isn't a Princess, and his Mother, the Prime Minister and some old Archbishop object." I didn't realise all that was involved and don't remember it being discussed at school. After his abdication speech one cold December night he left for France and my sympathy went with him.

My grandmother had been housebound for almost two years and bedridden for several months before she died in 1938. At that time I'd never heard of euthanasia but now it is often in my mind. Granny had lost the will to live and standing outside the bedroom door we'd often hear her plead "God have you forgotten me? I'm tired, so tired" There didn't seem to be any answer when she cried "Why was a fine young lad like Ian taken and a useless old woman like me left?"

Discussing it later Mum confessed she felt almost like a criminal, looking after Granny so carefully and tenderly, prolonging life against her will. Although my grandmother had been "The Boss" vital decisions about my welfare had been left to Mum. I now saw her in a different light more as a Head of the House than as an older sister. There remained a special bond between us. She was my best friend.

In 1938 we suddenly realised that in the wider world beyond our little island, sinister things were happening. When Chamberlain returned from Munich we were surprised by the tremendous relief shown by the adults on hearing him say "Out of this nettle danger we pluck this flower safety." With the wisdom and arrogance of youth we knew better – the crisis over Austria and Czechoslovakia was merely postponed. At school none of the teachers mentioned the trouble developing in Europe, and in fact we were never taught history beyond the First World War. It was as if current affairs didn't matter! I enjoyed school with English, History, Geography and French being my favourite subjects. Algebra didn't make much sense to me and I was a complete duffer at Art, and being the target of the Art Teacher's sarcasm didn't help.

We were jolted into reality on Sunday 3rd September 1939 with the Declaration of War, and especially with the arrival in Rothesay of Glasgow evacuees. Before the advent of T.V. we were unaccustomed to pictures of refugees, and the sight of bewildered young children with large identification labels and gasmasks in little cardboard boxes, slung around their necks was eternally fixed in my mind. A few carried brown paper parcels and less than one in ten had a small suitcase. I still remember a tear stained little chap tightly clutching a battered teddy bear almost as big as himself. Most Rothesay folk went to the Pavilion to help and Mum had blossomed into a billeting officer.

Several senior Academy pupils were given the task of filling bags with emergency rations (tea, sugar, biscuits, a tin of meat etc.) for each child to take to his new billet. One of the boys had the bright idea of piling the tins up into a tower and then knocking them down into outstretched bags. A grim faced adult rebuked us for skylarking. "Why is she so cross?" I wondered. "Surely we can't be expected not to laugh again."

At home that evening tired and emotionally drained, we realised we hadn't eaten since morning. Irene and I wolfed down the scrumptious scrambled egg Mum made. I've seldom had a more enjoyable supper. Thinking of all these children, now tucked up in strange beds far from home kept me from sleeping. The few accompanying mothers found Ardbeg too quiet and far from the bustle of town and many soon returned to Glasgow. Several children of course, stayed until the end of the War with a few eventually settling on the island.

Most of the evacuees had no previous experience of the country or the seaside and must have felt they had been transported to a foreign land, full of strange unexpected things. Rothesay, the only town on the Isle of Bute, a busy holiday resort in summer, relaxed and became a sleepy backwater in Autumn. Seeing the Victorian villas built by rich ship-owners and tobacco merchants made the newcomers uncomfortable and as if they'd strayed into Kelvinside or Pollokshields. It wasn't their scene at all.

Sitting on the promenade rail Mary Ann asked my mother "What's all that water for?" Her brother John scornfully muttered "Funny looking ducks here," as he watched the seagulls – some swimming, some gliding overhead and a great fat one actually walking along the pavement towards him.

We later heard about Alex gazing over the Port Bannatyne sea wall and saying to Peter his young brother, "I'm telling you there was water down there yesterday."
"There's none now see for yourself."
"I don't care I seen it, and they stones werena there."
Solemnly they regarded the mystery and grew even more confused and sceptical when old Duncan at the boat-slip explained about the tide being influenced by the moon. The moon? That big yellow thing in the sky? Did he think they were daft? They laughed at our anglised form of speech asking "Why do you talk so posh?" There was nothing posh about us with our west coast accents.

We were horrified to hear that the liner Athenia had been sunk on 4th September, realising that the German U Boat had been prowling the sea when War was declared, unfortunately choosing as a target a ship carrying defenceless children across the Atlantic. It was the first of many similar incidents.

Next day Irene and I seeing the local Territorial Army marching past the Skeoch Wood suddenly realised that boys we knew were going off to War to fight boys like themselves, boys they had never seen, from a country they didn't know. It seemed utterly senseless. Britain had viewed with complacency Hitler's fanatical hold on the people with jack-booted Nazis goose-stepping through Europe. We stupidly imagined War was something happening in books or films and in other countries, but War was here – all around us. The golden days of our childhood were over.

During the first four months of the War there was little action on land. From Germany "Lord Haw Haw" broadcast horrendous demoralising stories. By the spring all changed and even our own radio daily told of nightmare disasters with Holland, Belgium and Norway being overrun. After French resistance crumbled there was the famous miraculous evacuation of troops from Dunkirk in an armada of small boats. The Bute Battery, attached to the Highland Light Infantry, was not so fortunate. After fighting desperately at St. Valery-en-Caux it was devastating to find that the rescue boats were three miles away at Les Veules Roses. The chain of rifles linking man to man down the hazardous cliff face provided an easy target for the enemy. Many of the lads were shot or taken prisoner and a mere handful came home to Bute. The chilling consequence of War affected everyone in our small island community.

One autumn day a big grey ship anchored in the Bay and soon half a dozen sinister looking submarines huddled round her. It was the first time most of us had ever seen a submarine. Before long we learned that this ship – H.M.S. Cyclops, was the depot ship for the Seventh Submarine Flotilla and probably would be based in Rothesay for the duration of the War. The town was full of strangers. The evacuees came first, then the naval personnel (British, Dutch, Norwegian, French and Canadian), there were R.A.S.C. (Royal Army Service Corps) and Commando Companies in training.

A group of suave Polish Officers, rumoured to be high-ranking Government Officials, arrived. Quite a few local ladies succumbed to their charming manners, and indeed several weddings took place.

By that time I had left school to work in the office of the Kyles of Bute Hydro – a large spa type of hotel in Port Bannatyne. I'd worked there during the Easter holiday and was pleased to have been offered a permanent post. I didn't consider the option of further education, as we hadn't much money and even my small pay was welcome. Rheumatic fever had weakened Mum's heart, and unable to go out to work, she supplemented her income by letting rooms, as indeed Rothesay folk were encouraged to do. With the arrival of Cyclebox (as she was affectionately called) accommodation was at a premium. Just three weeks after Dunkirk, France capitulated and signed a formal surrender with the Germans on 21st June 1940. The situation was very grave.

Alan, a Chief ERA (Engine Room Artificer) in the French Navy had escaped to England after the fall of France. With a young English wife, and eventually a baby, he lived with us for a couple of years. After rigorous interrogation he had been eventually allowed to join the British Submarine Service, and to avoid reprisals against his family had been obliged to adopt another name. At school we'd been taught to translate Victor Hugo but little emphasis had been placed on conversation. Alan put us to shame as he chatted freely in a glorious mixture of Naval slang and good old Scots words. His culinary skills impressed us too, especially when he did unusual things like adding herbs and white wine to the rabbit stew. In those days using wine in cooking was regarded as extravagant. At first Alan was on a training submarine and slept at home most nights. As he left for work in the mornings I'd set off in the opposite direction for the Hydro.

Young and inexperienced I'd been awestruck when I went for the initial interview. The Hydro was a wonderful building – originally opened in 1879, extended and modernised after a fire in 1909. The large entrance hall with bright welcoming coal fires, banks of flowers, marble staircase with beautifully carved woodwork throughout was magnificent. Water was pumped up from the sea for the Salt Water Baths and small swimming pool. Russian and Turkish Baths were also available with qualified staff to give heat treatment and massage. Eighty of the eighty-eight bedrooms had sea views. There was a table tennis room, billiard room, badminton court, and a splendid ballroom with a stage and dressing room. In the surrounding grounds thick with rhododendrons, azaleas and other exotic shrubs, there were two tennis courts, two putting greens and a croquet lawn. Going straight from school into such a place was like stepping into the pages of a novel.

After taking private lessons in shorthand and typing from Miss Telfer in Castle Street, I was soon able to type menus and letters. At the beginning of the War the resident orchestra, and entertainment hostess left, and as the junior member of staff extra duties fell on me. I learned to organise concerts, dances, badminton and tennis tournaments, and the nightly military whist. I issued kitchen stores, kept stock sheets, arranged the dining room flowers. Being a general dogsbody was hectic but I loved the life. At first I wasn't allowed to alter anything in the Reservation Book. There were seldom vacancies but to enable anyone to extend a visit for a few days, involved a great deal of juggling on paper to avoid the necessity of the guest physically moving from room to room. Once I started working on the Booking Sheet I carefully checked and re-checked to avoid a disastrous mistake.

Daily I had unusual experiences, some quite unnerving. I tried not to panic when the stillroom maid had an epileptic fit and fell behind the dairy door trapping me inside, or when Mrs Adam wouldn't stop screaming when she was stuck in the lift. At the office window one old lady's wig came off with her hat and I looked away, pretending not to notice.

Most of the guests hoped to be able to stay in safety at the Hydro for the duration of the War. Ladies of the twin-set-and-pearl type reminisced over schooldays at St. Leonards or Rodean, others vied with each other to see who could first finish the crossword in the Times or the Herald. Another group sat in the library knitting furiously as if every soldier was in desperate need of a pair of socks. Old gentlemen snoozed in the comfort of the Billiard Room, with the crumpled Financial Times beside them, dreaming no doubt of their London Clubs. Outdoor types went fishing, played golf, tennis or putting. Frequent disagreement about the croquet rules downgraded it to the mad game in Alice in Wonderland!

Often a guest appeared in a new role – a Serviceman on a few days leave. One such person – Jack from Edinburgh, a tall handsome Pilot Officer came with his parents for a week. One evening after helping to sort out the flags from the Military Whist, he walked home with me. It was a starry night and the Plough and the Milky Way were clearly visible. A big bright moon peeped out from behind a cloud. He almost shouted "There's that dratted moon". He spoke strangely and the words almost exploded from him as he told me about his best friend's plane being shot down in bright moonlight over Hamburg. Suddenly letting out all his bottled up emotion, it was as if he was oblivious that I was there. I looked at the moon and realised that it was his enemy. Even now more than fifty years later that scene sometimes flashes – back when someone says "Isn't it a beautiful evening? Look at that wonderful silvery moon glittering on the water." He went on to tell me that he felt the holiday had been a horrible mistake. The trees he'd climbed as a boy, the tennis courts where he'd won tournaments remained the same, yet to his tired adult eyes they now appeared vastly different. The black blank curtains of the future obscured the happy memories of past holidays. He spoke almost bitterly and a shudder ran through me. No one had suspected that under the disguise of a devil-may-care fellow there was a tired young man who would have been happy to sit down quietly with a book and not have to fake jollity.

In September 1940 the Battle of Britain raged in the skies over the South of England, and twenty-two year old Jack was one of the many pilots who failed to return. When his parents came back to the Hydro in December they seemed much smaller, older and quieter. They said, "We are very glad we shared that last holiday with him – he was so relaxed and happy. He seemed so full of laughter, little jokes and surprises.

We've been coming here since he was a toddler, and that was one of the best holidays we ever had. Although we were worried about his job, he loved it, and we never let him suspect how we felt."

A lump in my throat made speaking difficult, so I just gave a little nod. It made me realise that all over the world, husbands and wives, sweethearts, friends, parents and children, and brothers and sisters would be trying to keep up the pretence of being confident about the future, hiding the dread of what might happen under a brave smile saying "Take care of yourself. Don't worry, I'll be alright. See you soon."

Chapter Two

Secret work in a submarine depot ship

I was greatly intrigued to hear that two older girls were working on board HMS Cyclops and presumably had joined the WRNS. One day I bumped into them on the pier, and in answer to my eager questioning they admitted that they worked in an office on the ship.
"You lucky things," I said "What exactly do you do?"
They exchanged glances and then Jean said "It is secret we aren't allowed to say."
Secret! That word had me hooked. I was perfectly happy at the Hydro, but I longed to do something mysterious, unusual and important. I had never considered what might happen if the War was prolonged, and at that time girls of my age were not being called up.

About a month later, to my surprise and delight, I received a letter from a local lady – Miss Dorothy Marshall, an archaeologist by profession, Commandant of the Red Cross and County Commissioner of the Girl Guides. As a prominent member of the local community she had been asked if she could recommend a young British girl whose family background was known to her, and whom she considered would be suitable to work with confidential material on the ship. She said that she understood there would shortly be a vacancy on the ship, and if I was interested, a Wren Office from Greenock would interview me in, (of all places!) the General Waiting Room on the Pier! Interested? Of course I was! Miss Marshall's father, a much respected doctor on the island had often had long talks with my grandfather, and of course she knew me from the Guides.

A few days later, trying to ignore the butterflies in my tummy, I arrived at the Pier Waiting Room in time to hear the Wren Officer in the voice of authority demand – "Will everyone please leave this room immediately? I have important Admiralty business to conduct."
The passengers all went out without questioning the order or muttering complaints. I doubted the legality of the order but was greatly impressed by the way they all obeyed promptly. The Wren Officer (who didn't

disclose her name) asked me numerous questions but was rather vague about the mysterious job. Later I realised that, as an Administrative Officer, she probably didn't know what it entailed.

Somewhat disappointed that she hadn't given definite assurance that I'd be working on the ship, I took the application form home. I waited impatiently for further instructions and eventually all was settled. I left the Hydro and on 7th July 1941 reported on board HMS Cyclops, where I was to be trained to be a C.B. Corrector (whatever that was!). Another phase of my life was beginning. It was hard to believe that I was actually going off to work on a submarine depot ship in the midst of a War. Round and round inside my head buzzed thoughts of spies and secret codes. Years before in our owl tree den Irene and I had invented a special language with all the words written backwards. Difficult to pronounce, it was soon abandoned. It will probably be something like that, I thought.

The work wasn't at all as I imagined. The Official Secrets Act precludes full description, although in the present computer age, everything must have changed radically. The office, aft and below deck, was somewhat like a library issuing signal. publications and confidential books to submarines and escort vessels. All day long we squeezed figures and letters into small spaces in codes and decodes, and inserted slips of paper about mines and wrecks etc. It was nerve racking to realise that writing FST instead of FTS could have disastrous consequences and we checked most meticulously. While a submarine is at sea there is no time to spare for fiddling paper work, so we aimed to have all the books corrected right up to date before a vessel left for sea. One of the first things I learned in this strange new world was that submarines were referred to as boats not ships. Our "Boss" was an R.N. Lieutenant Commander but having other duties he didn't work full time in the office. There was also an R.N.V.R. Sub Lieutenant, Jean, a Petty Officer and myself, a Wren rating.

Back in 1941 I wasn't familiar with the word chauvinist, but I was soon aware that Cyclops was full of chauvinistic men . The older Royal Naval types, officers and men alike, grumbled about us. Shocked at tradition being flaunted to the extent that women were actually working on board the ship, they protested loudly.

"Ships aren't suitable places for women."
"It is unlucky having women on board, and unthinkable to regard them as crew"

"What are things coming to? They are certain to cause disruption in the ship's routine."

"What exactly do they do in that little office?"

"They needn't expect any privileges here."

"They'd better not grumble about things."

"If we aren't careful they'll soon be swarming everywhere and taking over our jobs."

Maybe they sensed that great changes were taking place, although no one imagined all the upheaval that War would bring, and how much womens' place in the world would alter. The expression "neither fish, flesh nor good red herring" could have applied to us. Although we were ratings we weren't allowed on the Lower Deck, and weren't allowed in the Wardroom either. The only privilege accorded to us was being taken on and offshore in officers' boats, instead of in liberty boats packed with sailors. There was no necessity for the work we did in peace time, so fear about us taking over their jobs was unjustified.

Meal times presented a problem. At first the Wardroom Guest Room had been used, but that was a short-lived idea, bringing bellows of rage from the old R.N. brigade. They complained "It is bad enough having these women on board the ship, but it is quite preposterous allowing ratings to eat in the Guest Room. On the other hand they most certainly can't be allowed on the Lower Deck. They are causing problems already." A solution was found and a small cabin beside the ship's office, sometimes used by the Chaplain, was allocated to us over the mid-day meal time. Jimmie, the Jaunty's Messman was detailed to look after us. The Jaunty, we discovered was a kind of policeman and the Regulating Petty Officers who helped were Crushers.

We had no idea how far Jimmie had to come from the galley but somehow he managed to keep our meals hot with the plates tied up in a big cloth. Every week he collected our cigarette and chocolate ration from the NAAFI canteen. Again we had no idea where the Canteen was, or what was sold there. Jimmie knew we worked in an office but never questioned us about the work. Having been in the Navy for about 20 years he was glad of the "soft number."

He was our link with the Lower Deck and told us he'd tried to convince the boys that
we were nice ordinary girls and not at all toffee-nosed as was alleged. The reputation we had of only being interested in Gold Braid was

undeserved. Only submarine officers concerned with the C.Bs. were allowed in the offices, and we had almost no contact with ratings. Even the messenger from the S.D.O. (Signed Distribution Office) stood outside in the alleyway and handed in the coded messages through the open door.

It didn't take long for it to dawn on me that had I been slim and glamorous I probably wouldn't have been considered for the job, but they seem to have concluded that I was a good solid type, unlikely to cause any disturbance amongst the men. I was a strange young girl, instead of thinking of all the prospective boyfriends there would be, I thought, "Help! All these men! How will I cope?" Being self-conscious it was an ordeal for me every morning to clamber up the wobbly wooden steps against the ship's side (strangely called a gangway) and, on arrival at the top salute the quarter deck. An alarming number of people were assembled there – the Officer of the Watch, a sailor with the grand title "Corporal of the Gangway" a messenger, and often a midshipman too. My next problem was the Keyboard Sentry, a young sailor, grinning broadly with pleasure at the brief interlude in his boring job. He'd sometimes sing so quietly it was barely audible to the tune of a popular ditty "Hey, hey, hey, little Wren when when when will you come to the pictures with me?" Trying not to blush, I'd sign for the office key and scuttle past him.

Negotiating our way astern on the open deck over coils of rope and steel hawsers was hazardous, especially as the crane was operating while a working party loaded torpedoes into a submarine. Stepping inside the accommodation we then had to climb down a couple of steep ladders before we reached the cabin flat, where the office was situated "below deck and between decks." No one with claustrophobic tendencies could have worked there all day, under electric light and in a stuffy unhealthy atmosphere. Security was paramount – hence the location of the office amidships. The books were housed in steel safes bolted to the deck and bulkhead. In an emergency secret matter had to be easily jettisoned and some code books had bars of lead inserted in their covers to ensure that they'd sink easily if thrown from the ship's bridge and not fall into enemy hands. Once I dropped a Naval Code on my foot and for ages had a very black, very sore toe!

Now that I was "in the Navy" a whole new vocabulary had to be understood. Brought up by the sea, and able to row a boat at an early age I had no trouble with basic things like bow, stern, deck. I soon realised that port was the left side facing the bow and starboard the right, and of course it was never "upstairs" but always "up top and down below". Hydro words – booking, hotplate, dining room station, ration books, P.A.Y.E. forms all moved to the back of my mind. I often made a faux-pas. About 11.50 a.m. on hearing the shrill pipe "Cooks to the Galley" and ten minutes later "Hands to Dinner" I couldn't help saying "That's silly. No one could possibly have cooked a meal in such a short time." Choking with laughter, Iain (the subby.) explained that the first pipe meant that the sailor designated as cook in each mess had to go and collect the meals cooked in the main galley.

At first, coming up on deck ready to catch the 1730 boat for shore I blinked in surprise seeing buses going along Ardbeg or past the Glenburn Hotel on the opposite shore. It was akin to the feeling one gets emerging from a crowded cinema after a good film, and realising it is no longer the American West or back in Victorian times. For a submariner it must be even stranger, stuck down below for so long, stepping up onto the casing at Harbour Stations, gulping in fresh air, and seeing other submarines with the depot ship towering above.

Like a mother hen, Cyclops usually had several boats huddled round her – each linked by what seemed an insecure-looking plank. We weren't too happy if the Corporal of the Gangway warned "She is outboard of four" signifying that the shore-going motorboat was tied up alongside the outside submarine. Crossing over those wobbly connecting gangways and along slippery submarine casings was scary especially in the blackout. It is surprising that we avoided landing "in the drink." Fortunately the motor-boat was usually at the foot of the main gangway.

One day A.V. Alexander, First Lord of the Admiralty came on an official visit, and to our great indignation the Boss locked us inside the office. Apparently although Admiral (Submarines) Max Horton and the Director (Wrens) knew we worked on the ship "My Lords," the Admiralty hadn't given special permission. A.V. Alexander met the ship's company inspected Sea Cadets and Dutch sailors, but we were hidden out of sight. No doubt it was made official after that, but to get proper recognition these things seemed to take ages, wads of paper, and, almost an Act of Parliament. If we had been on view the First Lord would almost certainly have spoken to us. As the crew kept a watchful eye in case we were accorded any favours,

it was probably just
as well we weren't visible.

Although suspecting that sometimes we were considered a nuisance, we were tolerated because we worked quietly and efficiently and kept a low profile. We were proud to be in the submarine service and found the submariners to be a great bunch of lads who appreciated the work we did. There's a unique bond of comradeship between the officers and men of the submarine service. A man wasn't merely Brian, Tom or Jim but someone in charge of the radio, a pump or a valve. Every man was a specialist and yet each one was capable of doing the other's job. Most of them were emphatic that they much preferred the dim life under the sea to being in General Service, saying "Brave chaps up there on the top we are safer hiding below!"

When the Commander was teaching us to sail I really blotted my copy book. Jean was at the tiller and I was for'ard when the order came "Put that sheet round the cleat" I was stumped. Gazing up at the sails, I asked what I thought was a sensible question "Which Cleat?" Back came the reply "On the thwart" There was nothing for it – I had to ask
"What's a thwart?"
"You are sitting on the dammed thing."
I foolishly replied "Oh you mean – put that rope round the hook on the seat."

The Commander was not amused and decreed that we would not be allowed to go sailing again until we studied the Seamanship Manual. Before the next weekend I had added "guff, peak, stay, tacking and luffing" to my vocabulary. Soon we could sail as capable as any one of the ship's company.

One Sunday we went for a picnic with the Commander, Ken, the Engine-room Commander's eight year old son and his little friend Winnie. We sailed round to the boat slip at Port Bannatyne. There we picked up the three sons of the Earl and Countess of Dumfries. The Earl (who subsequently became the fifth Marquis of Bute) was a very capable Cypher Officer on Cyclops, serving as Lieutenant John Dumfries RNVR. The twins, John and David and little brother Jimmy (James) in their usual kilted garb had walked down to the slip from their home at Kames Castle, leaving baby sister Fiona at home.

The beach at Toward (HMS Brontosaurus) was used for Commando landing practice, but we had special permission to land on an unmined section. Carefully we navigated the boat across to the right spot and scrambled ashore. As soon as the picnic basket was unpacked we sent the boys off gathering firewood. First John got tar on his socks and enterprisingly tried to wash it off in the sea. A buckle came off David's shoe and Jimmy caught his jersey on a barbed wire fence. The Commander was busy frying sausage and eggs, and I was buttering the bread when wee Winnie's Glasgow voice piped up "Hey Commando is the eggs no ready yet?" Jimmy asked me "What did she say?" and wasn't satisfied with my reply "Oh Commander, are the eggs not ready yet?" He practised "Hey Commando . . . . " all the way home and later we were told it became the in-phrase at the Castle.

Back at Cyclops we sent the boys up to the quarter-deck, with instructions that they were to wait there quietly while we stowed away the sails. It wasn't an easy job to fold them correctly and squeeze them into the little canvas bag but we had to leave the boat in good order as any male crew member would do.

Once ashore we made for the taxi queue and soon three dirty, dishevelled but happy boys were delivered back to Kames Castle. Next day Lt. Dumfries told us that they had all declared they had a "spiffing time." Forty years later John, then the sixth Marquis of Bute, introduced to me at a Scout meeting, said that it remained clearly as one of the Red Letter days of his youth.

We had heaps of dates and my Mother felt I went out with too many different boys but it was all very innocent. Often two or three boys would tag along with the one who had originally asked me out. I remember we once hired bikes, cycled to Dunagoil and picnicked at St Blane's Chapel. Another day four of us climbed Barone Hill, but usually we weren't so energetic and went out to dinner, to the cinema or to
dance. The Pavilion, just opened in 1938, was filled to capacity most nights. Tuesday, Scottish Country Dancing Night was no exception. The Commander, a Scot, and an energetic member of the Country Dance Society used to bring a party of boys ashore with him. For a few Royal Navy Officers "Hamilton House", the "Duke of Perth" and even "The Glasgow Highlanders", presented no problem, but others were quite bewildered by shouted instructions. "Turn the Corners", Poussette", and "Allemande". "Cast off two" set them off into fits of laughter – all totally new words for them to learn. The set usually ended in confusion.

Again the Commander was NOT amused and organised practice classes in Bishop Street Hall on a Monday night so that all would be simplified for the less able ones. A couple of local girls, Country Dance experts, came to help us teach them. Starting off with little idea of even how to do a pas-de-bas they soon progressed from "Petronella" and "Corn Riggs" to the "Eight Men of Moidart" and energetic dances like "Quadrilles." They no longer thought that "casting off" was something to do with knitting!

"The Seventh" was a training flotilla and in 1941 had Oberon, Otway, L26, L27, the old H Class, the Dutch submarines 0 9 and 0 10 attached as were the Norwegian's B1 and Polish "Wilk". In December 1941 the Admiralty, desperate to prevent the German pocket battleships Scharnhorst and Gneisenau from escaping into the Atlantic, even sent our ancient submarines to help form an iron ring round Brest. I was shocked on Boxing Day when the Subby announced bluntly "H31 has been sunk. Prepare destruction certificates for the books on charge, and allocate their pigeon-hole to P555, a lease-lend boat coming from America." Horrified at the casual way the news was broken to us I protested and was told "There is a War on. Lots of people are going to die, many boats will be lost, if you girls are going to be sentimental and emotionally involved you'll be no use here. That confirms what people thought about women being employed on a ship. I'm off to the Wardroom for a gin." Again I realised how War was utterly stupid and a useless waste of young lives.

Later when I worked on board HMS Forth (3rd s/M Flotilla) a boat quite often failed to return from patrol and we learned that life had to go on as before. For the sake of the next submarine due out on a hazardous patrol we all had to act as if we believed no further tragedies could occur. A dance was usually held in the village hall the night the loss of a boat was confirmed and everyone was expected to attend. It was a dangerous life – submariners lived for the day and daren't think or plan too far ahead. Few of us ever dreamt of life after the War. We never wished the boys good luck or watched the boat out of sight. Off they went with a "Cheerio. See you soon."

Rumours went round Rothesay that Cyclops was going to Dry Dock in Glasgow. I was shocked when Mum told me that she had heard this from the baker's van man, who said he "had it on good authority." As the days passed it became evident that it was more than just a rumour. "What will happen to us?" we asked the Subby. "A dry dock is not a place for women. You will certainly never be allowed to go there" he pronounced. "We'll probably be put on one of the escort vessels, or maybe they'll make us take leave."

In the end it was decided that he could stay in Rothesay, and we would go with the ship and carry on with the correcting. It wasn't really practical to transfer a quantity of books to a small escort vessel. Furthermore the escorts accompanying the submarines were sometimes away overnight at Campbeltown or even Londonderry, so it was unthinkable that we went on one of them! My aunt, who worked in the Censor's office in Glasgow was rather peeved when she was subject to investigation before it was deemed suitable for us two Wrens to stay with her.

On sailing day we had to be on board an hour earlier than usual, as the ship was due to weigh anchor around 7.00 a.m. As the "Boss" was also the ship's Navigator and on duty on the Bridge we were on our own. Up top all seemed hustle and bustle, but it was strangely quiet down in the cabin flat, where our office was situated. They had long since stopped piping orders down to our deck, as most of them had nothing to do with us, but we listened carefully for "Away Boats Crew" which was the signal for the shore-going motor boat to come alongside. At first we had been constantly interrupted by a voice calling for the driver for the crane, or commanding a working party to "fall in." The favourite pipe with the men was "Up spirits" when the tots of rum were being given out, but of course, that didn't apply to us either. That morning we could hear distant instructions for the ship to prepare for sea. I vaguely heard the order "Close all Z and Y doors" but didn't pay attention thinking it had nothing to do with us, but we soon found that it did.

Curious to see what it was like to be "at sea" we decided to lock the office and venture up on deck for a few moments. We realised then that the water-tight doors had been closed, and unable to get through our usual exit to the upper deck, were imprisoned below! We went exploring and eventually found an emergency ladder, and up we went emerging on the deck near the ship's office. It was cold, grey and misty and there was nothing special to see at all – an anticlimax.

Instructions had been issued that once we were ashore we were not to disclose the ship's name but to say that we were from Job 1381. I didn't really see how the ship's identity could be concealed when the whole of Rothesay knew the ship had gone to dock, and it was difficult to imagine sailors ashore in pubs, not mentioning the ship's name. No one explained the dock's location to us, and incredible as it now seems, we never thought of asking. At 1730 we went ashore through the dock-yard to the gatehouse. When we asked the name of the yard the duty clerk eyed us with great surprise and suspicion. He cross-examined us thoroughly before grunting "Barclay Curle." We still weren't any wiser, but found our way up to Dumbarton Road. We studied the tramcars and were surprised to find that Auchenshuggle actually seemed to be a place. Unfortunately, my aunt had moved a few months before from the West End to Mount Florida, miles away, on the south side of the city. All evening we worried about the Officer of the Watch's parting shot "Remember the 0800 boat as usual in the morning." To miss the boat, to be a minute late, and "adrift" was unthinkable.

It was very dark, very cold and very early when we set out next morning.

The ship looked huge in the dry dock with an incredibly dirty mussel-encrusted hull. We had our first encounter with dock workers – a noisy cheery bunch with colourful language. None of them expected to find two females working away at the bottom of the ship and if they had just let out a choice mouthful as we appeared they gaped at us, but immediately muttered "Sorry Miss." Used to strict naval discipline I was astonished when I came across a group playing cards in the cabin flat, when they were supposed to be working.

One of the problems of course was lack of water. As the Captain was in hospital undergoing an appendix operation, the Commander was in charge. He had warned us "There will be no water – even for Sanitary purposes, and there are no special facilities for females in a dockyard. You may have the use of the lavatory ashore designated for ship's masters. I'll leave the key with the Keyboard Sentry." (gasp of horror from me!). He reconsidered, "No there may not be a key specially allocated for this ship – just ask at the Gatehouse for the key of the Captain's lavatory Job No.1381." I didn't like that idea either and imagined the red-headed clerk in the office making all kinds of wisecracks but eventually I tagged along behind Jean and let her deal with the matter. At lunch time we carried a towel and a sponge bag with us, as if we were only going for a good wash! Crossing the Quarter Deck we half expected to be told that there wasn't another boat ashore for thirty minutes.

Even when we weren't in Dry Dock I'd found the whole thing a bit of a problem on the ship. Near the C.B. office there was a row of lavatories called "the Heads", for the use of officers in the cabin flats. For some perverse reason the one allocated to us was not the first but the second one in the row. Once I'd been there when the pipe went announcing the approach of Captain's Rounds – a kind of inspection party. A great line of Officials came along, with the Captain and other Departmental Heads all wearing white gloves. Cyclops was an old coal-burning ship and, when she was fuelling, dust even got inside the accommodation. The unfortunate sailors who had to clean the ladders and alleyways had a difficult task as all the paintwork had to be washed and the ropes attached to the ladders scrubbed clean. The white gloves were supposed to remain spotless until the Rounds had been completed. That morning hearing the pipe, I stupidly panicked and stayed inside. I presumed it was the Captain who said, "Why aren't all the doors open?" Someone muttered an explanation and they moved away. Afterwards I was told that my black legs were visible through the gap at the bottom of the door. I was most embarrassed, and now there was a problem in dry dock!

One bitterly cold foggy November morning we arrived in the dock-yard and were startled to realise that the ship, with steaming lights on and a couple of tugs fussing round, had moved into the river. We anxiously checked our watches to make sure we weren't late. A muffled voice through a loud hailer told us to go away and return in two or three hour's time. One of the Dockies explained that she was "turning in the river." Stupidly we didn't believe it could possibly take so long, and in any case we had nowhere to go. It would have taken ages to return to Glasgow, and we never thought about going by tram-car into Clydebank. The dockside at eight in the morning was very cheerless but we stood about for ages and then walked up and down the cobbled street outside the gate.

When the ship tied up and eventually lowered a gangway we were nearly frozen and far from happy. If we had only been told about the undocking we could have been there an hour earlier or two or three hours later. We daren't grumble as we had been warned that there would be some hardships. Any derogatory comment we made was always greeted with "We keep saying a ship is no place for women." Eventually all the work was completed and we sailed for home. When we reached Helensburgh the ship reduced speed and went round the Degaussing Range.

It was a long day and we grew red-eyed and weary poring over our work and constantly checking the tiny letters and figures. We took it for granted but we never ever stopped for a tea-break or "stand easy" like the men. Finally we realised, by the distant orders and clanging sounds that we must be approaching Rothesay Bay. It was frustrating with no porthole not to be able to see what was happening up top.

The hour was late and no shore leave was granted, but of course it was unthinkable that we were allowed to stay on board overnight. A gangway was lowered, the motor boat's crew specially called out, and we were duly dumped ashore at the King's steps. It niggled more than a little that we were landed there in the blackout's inky darkness after the last bus had departed. No one seemed to care what happened to us (not that murder or rape was so common then!). The priority had been to get rid of us two females, and the cry must have been "It is night time they should be off the ship."

The next morning when we reached the Pier at 7.50 a.m. there was no sign of the motor boat. One of the Pier staff told us "Cyclops sailed before seven this morning." We were sure he must be mistaken and went along to the Boom Defence Office to make enquiries. The officer-in-charge told us that Cyclops had gone to swing her compass and do sea-trials off Inchmarnock and suggested we took the rest of the day off. We weren't too confident about this and were sure that "Breda" the escort vessel, would send a boat for us, or at least signal instructions. How wrong we were! When full daylight came we saw an empty bay – not a submarine or escort vessel in sight. We realised that we really had been left behind. It was the last straw, especially after they'd landed us ashore so late the previous evening.

Sitting by a window in the Regal Café most of the day drinking lots of cups of tea looking out at the empty bay, we grew more indignant by the hour! It had been a completely wasted day, and about 4.00 p.m. very disgruntled we went home. The next morning the motor boat came for us as usual. In that male dominated world a Petty Officer and a Wren didn't seem of much account, but we felt at least they could have told us what was going to happen. It almost seemed as if they had forgotten us altogether – and we felt mutiny had often occurred with less cause!

The submariners, however, appreciated the work we did and were always grateful for our help. That evening still fuming about it, I had dinner with Peter and told him the whole story. He said that the other submariners had been discussing it, and thought that the depot ship staff had been jolly rotten to treat us like that. Peter quite a heart-throb – six feet tall, dark and handsome came from Durban. I only went out with him twice before he moved to another flotilla. Like so many others he was lost in the Mediterranean about six months later.

Shortly after that a most unusual thing happened – a Wren Officer appeared from the Greenock base – HMS Orlando! We viewed with scorn shore establishments that bore ship's names, and felt that they weren't in the Navy like we were! Knowing nothing about the Wrens we were surprised that this Third Officer suddenly seemed concerned about our welfare. She wanted to see our rest room, and our recreation room! Blank expressions appeared on the faces of all the senior officers – such things hadn't been considered. Cyclops was an old ship and space was at a premium. She insisted that, at least, they allocated some place where we'd be able to change our stockings and even our skirts if we got wet coming on board. A notice was then printed on the bathroom door next to the office. In large black lettering it read "For the use of WRNS only between the hours of 0800 and 1730." By no stretch of imagination could it have been called a rest room but it was better than nothing. Previously we'd hung our coats behind the office door and kept spare clothing in a suitcase there. Now we could move the case each morning, comb our hair in front of a mirror, even wash our faces, sit on the edge of the bath and chat at lunch-time.

We were also told that if we wanted exercise after the midday meal we'd be allowed to walk on the starboard side of the boat deck, while the Commander might be on the port side but no one else was to be allowed to use the deck at that time. It was great to be able to get some fresh air after spending hours in the stuffy office. "Maybe, after all," we thought, "Wren Officers are useful." Thinking back, I reckon it was sheer good luck that we hadn't had an accident, or complained of feeling ill, because they certainly hadn't made any provision for such emergencies. There was, of course, a Doctor on board but sick bay was for'ard down a particularly steep slippery ladder, quite a distance from our office.

One rainy day Jean had to go for an inoculation. It meant climbing up a couple of ladders, crossing out in the open and going down again for'ard. Suddenly remembering how we'd found another exit when we went to Dry Dock, she decided to explore and found a way through the main alleyway to the Sick Bay. It was quite against the rules but it seemed to her more sensible to take this route and it certainly was quicker and avoided the rain. When she came back she told me of this daring exploit but said no-one had challenged her.

Ten minutes later the Engineer Commander 'phoned and demanded her presence in his Day Cabin. "Engineer Commander?" she queried, "What has he got to do with us?" She soon found out. When she saw him sitting grim-faced behind his desk she realised she was "in the rattle" (in trouble). He roared at her "There has been a very serious complaint. This afternoon you were well out of bounds and passed by
while ten stokers were showering. This grave matter must not occur again. Understand?" In response to her muttered "Yes, sir", he thundered on; "Any more trouble and you will no longer be considered a suitable person to work on the ship, and will be transferred to a shore establishment immediately. That is all. Go now."

Duly crestfallen she came back to the office. Although she insisted she hadn't even glimpsed one of the naked men, obviously they had seen her and rushed to report the matter. She didn't try again, and I certainly wouldn't have dared to wander like that. We knew that we were restricted to very few parts of the ship, but it seemed rather a stupid fuss for men to make in the middle of a War!

I still felt apprehensive when I came onto the ship – it wasn't just negotiating the jerky, swaying gangway, but the whole rigmarole – saluting the quarter-deck, signing for the key, and going along the Wardroom Passageway past the Maltese stewards, peeping out of the pantry doorways. It was worse when Jean was on leave and it was then that a most embarrassing thing happened. When I went into the bathroom to hang up my greatcoat and respirator something made me turn from the back of the door, and there, in wide-eyed astonishment, sat a man in the bath. I let out a yell and rushed out slamming the door behind me. Our Subby, Iain, emerged from his cabin nearby. I gasped "There's a man in the bath". "A man," said he, "Is he an officer?" (As if that made any difference) "I don't know," I answered, and like an idiot "He hadn't on his uniform." Iain went to investigate and hoots of laughter ensued. When he came back to the office, he tried to reassure me. "Oh", he said, "It is alright. It is only old 0-". "Who is he?" I queried. "The C.O. of H.28." "Well he has no business in our bathroom. I hope you told him so."

Later I heard that the culprit had related the tale with relish and much embroidery, over the lunch-time gins in the wardroom. He'd just come back from sea, as the door was open he hadn't seen the notice and certainly didn't know there were any females on board. His version was on these lines:- "I was lying back half asleep soaking in the bath, when this gorgeous creature came in. She took off her hat, she unhooked her respirator, then she took off her greatcoat and her jacket and was just going to take off her shirt, but, alas, in my excitement I must have moved, because she let out a terrible shriek and fled."

I was most upset and imagined all the jokes that were going around. I had long since learnt that men are terrible gossips, and usually everything we said and did the previous evening was known on the ship early the next morning! It didn't strike me as funny, and I told Iain that I expected him to contradict the story and give the correct version. We did, in fact, often take our jackets off and roll up our sleeves as it was very hot in the office.

Many years later, after the War, at a cocktail party on board the "Adamant", I met old '0' – a Lieut. Commander R.N. With a charming smile, and pink gin in hand, he tried the usual line of patter, "Hullo! We've met before." I stared blankly, but he persisted – "Weren't you a Third Officer WRNS out in Trinco?"

"No, I've never been to Trincomalee." "Oh, sorry – I'm mixed-up but I'm sure it was during the War. Were you a Q.A. (Queen Alexandra's Nurse) out in Alex?" I denied this too and tried to involve someone else in the conversation. Then suddenly he burst out; "Good God, I remember – the Wren in the bath!" Being older and more astute, I was able to cope and retorted, "Better rephrase that – the man in the bath you mean!" Of course everyone wanted to hear the story – my line had been quite a stopper to the usual trivial cocktail party chatter. This time I was well able to join in the laughter suspecting "old 0" had dined out on it quite often.

But I digress – back to Cyclops days.

One stormy day normal boat service was suspended, all shore leave was cancelled and the eternal problem arose "What will we do with the Wrens?" Most of the submarines were at sea and consequently there were lots of empty officers' cabins in the alleyway beside the office, but it was never considered that we stayed overnight. It was deemed far too stormy for any boat to get alongside the main gangway to allow any of the men ashore, - but they had to get rid of us! As the Captain's little planing dinghy could be manoeuvred under the stern, it was decided to get us ashore that way.

After we'd been out sailing we had sometimes come inboard by the boom, but going off in a gale was a different matter. Different and difficult! As we didn't want to be "in the drink" we obeyed instructions and, with thumping hearts, jumped into the planing dinghy exactly when the coxswain told us. The sea seemed very angry, cold grey and menacing.

Next morning we told the Commander how awkward it had been, and that it seemed quite ridiculous that we weren't allowed to wear trousers. In order to get the required leg room we had had to tie string round our waists, and hitch the wretched skirts up above our knees in a most unlady like fashion. He agreed to ask the Captain if at least he'd allow us to make pleated skirts. Surprisingly our request was granted, on condition that we used the regulation serge. We were delighted and from then on wore pleated skirts. No one dreamt of consulting or even informing any Wren Authority about this. Apart from the brief visit from the Greenock Third Officer, we'd had no contact with any others. We were on the ship's books, directly under the command of Captain S/M 7, The Seventh Submarine Flotilla.

A signal came inviting us to a party on board the Princess Iris, a Combined Operations Headquarters ship stationed at Toward. They were apparently celebrating the anniversary of her commissioning. To everyone's amazement, and the annoyance
of some, we accepted the invitation. We felt it would be something different and we'd see how another branch of the Navy operated. The boys made derisive remarks:
"It doesn't even look like a ship – used to be a train ferry."
"Haven't you enough boy-friends here? What's wrong with us?"
"Goodness knows what kind of a "do" it will be."
"What on earth are you thinking about – going there?"
"Remember combined-operation types aren't like the submarine service."
When someone actually said "Maybe they won't treat you

properly, like we do" – that did it – that finally made up our minds. Off we went, regardless of their criticism and still mindful of the way they had sailed off and left us behind!

There were several Wrens there from Toward – HMS Brontosaurus and from HMS Osprey, the Dunoon base. It was our first experience of being part of a group of Wrens. I was dancing around quite happily, when a red-faced Wren Officer put her hand on my shoulder demanding "Girl, why aren't you in uniform? Where do you come from?" She didn't seem to have heard of the Cyclops and was further enraged when she saw Jean, a Petty Officer, dressed in similar fashion. We had become so accustomed to wearing the pleated skirts everyone had forgotten that it wasn't regulation uniform. As far as were concerned the Captain's word was law and took precedence over some unseen and unknown Wren officials. "There will be trouble about this. Serious trouble," she vowed, and demanded our official numbers. Mine was 23456 – I'm sure she didn't believe me at first. It did cause trouble but not serious trouble.

Chief Officer Clyde Area sent a signal of complaint and two days later a Third Officer from Greenock came to discuss this outrageous occurrence. The Royal Navy Captain in charge of a Submarine Flotilla had more serious things to worry about than Wrens' skirts and certainly wouldn't tolerate his authority being challenged. He entertained her in his Day Cabin and after a good lunch and probably a couple of gins they discussed the matter. We were sent for and told we now had official permission to wear the offending skirts but only for going off and on the ship. "Never ashore, and never, never at any other time", she told us quite sternly. "Is that clear?" We were uncertain if she meant us to change in the motor boat on the way ashore, or in the General Waiting Room! – Needless to say we didn't ask, paid no attention and carried on as before. Eventually more Wrens came to work on board (there were six in 1942, and more later) and the concession of wearing pleated skirts was withdrawn.

A couple of months later we were actually allowed to go out to sea on a day exercise. We had no illusions – it wasn't done to appease or please us. It suited them to take us, and was part of the crew's training. They planned that Cyclops would sail early one evening, and the Wrens would join HMS Titania (an auxiliary Submarine Depot Ship) the following day at 8.00 a.m. Not having any Wrens in their complement at that time they treated us with great courtesy. We were surprised when they provided us with coffee and hot buttered toast and let us look over the side and see what was happening.

At a pre-arranged rendezvous the two ships reduced speed to the absolute minimum. Burdened with life jackets and hampered by skirts we clambered on to a whaler from Cyclops and were rowed across from Titania by great burly sailors. The boat was hoisted on the falls and we climbed down scrambling nets onto the boat deck. It attracted a lot of gawping spectators, but a roar from the Bridge "get your heads in from those bloody scuttles" (port-holes) soon settled them. At least this time we weren't on the shore feeling forgotten and neglected! Could it possibly be that they were beginning to accept us, and realise that as the War progressed there would be lots more of us?

Chapter Three

Wrens swarming everywhere

When I got my hook – that is became a Leading Wren, I was drafted to H.M.S. Forth, the depot ship of the Third Submarine Flotilla. She was anchored in the Holy Loch and I lived ashore in the requisitioned Ardnadam Hotel. Later as more Wrens arrived two large private houses – Cairnryan, then Cromlech, were requisitioned and I was moved along, first to one and then to the other.

It was a different set-up altogether. There were Wrens everywhere – W/T and Teleprinter Operators, writers in the pay and Captain's office, Wrens in "slops", (clothing store), Attack Teacher Wrens, and several M.T. Drivers. A great many Boats' Crew Wrens operated round the area and eventually all the Boats' Crew training for the Clyde area was undertaken by H.M.S. Forth with a senior P.O. Wren Coxswain in charge. Just as their male counterparts did, regardless of the weather, these bell-bottomed girls had to go into the boat via the iron boom ladder, out along the quarter boom and then down the jumping boom ladder.

Despite being a Leading Wren and being fairly knowledgeable about submarines, I felt a bit of a "rookie", and kept quiet about my unusual early service days. The other girls all seemed to have had several weeks training at Mill Hill London or Blundell Sands near Liverpool. There they had been taught about Naval customs and traditions. I learned they also had lots of squad drill and scrubbed floors etc. – throughout my time in the Service I never had to do either. Instead of squad drill we eventually did exercises on board Forth with the Physical Training Instructor.

The C.B. Office was still amidships but being nearer the main deck than the one on Cyclops it wasn't nearly so stuffy. The office staff consisted of an RNVR Lieut. Commander, a P.O. Wren, five Wren ratings and myself, a Leading Wren. The Chart Correctors had a separate office. As there were lots of other girls on the ship I no longer felt conspicuous as I rattled up the gangway and made my way to the office. On Cyclops we had been the first invaders of a male bastion, and had had to go very warily to avoid resentment or criticism. The general attitude towards the girls on the Forth was totally different, although we had to obey the rules laid down in KR & AI (Kings Regulation and Admiralty Instructions), in the same way as it applied to the men.

The Third Flotilla was operational, with many boats patrolling Norwegian waters and the North Sea, or going on Atlantic Convoy duties. Newly commissioned Submarines "worked up" before going to the Med. or the Fast East. The War seemed much nearer and alarmingly real. To-day's huge nuclear submarines are totally different creatures and luxuriously equipped compared to those of fifty years ago. In the early days most of the boats were known by number, but in S.3 they all had names. Those uppermost in my mind are Storm, Stoic, Stubborn, Syrtis, Stonehenge, Safari, Seraph, Seanymph, Sceptre, Graph (a captured U boat) Tempest, Triptoe, Telemachus, Templar, Tallyho, Tantivy, Trusty, Truculent, Tantalus, Uproar, Utmost, Upright, Unrivalled, Upstart, Untiring, Untamed, Venturer and Vandal, but there were many others.

I'd heard about the Jolly Roger, but had never seen one until I went to the Holy Loch. Every submarine took one on patrol – a real black pirate flag complete with white-painted skull and crossbones! The morale of the whole flotilla was boosted when a submarine returned flying its Roger. A white bar was sewn for every enemy ship sunk by torpedo, and a star signified that one had been sunk by gunfire. A dagger denoted the completion of a special mission – that was real spy stuff, often involving landing agents, leaking false plans, or bringing people out of enemy occupied land.

I particularly remember the day that Safari came back from the Mediterranean after an adventurous eighteen months with the sinking of forty enemy ships. When the order came through the tannoy "Clear the Lower Deck. Clear the Lower Deck" we all rushed up top. The other submarines left the depot ship in a manoeuvre called a "Trot fob" as Safari glided in slowly. The escorting frigate moved away to her mooring buoy and soon Safari tied up alongside Forth, her mother ship. It was a great thrill for us to see the white sweatered crew standing proudly on the casing at harbour stations with the large Roger flying from her conning tower. The Captain called "Well Forth, let us give three hearty cheers for His Majesty's Submarine Safari on successful return from war patrol." A great buzz of excitement went through the ship as he raised his gold braided cap and led the cheers. It was an especially poignant moment for Commander Ben Bryant as it was one of his old submarines, and he had actually been in command on ten of her fourteen patrols.

The men were home safely at last – to meet their loved ones, to baths, proper beds, ordinary food, to relax and forget all the strain of living and fighting in what was literally a small steel box. Somehow the close comradeship among them compensated for the cramped uncomfortable living conditions, and there were very seldom any requests to return to General Service. Unlike the aeroplane with a raid lasting only for a few hours a submarine patrol often went on for weeks. A boat could be involved in an incident in a deep mine-infested area with no news filtering back for a long time. It must have been particularly worrying for families ashore waiting in ignorance of the outcome of a patrol. Once or twice several women clustered round us as we came ashore at Ardnadam and asked if there was any news of a particular submarine. We always denied knowing anything at all but I hated these encounters more especially if I knew a boat was overdue.

Strangely no one ever used the word stress in those days but stress there most certainly was for us all. As for counselling – the whole concept was unknown. Submariners relaxing ashore, outwardly carefree were in someway like public school boys on holiday. When a sister submarine was lost they gave the impression of almost indifference. It took me some time to understand their attitude and to realise that they were far from unfeeling but seemed infected, almost protected, by a strange brand of fatalism.

On 21st February 1943 the whole Flotilla was stunned by the disappearance in home waters of Vandal without trace, and again on the 30th May by the loss of Untamed.

Vandal was not found until 1994, she lies in an area off Lochranza Arran, now declared an official war grave. Untamed was salvaged, refitted, and eventually renamed Vitality, with superstition haunting those who had to sail in her. As they were both new boats, still "working up", and neither loss was due to enemy action, there was disbelief that such disasters could have happened in the Firth of Clyde.

The month of May had started off so happily for me, and ended in personal tragedy when Geoff was lost on Untamed. We had been instantly attracted to each other, and seemed to be on the same wavelength. Although we hadn't known each other very long, we hoped, if we were spared to have a future, that it would be together.

Perhaps it wouldn't have worked – we didn't get the chance to find out. Falling in love isn't just the chemistry between two people, there's more to it than that – a kind of magic all-consuming mystery. Being in love in Wartime is a very risky exercise and many romances didn't develop into happy marriages. Thinking back I don't suppose we had given any serious thought to all that would be involved in making a life commitment.

That last evening we had a meal in MacColls Hotel, Dunoon. Wanting to avoid being involved in idle chatter with others from the Flotilla, we set out to walk along the back road to Ardnadam. It was a beautiful evening, and the Wedgewood blue sky was just fading to a paler blue as we strolled down the lane that to this day passes Cromlech on its way to the sea front. We stopped for a while and sat on a log in the little wood, and somehow a special feeling sparked off between us after only a few passionate kisses. It seems incredibly foolhardy now but despite our brief acquaintance we began to plan the immediate future. It was uncharacteristic of my normal behaviour, and afterwards I wondered how quickly I would have felt that it was all unrealistic nonsense. Forthcoming events crowded in on me.

Untamed was sailing the next morning, probably only to Campbeltown for a day or two. We both expected to be off duty the following Saturday and hoped to go to Glasgow. In the evening we would phone our respective homes and announce that we had been engagement-ring shopping. We daren't plan for the future – that was a vague uncertain state. The word death was never mentioned but lurked in the dismal dark corners of our minds.

The netted boom across the Clyde prevented direct traffic between Dunoon and Rothesay but, I found that by taking the bus to Sandy Beach, Innellan and walking to Toward, I could avoid the circuitous route home. The R.A.S.C. ran boats from Hoppers Pier right into Rothesay Harbour, and it was easy to scrounge a lift. As we'd probably only have a few hours to spare I planned to take Geoff home that way to meet Mum. It was all "ifs" and "buts" but life was like that.

Normally, regardless of whether we were aged eighteen or twenty-eight, we had to be in quarters by 10.30 p.m. Twice a week we were entitled to a late pass – until 11.00 p.m. If we were all invited in a group to a dance, or party in another establishment, an extra general pass would be allowed until midnight. On these rare occasions we all had to go out and return together in naval transport. None of us objected to the rules as they applied to everyone, but the boys grumbled, often having to hang about Ardnadam Pier waiting for the boat to take them offshore.

I shared a little cabin above the side door of Cairnryan with another two girls. That night I had a late pass. Peggy was asleep when I got back to the cabin, but I whispered my news to Jean. I swore her to secrecy as we had decided not to tell anyone until we'd been to Glasgow. Afterwards I was glad I hadn't broadcast it round the Wrennery. Jean was delighted for me and we lay whispering to each other after "lights out". She was one of the few girls who didn't work on board Forth but in Sandbank at the office of Captain M/L (Motor Launches). Peggy had been married for a few months and didn't go out very often, even to the cinema with any of the other girls. She lived in constant dread that she'd get some awful news about Jim's ship – he was on a corvette mostly employed on Russian convoy duties. Peggy spent a lot of time in the recreation room, listening to the radio, worrying and dropping tears on her letters. She was the only girl I knew who was discharged as being psycho-neurotic. The others in the office impatiently said "She cried her way out to civvie street", but I liked her very much. Before she came to the Forth she had been amongst a group of Wrens in Lowestoft who had been attacked by a German dive bomber and understandably that must have shattered her nerves. Later, when I went to visit her in Gillingham Kent I found her to be bright and happy.

The next morning Untamed had sailed before I went along to Ardnadam where meals were cooked for all three Wrens' Quarters. Outside the door I almost fell over Beryl a stoker in one of the motor boats who was poking frantically about the gravel path. As a Boats' Crew Wren she worked in watches, as did the W/T and Teleprinter Wrens. We didn't mix so much with them as we did with the girls in our office, or our cabin-mates. I vaguely knew that she'd been engaged for a couple of months, and that John had recently been transferred to

Untamed. Apparently after a stupid quarrel the previous evening, she had thrown her engagement ring at John, who had stormed off without picking it up. Suddenly "Found it" she whooped, greatly relieved. She couldn't wait to say sorry to him, but it was too late, she never got the chance to "make it up".

I never could remember who first told me that the escort had reported back that Untamed had failed to resurface, and seemed to be stuck on the sea-bed or on a ledge. Grim-faced, the older crew members on Forth were the first to realise that something seriously wrong was preventing her blowing the ballast tanks and coming back up to the surface. As the hours crawled past the news filtered through that the rescue vessels were unable to fix grappling irons and lift her. Although it was May, the weather had rapidly deteriorated, and a strong wind and choppy seas were hampering matters. No one emerged through the Davies Escape Hatch,, and the divers reported there was no response whatsoever to their knocking on the hull. All was silent inside
their steel prison below the sea. There was no hope.

All night I sat by the cabin window and wondered if the sea water seeped quickly into the batteries, and the dreaded deadly chlorine gas escaped immediately, or if it had been a slow business. I tried not to think how ghastly it would be to be the last person overcome by the fumes and see everyone else dead. These horrific thoughts crowded out everything else. I thought about Leppy, the little kitten smuggled onboard as a mascot. He was named Leppy because of his leopard-like markings, not his fierce habits. I imagined Geoff cuddling him. Maybe they fell asleep together. Maybe . . . . . .

For me it was a nightmare but I tried to remember it as a shattered dream.

In the weeks that followed Eddie, the bugler on Forth, practised the Last Post almost nightly. It echoed round the hills in a horrible haunting way. There was no escape and I desperately tried to stifle the cry within me "Why" "Why". "What is the use of it all?" I've long forgotten the sound of Geoff's voice, and infectious chuckle. Indeed even the memory of his face seems blotted out of my mind alarmingly quickly. My grief turned to rage at the senseless stupidity of War, and how it all seemed such an unexplained needless waste of young lives. The awful way that they died trapped in that tin box made it all seem doubly tragic. I mourned for all submariners – all those lost, and all who would be lost in the future.

The thirty-seven boys, in leaded coffins were eventually buried together in Dunoon. Grim reminder of War, they lie, under simple white crosses in that quiet little cemetery

Unable to face all the drama and distress of the funeral, I went home on leave, but later pieced together snippets of information about it. No one involved would ever forget the sombre, emotional event. It must have been particularly distressing for the sorrowing next of kin and very difficult for the Naval Personnel who had to try and maintain a stiff upper lip. A Naval band, playing solemn slow marches led the funeral procession from Ardnadam to Dunoon. Officials from Admiralty as well as the Forth were there; twelve Wrens were detailed to attend and an entire submarine crew from another U class submarine. It was hard to imagine how they felt when they were marched back after the ceremony to quick rousing tunes. The echoing thought "which boat will be next?" must have drummed through their heads almost swamping the sound of "Life on the Ocean Wave." It was a sad, sad time for all.

I had more or less decided not to go out with a submariner again, as I didn't want to let anyone get close to me. I was grieving for all submariners not just Geoff. Civilians were thin on the ground, but I didn't care. It was Phil who pointed out to me the selfishness and stupidity of my reaction. "Nothing can alter the past," he said. "There's a lot we don't understand but we all have to get on with living and the job on hand." His words were true. We had to pretend that things were normal, hide our true feelings, although it wasn't easy to ignore the danger waiting to pounce round the corner.

I went out with him to the cinema and dances, at first rather half-heartedly. We both enjoyed walking and didn't just go to the Cot House or along the shores of Loch Eck to the Coylet, but sometimes climbed up into the hills. With a glorious view spread out before us we momentarily forgot the world of torpedoes and trot fobs, CBs and SPs. I fear I must have been a dull companion because for a time my zest for living had been somewhat dimmed. Like most of the other boats in the Flotilla his submarine soon left and went out to the Far East.

After the War I was saddened to hear that, having contracted Polio, Phil, wheelchair bound, had been invalided out of the Navy. It was ironic to think that he had come safely through the War and then been struck down in such a way. It must have been a bitter blow as he had been in the Service since he went to Dartmouth at the age of thirteen and a half, had his Command and recently been married. Fate really was cruel. Recently I was pleased to discover that he had been able to lead a full and happy family life in the Highlands. Miraculously he had found the courage to ignore physical disabilities and whizzing around in his hand-controlled car had kept himself busy helping other people without complaining about his "rotten luck."

After Untamed was lost Beryl, doubly heartbroken that John and she had parted angrily, devoted her time to trying to make everyone patch up quarrels. "Don't tell me you two girls are arguing over some kirbigrips when serious things are happening?" She'd always insist that apologies were given. "Never let the sun go down on your wrath" she'd say – I'm sure she went on saying it all her life. She loathed confrontation and always preferred agreement to disagreement. I've often wondered what happened to her and if she ever went back to the Holy Loch.

A lifetime ago in the Hydro, wearing high heels and a dash of lipstick I'd fondly thought I was an adult at last. At that time no one could have vaguely imagined what lay ahead and what fate decreed. I reckon all of us attached to the Third Submarine Flotilla REALLY did grow up quickly. It seemed as if the War would never end, and we learned to deal with life on a daily basis. We dare not look beyond, and acted our parts as gaily as we could for tomorrow was a blurred uncertainty. Sometimes in the dead of night, unable to sleep, I'd wonder how many more thousands would be wounded, buried alive, burnt, shot, starved, suffocated, imprisoned or drowned before it all ended. It seemed so senseless. Perhaps selfishly, but naturally, our chief concern was the part of the War in which we were involved. In the middle of things ourselves, we seldom hung around quarters waiting for the radio news bulletins of progress in other sections.

The boys were up to all sorts of mad tricks. One evening, I think it was someone's birthday, half a dozen of us were having dinner in MacColl's Hotel and Jack accepted the dare to eat all the daffodils from the flower vase. Generously sprinkling them with salt and some pepper he devoured the lot! It really put the elderly couple at the next table off their meal. They looked a trifle horrified and probably thought "These silly youngsters are surely drunk" whereas it was just a typical mad caper.

None of the old ladies battling with the weeds in the Ardnadam gardens and startled by the sound of a hunting horn being blown in the back lanes ever suspected that it was just boys from Tallyho skylarking, and that they were off to the Mediterranean in the morning – probably to death and destruction. It wasn't boredom but the release of pent-up feelings that led them into boyish pranks, and never the mindless vandalism of the present time. Conscious of the posters warning "Careless talk cost lives" we seldom spoke of work within our peer group, far less to civilians.

Life is a woven pattern with one thread leading on, or twisting back to another – a kind of patchwork quilt. The Kyles Hydro came back into the pattern with more grey and black threads than had been in the first bright patch. Requisitioned by the Navy in 1942, named H.M.S. Varbel, it was transformed into the headquarters of the Twelfth Submarine Flotilla. This, newest branch of the Service, was set up specially to train personnel for midget submarines and human torpedoes. A secondary base, Varbell II, was in Ardtarig, a house in a remote spot at the head of Loch Striven, ideally situated for the vigorous training for these new ugly-looking craft. Ugly, deadly and very secret.

The Forth Wrens were sometimes invited to dances at Ardtarig. It was a long way from civilisation, and involved a bumpy ride in a Naval truck along a narrow moor road from Sandbank. In the blackout most of the girls had no idea where the transport was going. Life in midgets was even more precarious than in conventional submarines. They all had the same attitude – "Let's enjoy this moment – who knows what tomorrow will bring?" They worked hard and played hard. Now more than fifty years later, Ardtarig is a fish farm, but the moor road is still for the most part a single track, and sometimes as I sit in my car in a lay-by, waiting for a couple of tourists' cars to pass, I wonder if the laughing ghost of the past still runs through the rooms at Ardtarig. He'd certainly laugh to see those of us who are left, now old and arthritic, but going on as best we can, trying not to repeat ourselves, or bore the young with tales of long ago!

A strong thread from Varbel twisted back and linked to our office on Forth. In addition to the Signal Publications we had C.Bs. (Confidential Books) which were kept up to date from the reports of Fleet Air Arm Reconnaissance Planes etc. The C.Bs also had little mysterious bits of information more like the "secret" stuff I'd dreamt about. Before a special Mission the Submarine's Commanding Officer would be briefed by Forth's Staff Officer, and if relevant come down to our office to study a C.B. It was absolutely forbidden for any notes to be taken, so all reports had to be read over and over again until every detail was familiar.

Some of the boxes dealt with Norway; and Alten Fiord turned out to be particularly important. The Germans felt that their prize 41,000 ton battleship Tirpitz lurking there, so far from the open sea was quite safe, as it seemed impossible for a submarine to get through all the protecting nets and mines; furthermore it would be too far for small craft to make such a long hazardous journey. A new plan evolved for the parent submarines from Forth to tow the midgets for several hundred miles.

Admiral (Submarines) came up from Northways, himself and "Cleared the Lower Deck." He emphasised to the depot ship crew the importance of secrecy. It was almost a suicide mission, if they reached the target they would either be lost or taken prisoner. With great trepidation we awaited some news and the return of the S.3 submarines involved, Truculent, Thrasher, Syrtis, Sea-nymph, Stubborn and Sceptre. We were still sworn to secrecy and, even after the raid, had to ensure that the Third Submarine Flotilla's involvement was not leaked. The story of the gallantry of the X Craft Personnel cannot be condensed into a few pages, but has been immortalised in several books.

A brief statement was released to the media on 12th October 1943 stating that on the 22nd September British Midget Submarines had daringly penetrated Alten Fiord, 200 miles within the Arctic Circle, attacking and grievously wounded the Tirpitz. Few people even in the Navy knew that British Midget Submarines existed. It had been a well kept secret. Several years later the full story of Operation Source was revealed and the "Supreme endurance and contempt for danger" of these boys was realised.

Chapter Four

Damp squib at D-Day

On May 19th 1944 I was promoted to the rank of Petty Officer and told that I'd be drafted the following day to Portsmouth for onward placing. Panic stations! As soon as I was ashore I telephoned Mum, gobbled down the evening meal, and rushed up to Cromlech to pack and make all the necessary uniform changes. In Naval jargon I had "got my buttons" and all the black uniform buttons had to be exchanged for brass ones. The Leading Wren's hook had to be unpicked and replaced by the Petty Officer's badge on jacket sleeves and great coat. I was about to sew the P.Os badge on my new tricorn hat when Mary snatched it from me, grabbing the scissors as she said "That thing is like a pudding basin. You certainly can't go off looking like that." Brushing aside my protests she cut a chunk off the crown.

"Don't worry" she said "I used to be a milliner in civvies street." She made a splendid job of reassembling it without leaving the seam showing, and the finished result was a distinct improvement.

The original Wren's hats had been old-fashioned frumpish creations and we had all been delighted when an Admiralty Fleet Order was issued regarding our uniform. The hats were changed to a much more attractive style a cross between a beret and a matelot's cap. With the help of the sailors we all sported a "tiddley bow" with a sixpence inside, an old trick to make the bow stand up properly. Unfortunately no photograph exists of me in anything but the old dowdy hat. After that AFO came out we were allowed to wear plain clothes for recreational purposes, and when off duty quickly changed into civilian clothes. Bending the rules a little we reckoned almost everywhere we went everything we did could be classed as recreational.

Travelling during wartime was quite hazardous and trains often had long unexplained delays. The Glasgow to London train was very crowded and I was very lucky to get a seat. Soon the corridors, noisy and smoky were blocked with Service men and women, kit bags, respirators, and some battered suitcases. Memories flashed back to 1942 – Before I left Cyclops I had turned down the opportunity of promotion and gaining the tricorn hat of a Wren Officer. Having been recommended for a Commission I was interviewed in Greenock by three Senior Wren Officers. Questions about my friends, hobbies, favourite piece of music and holiday venues presented little difficulty, but I was somewhat nonplussed when asked "What do you think of communal washing?" The idea didn't appeal to me but I evaded a direct answer by saying "I don't suppose it would be very different from a Girl Guide Camp".

They consulted for a few moments, and then told me that as C.B. Officers had tremendous responsibilities it was unusual to give a Commission in this category to a Wren under the age of 22. They were, however, sure that I had the potential for a good Cypher Officer. To their surprise, I thanked them but declined the offer explaining that I felt cyphering would soon become a monotonous boring job and I'd rather stay in a C.B. Office and, in fact was quite happy as a rating. I never regretted that decision although was pleased to have changed my rating's hat for the new shape. Since then I have been sorry that I never had even one snapshot of me in the tricorn!It was strange to have to move away from all my friends and stranger still after just one day in Portsmouth to go to work in H.M.S. Shrapnel, a shore base in Southampton. A Lloyds Bank Building near the docks had been requisitioned – rumour had it that they were only given twenty-four hours notice to quit. The Bank building was ideal with large walk-in vaults where hopefully all the secret material would be buried safely underground when a large scale air raid took place.

This time I didn't feel in the least like a new girl, as we were all starting afresh having been drafted from all over the country and actually moved in with the furniture. There were about twenty girls. Freda another P.O., three or four Leading Wrens, two Sub-Lieutenants, a Wren Second Officer, a couple of messengers, a motor cycle dispatch rider, two M.T. Wrens and an R.N.V.R. Lieutenant Commander with the amazing name – Rex de Mountjoy Rudolf! in overall charge. He was a terrific organiser and divided up jobs with apparent random and yet with care to have an experienced person in each group.

Southampton Water was alive with ships, and I had quickly to switch my mind from submarines to M.T.Bs, Minesweepers, Corvettes and all manner of landing craft – L.C.Ts, L.S.Ts, L.C.Hs etc. I knew that L.C.T. stood for Landing Craft (Troops) but the rest I had to work out for myself. It was, of course, very hush-hush, and we weren't allowed to make 'phone calls or post letters. Looking back, the days in the week leading up to D.Day blur together into work and sleep. Off duty we couldn't even enjoy the luxury of soaking in a hot bath, as a black line painted about five inches from the bottom indicated the maximum amount of water we were supposed to use! Every drop of water had to be conserved for hospital ships and other essential purposes, and most days not even a trickle of water came out of the hot tap!

American Military Police, (nicknamed "Snowdrops") controlled the traffic in the streets round Southampton's dockland, to let the convoys through. Everyone in Hampshire speculated about the large scale manoeuvre obviously afoot, with troops, lorries and tanks moving in all directions. It was later revealed that many false plans had been deliberately leaked to the enemy; leading them to expect an invasion in the Pas de Calais, or even in Norway. Wrens from the D.A. were to be based on all the main loading hards in Southampton, Lymington, Lepe etc. I was put in charge of a night watch on Town Quay. The plan was that waves of assault craft would land troops on the beaches, pull out quickly and hopefully return to the home base. Although these small vessels carried very little in the way of confidential matter, it had all to be kept up to date. As the ships' officers responsible would have no time to come to the D.A. the craft had to be physically boarded each time they came into port. This was the job allocated to us, with twelve hour watches being worked in the first critical days.

The messengers, drivers and motor dispatch riders, not being so directly involved, were put out of the office. Then Lt. Cmdr. R. stood up on one of the long tables normally used by the correctors and said:-

"Well girls, this is it. To-morrow is D Day. This is why we have all been working so hard. Let us hope this is the beginning of the end of this ghastly War. These are proud moments, but make no mistake it isn't over yet by a long chalk. There's still a lot of blood, sweat and tears to come – but we'll get there." He went on to ask those in charge of watches to go to the loading hards, study the area and walk slowly back to quarters. Then he told us to go back to the hard, and then walk slowly to the administrative headquarters in Bugle Street.

He emphasised that we had to ensure we were thoroughly familiar with the route as immediately after H hour D.Day, it was expected that the Germans would retaliate with a fierce air bombardment - concentrated on Portsmouth and Southampton, and in particular on the loading hards. Fallen buildings and rubble would distort the whole face of the landscape. He continued:-

"No one will have time to help if you are lost, so make absolutely sure you can find alternative routes. As all probability the Admin. Offices in Bugle Street will be bombed, and records destroyed, I suggest that those in charge of the watches carry with them at all times, a duplicate list of next-to-kin. See to all that now."

He ended with the chilling words:-

"I'll move from place to place and help where needed. Second Officer and a group of girls will man the office. If I am killed she will take over, and if she too is killed the Petty Officers will be in charge. Heaven help us if they too are all killed. Don't forget the Bank Vaults – the contents will surely be alright and you'll be safe there too in a heavy air-raid. Good luck." A shiver ran down my spine more of excitement than fear. Disregarding our vulnerable position I thought "This can't be real. I'm watching a film."

Off we went trying to visualise how the area might be altered by shattered gas and water mains and fallen masonry. As our job involved boarding each craft, it was suggested that since the ramps were often under a foot of water, it would be sensible to hitch a lift across on the running board of a lorry. No thought had been given to the return journey and without Wellingtons I reckoned we'd have very wet feet for the best part of twelve hours every day.

That evening I sat in the Recreation Room taking up my bellbottoms. (issued to us at last). Frankie, one of the oldest girls – probably over thirty, studied me closely and remarked that I had a very red face. "Are you awfully hot?" she asked. I hoped all the excitement wasn't showing in my face. Some others gathered round declaring that I'd come out in spots. Ignoring my loud protests Frankie marched me down to Sick Bay. The duty Q.A. (Queen Alexandra's Nurse) diagnosed measles and the doctor confirmed it. "German Measles" he said. I was most upset, especially as I didn't feel ill at all. I asked him to 'phone Lt. Cmdr. R. and get his assurance that we were up to the eyes in work, and I couldn't be spared from the office.

"Where do you work?" he queried.

"In the D.A."

"D.A. What's that?"

"The Distributing Authority"

"Distributing Authority? What do you distribute?"

"I'm not really allowed to say, but books and maps, things like that."

"Good grief – just the things to transmit germs. Oh, well it can't be helped. It is only a mild attack. Have you been in contact with any ships lately?"

He was flabbergasted when I explained that at least a dozen C.B. Officers from the larger ships lying in Southampton Water had called at the office the previous day, or had had books delivered out to them. Despite all my protests he said I had to be quarantined immediately, and wouldn't even let me go back to the cabin to collect my things, but agreed that as I'd only be off duty for a few days I could stay in the Sick Bay. In this respect I was lucky as all hospitals in the Southampton and Portsmouth areas had already been evacuated inland to make immediate bed space available for air raid casualties and clearing stations for the hospital ships.

About half an hour later Matron popped her head round the door and, in rather a disgusted tone said:-

"Oh, you are the infectious case. You won't be allowed in the air raid shelter. When the warning goes, just get up and lie under the bed. You will be as safe there as anywhere."

To everyone's amazement the dreadful bombardment over the town didn't materialise, and the air raid warning never went all night. Southampton already bore many scars of previous raids with the main shopping street, the Bargate, having been more or less been obliterated. I had more than my usual trouble in getting to sleep that night – it wasn't the spots that bothered me but I visualised half of the Navy being struck down with measles and the invasion would be a failure! No doubt I wasn't an isolated case, but I never heard of anyone else similarly affected, or found out how I caught it!

In the morning the V.A.D. taking the blackout shutter down told me that it had just been announced on the radio that the Allies had landed on the Normandy coast. Choking back tears of frustration I mumbled "Have they?" It really was the last straw to be stuck in bed on that most important day. My mother received a telegram "Your daughter is safe and well but unable to communicate." She rushed round to tell Jenny that she thought I'd been sent to France – some hope!

I was pleased when I later learned that two midget submarines X20 and X23 had lain off the beaches for a couple of days before D Day and had led the British and Canadian forces ashore. As their mission was code-named "Gambit" they weren't exactly reassured to discover that this was the term for a throwaway move in chess, where a piece or person was sacrificed to secure an advantage. It was all the more difficult, as, with the twenty-four hour postponement their oxygen supply was in danger of running out. Submarines still held a special place in my heart, and I was always proud that I'd worked with them for several years. Although soon released from hospital I felt cheated at not being part of D Day itself. Years later I grimaced when I heard it referred to as the longest day. It was certainly so for me – a very long, long miserable day.

When the craft returned from France the boys grumbled "It is just like running a ruddy bus service," complaining "We don't know what is happening. Tell us – how is the War going?" They were desperate for news and devoured all the newspapers we could get. It seemed incredible that they didn't know what was happening, or how the troops had fared after they had landed on the beaches.

For most people 55BC and 1066 are memorable dates, and all true Scots also know 1314, 1603 and 1745. Here we were, taking part in Operation Neptune and not fully realising that 6th June 1944 would become a most important date too. Even the dullest of lives threaded through the patchwork pattern of history. As the beach heads were quickly established, watch-keeping hours were abandoned and everyone was recalled to the office. Seeing thousands of Canadians and Americans on the way to France, I thought how remote their homeland must seem too them. I felt very far away from the hills and lochs of Western Scotland but if I shut my eyes tightly I could see it all clearly, all so beautiful, so quiet, and far removed from this ghastly world of men, machines, tanks and troops. When a major port like Cherbourg came into allied hands, there was great excitement – but also quite a flap in the office. More staff arrived and additional space acquired. Ideally situated down a side road near the Lloyds Bank office, Ocean Trading Company's store was requisitioned. R. moved across and I was sent there too with a group of Wrens. The main benefit was gained from the huge underground cellars, partly under a

Pub, but with the innermost part under a Public Lavatory. We didn't linger down below any longer than we had to, as we were never too sure which smells came from where!

Anyone passing the big wooden door in the lane couldn't have had any idea that anything out of the ordinary lay behind its flaking grey painted exterior. Hidden from view, inside the cobbled courtyard the sentry in response to a knock on a certain panel, activated the door electronically. This unfortunate sailor (usually an old three-badge long service man) must have been terribly bored. He didn't know what we were doing, or what he was guarding. Hour after hour he must have thought "Can this be why I joined the Navy?" I wondered what he'd tell his pals in the pub at home! Maybe he was pleased to have a "quiet number" but I doubt it. None of us visualised that in years ahead garage doors and T.V. sets could be operated by remote control, and things like mobile phones would be taken for granted.

As the distance between the office and the Continental ports grew, distribution from the office became more difficult. SHAEF (Supreme Headquarters, Allied Expeditionary Force) had a boat crossing the Channel daily, and we took urgent material to Fort Southwick for onward transmission. Once Lyn, one of our M.T. drivers, and I were delayed when a Royal Marine motor-cyclist flagged us down and insisted we waited until some V.I.Ps passed down from the Fort. Vainly we protested we had "Red Priority" and should be allowed through immediately. We'd already travelled along a nightmare section of road almost jammed with lorries and troops on the move between Portsmouth and Southampton, and were almost at our destination.

I remember grumbling "V.I.Ps? – huh. You'd think they were in a different War from us. We've got to get through." Soon down the road came a staff car with Winston Churchill and General Montgomery, followed by another one with General Eisenhower. At the Despatch Office, Jill, the duty P.O. told me that Churchill had asked a few pertinent questions, and seemed to appreciate the problems we had serving these newly established bases. If we had been five or ten minutes earlier he'd certainly have spoken to me. So that's the story of how Churchill didn't speak to me – just as I missed out on D.Day – damp squibs both of them. Both areas of grey thread in the patchwork of my life.

Off duty we didn't hang around quarters for long – we had a

hectic social life. Frequently there would be an invitation for a group of us to attend a dance at an RAF base, a transit camp or a hospital, so we met a cross-section of all ranks and services. It was at one of these dances I met Steve – he was in the Fleet Air Arm stationed at Eastleigh. I was really startled a few weeks later when he asked me to marry him. It was totally unexpected, and unrealistic. Although I liked him a lot, I didn't really know him very well, and our relationship hadn't, in my opinion, developed to anything like that stage. I certainly wasn't ready or anxious to be anyone's wife! I managed to refuse him firmly but kindly. He was awaiting an overseas posting, so probably that had something to do with it.

I was surprised when Graham from the Princess Iris sought me out. I'd only met him twice and that was away back in Cyclops days. I barely remembered him. We took the ferry across to Bitterne and spent a pleasant evening chatting in a little pub there. We were both off duty on the Saturday and went by bus to Romsey in the New Forest.

After lunch we were wandering aimlessly round the shops when, to my amazement, he stopped at a jeweller's window and suggested I chose an engagement ring. I was astonished, utterly astonished and almost laughed at the absurdity of the idea. I really was tempted to give the traditional "This is so sudden" reply. It was ridiculous – we were only casual acquaintances, and of course I rejected his suggestion.

It didn't just happen to me. Rene my cabin mate and I discussed it and tried to decide why so many girls were getting proposals. Mostly we'd been to parties, cinemas or dances with the boys and hadn't spent long enough alone with them to find out what made them tick. Facing an unknown posting they had time to brood and think about things. Although they'd never admit it and hiding under outward bravado they were alternatively scared stiff or bored. They wanted as an anchor in their topsy-turvy world, someone who could understand it. Family and the girl-next-door belonged to another life. I'm sure they never thought clearly of all the implications of "marrying in haste." Incredible as it seems in today's world, moral standards were totally different and the boys never suggested to a "nice girl" that they slept together. In all fairness, the opportunities didn't readily present themselves, and it was before the advent of the Pill or perhaps we would all have acted differently.

We girls were also far from home and trapped by the ugly war machine. The past was remote, the future just a hazy dream, only the present was real. War-time friendships were strange. Often we knew nothing of each other's family background, yet in conversation little intimate things would creep in. Regrets at things undone and time wasted would be revealed – dreams and hopes too.

Not surprisingly there were several broken romances. Freda's engagement to Jim, a rear gunner in the RAF, came to an abrupt end. He wrote from the Middle East to say he'd fallen in love with a WAAF and as soon as they had the necessary permission they were going to be married. Hazel a really vivacious red-haired chart corrector and Hank her American boyfriend appeared to be ideally suited. A special aura of happiness around them somehow set them apart. We were all surprised when he confessed one day that he was married. Hazel's world fell apart. She refused to listen to his pleas that his marriage had been over and that he had planned to get a divorce long before he met her. Feeling cheated, she said she'd never trust anyone again, she stopped seeing him, wouldn't answer his phone calls – tore up his letters, and went around stony-faced. Shortly afterwards she went on an overseas posting so we never learned how her story ended. I still keep in touch with Rena – now happily married and living in Canada, but in the Southampton days she had been engaged to Derry – a midshipman about five years younger than she was. It all ended in tears when he wrote to say it had been a mistake – he had rashly become engaged before he left the U.K. but now, three months later, saw things differently. He realised he didn't want to get married to anyone for years and years. There was too many places yet unseen, many people still to meet, books to read, pictures to paint, songs to sing – and lots of things to do before he thought of settling down. I felt he had written very honestly but Rena was terribly upset. In a way it was exactly the way I felt myself. I'd already had some unusual experiences but there was still much left undone. I had tried to explain this to Steve, Graham and others who came along with similar aspirations. At that stage I wouldn't have made a very good wife with little experience of running a house and other people had cooked all my meals ever since I left school. I expect that, years later, they were all glad I'd said "no" and reckoned they had had a lucky escape!

It had been different in a Submarine Flotilla, where we were all like a huge family, sharing joys, hopes and sorrow too. Very few of the boys were married and those who were usually had wives and children living around the Holy Loch. Many of the wives didn't have an inkling of how insecure the future was, or realise that their happiness was so delicately balanced. They appeared deceived by all the talk of "It is much safer under the sea" and usually swallowed the story "We are only going exercising off the North of Scotland." In the same way as Jack at the Hydro had fooled his parents, the boys used those cover-up tales to avoid their home lives being threatened by the nightmare of dangers ahead. Or were they fooled? ..... I wonder ....

The shuttle moves and threads run back to the moon. It has always fascinated me, but since Jack's reaction at the Hydro, I'd felt somewhat differently about it. Thinking back to Ardnadam – the moon was Claire's undoing. Second Officer saw her clearly one bright night, when the world was silver in the moonlight, and the shadows of the hills on the water dark and black. She was standing at Cairnyan's gate, arms entwined round a married naval officer. Up until then there had just been a whisper about this Boat's Crew Wren's romance, but I suspect some of her cabin mates knew about it. We had all been well warned that no breath of scandal would be tolerated and that good-night kiss was enough for Second Officer to take action. Within about three days Clare was drafted to Plymouth, where, conveniently it seemed a Motor Boat Coxswain was urgently required. There were plenty of single men to choose from, and while I was there I only heard of this one incident.

It was different in Southampton off duty we all went our separate ways. With no common link of understanding between us, we weren't involved in each other's emotional experiences. On Forth the loss of a submarine affected the whole Flotilla, but in H.M.S. Shrapnel a missing soldier, the non return of a craft, or a shot down plane only mattered to those personally concerned.

There was a seedy looking café next to the main office, nicknamed the Greasy Spoon. A sleepy cat sat in front of a blackboard in the window. Now and again it stirred to chase one of the many flies not yet trapped by the revolting strips of gluey paper that hung from the ceiling. On the blackboard an illiterate type scrawl announced "To-day's special" which, amazingly, was often Roast Beef or Steak Pie. Despite its unsavoury appearance it was a very popular meeting-place for service-men, particularly Americans. I was convinced the café owners were in the Black Market, probably getting supplies from a nearby USA camp. Every forenoon the Wren Messenger brought across a tray of steaming hot tea and a scrumptious half slice of hot buttered toast for each of us and we paid something like 1p. each. One day there was no toast. R. had a little office at the far end of the big room where a dozen correctors worked and I sat at a desk facing down the room. When he wanted something he seldom used the internal 'phone but just leant back in his chair and bellowed "P.O." to summon me.

He'd been on an outside call when the tea arrived and complained "That fool girl has forgotten my toast." "Yes", I said, "She told me that there was none because the Greasy Spoon has been raided."

"I knew the Police would get them soon or later." he replied.

"Yes, they were in the Black Market."

He roared with laughter and nearly choked as I went on with my theory about the popularity of the place, and how huge trucks used to pull up outside. I'd never actually seen them carrying in sides of beef but imagined they waited for cover of the blackout. Our conversation ended as someone came into the office and I went back to my desk, giving it no further thought.

Later I called R. down the cellar to see a leak in the roof. Dripping water was obliterating copy numbers on special books made of a new kind of litmus type paper. This was a serious matter, as they were all "on charge" and a very strict record kept. When a ship was lost with all the books on board a great deal of paper work was involved, and destruction certificates had to be sent off to Admiralty. To lose a book from the office stock was equally serious.

After he dealt with it he said to me:-

"Were you pulling my leg, or do you really not know why that place was raided?" I repeated my theory.

"Good grief," he said, "You had better get back to that little island. This wicked world is no place for you." I hadn't the faintest idea what he was talking about and was totally unprepared when, in response to my queries, Moira, my little Cockney typist said, "Why, P.O. it is a brothel – everyone knew that!"

A brothel! I was astonished. Reading about brothels had given me a vague idea that they were in Paris, or flashy West End London spots. It seems quite unbelievable now, but I certainly didn't imagine that a flat, attached to a café, at a busy street corner could be one.

It's quite obvious now that it wasn't food that drew the customers in like a magnet! Up until then I had thought prostitutes would be young glamorous types with model girl figures. I'd never noticed any females around before but when the café eventually reopened I saw several middle-aged, rather shabby looking females hanging around. Can they be "the girls?" I wondered.

Telling the story against myself some years later someone said "You weren't just innocent, you were plain dumb." How could I have been so daft? I was incredibly naïve. R. of course thought it was a huge joke and kept bringing it up at every opportunity. He told me; "I bet what you think is a nice tea-room in that place in Scotland is a hot-bed of vice."

I didn't really believe him, but when I came home on leave I eyed with suspicion the Town Councillors and others who seemed to be eternally drinking coffee in Allans! But "No," I thought "He is wrong – it is also full of couples and old ladies." It was indeed all it seemed to be – a genuinely respectable establishment. I never investigated the exact location of any Rothesay "den of iniquity" but now I realise there probably were several. I had read too many books and still lived in cloud-cuckoo land, but slowly was beginning to realise that people and places are very often not what they seem at first sight. R. teased me unmercifully and lost no opportunity to tell people how I came from a little island in Scotland where there was no vice.

Rena, my cabin mate and I got on like a house on fire and we were both friendly with Freda, the P.O. Wren in the main office of the D.A. On our days off we often went to Winchester and once saw the Ballet Rambert in Salisbury. It was a great treat for me as there's little opportunity to see ballet in Bute. Zena, a P.O. in the Fleet Mail Office had a small cottage in Minstead in the depth of the New Forest and the four of us once spent a marvellous weekend there. It was a picture-postcard cottage complete with thatched roof, raftered rooms and even roses round the door. It was wonderful to be able to relax far from the sight of bombed out buildings, and ugly gap sights. Streets of buildings have never been my scene and often in quiet moments before I went to sleep I'd think of a lovely peaceful spot like Scalpsie Bay with Goatfell on Arran looming high in the background.

Much of Southampton had been destroyed in air raids but surprisingly the Guildhall had escaped the German Bombers' attention.

One concert in particular held in the Guildhall lingered in my mind for a long time. Coming out after having been quite lost in Debussy's "Prelude a L'après midi d'une faune" I blinked when I was abruptly brought back to reality by the sight of the rubbish strewn bomb craters. Threads pulled back to the Old Cyclops days and the surprise view of the town after a day spent below deck. "All that was years ago, in another world," I thought.

No matter how tired I was, or how busy, I usually managed to read a chapter or two of a book, although I no longer devoured books as previously had been my habit. I wrote a few letters too – more scrappy notes than letters. I wrote home frequently and, in return Mum sent long newsy letters, and the local paper, the Buteman. Most of my peers were in the services by this time – Betty in the WAAF, Jean with the Army Nursing Service in Burma, Netta in a Munitions Factory, Cathie was in the Fire Service, Margaret was a medical student and Irene was in the A.T.S. I used to keep in touch by scribbling notes at odd moments, and in odd places – sometimes I'd write amongst the dirty tea-cups in a café, or on a train or even on a bus. Nowadays when I get complaints about the illegibility of my handwriting, I blame it on all the hurried scribbles I sent off in wartime.

Irene and I hadn't met for ages, but eventually when she was stationed near Aldershot, we managed to get weekend passes and went off to Bournemouth. The town was very busy and we tried vainly to get into the Y.W.C.A. Only the very ritzy hotels had vacancies and we couldn't afford anything grand, but had to be content with a back
street bed-and-breakfast house. It didn't look too bad on the outside but it certainly wasn't very welcoming. The bedroom walls were plastered with notices. They warned:-

No smoking - No food or drink allowed in the room No washing to be hung up

No lights on after 11.00 p.m. No baths unless by prior arrangement 2/6d each.

As the landlady hadn't put up a "No talking" notice, we sat on the lumpy bed and chatted madly for half the night; exchanging news and talked over some of the escapades we had had away back in beautiful Bute.

We wondered if children still played by the burn and crawled under the road on to the Pointhouse shore. Was there still a sea of bluebells on the Kildavannan Hill, and was the shore there still covered with white chuckies? Would it all look the same to us when we returned with older, sadder eyes? We hoped so. In the meantime we both worked with people who had never heard the word chuckies for stones, and laughed at us when we called our little fingers pinkies! We had grown to realise we were bi-lingual and spoke Scots and English too! The War was over before we met again and our lives went in totally different directions. To this day we are still the best of friends.

Chapter Five

Peace and the party pooper

T hirty of us were invited to a dance in a remote part of Salisbury Plain, one night in September 1944. It proved to be a super affair with a good band, and handsome paratroopers as partners. They had gone to a lot of trouble decorating a large aircraft hanger with giant gaily coloured parachutes. Three days later we heard the dreadful news about Arnhem and how many lives were sacrificed by being sent "a bridge too far". Most of the happy boys we met never came back.

The Allies were making steady progress but the Germans, determined to keep every mile, fought on. Their secret weapon – V.1 – the flying bomb came in slowly, but when the engine cut out a weapon of destruction fell to the ground. When they launched V.2 rockets they travelled ahead of their second waves and without warning rushed sinisterly earthwards causing unbelievable damage. Still the War dragged on – would it never end?

Plans were afoot for me to go with six Wrens to Rotterdam, but the idea was abandoned when the Sub. Lieut. sent to requisition quarters, was killed in a "buzz-bomb" raid. As far as I can remember Director WRNS was still willing to let us go, but C.-in-C. Portsmouth disagreed, or perhaps it was those faceless Admiralty officials who raised objections?

Later it was planned to set up a C.B. Office in Hamburg and I enthusiastically went to Southampton University on a crash course in German. Having learnt it all so quickly I have retained very little. Our cabin had en-suite facilities, and with the end of water rationing I used to delight in lolling in the bath. Nightly I muttered German irregular verbs or rolled my tongue round phrases like "Der strassenbanwagon kommit und wir steigen ein" Rena used to complain "Stop muttering and come out of there." The War ended before the Hamburg office was established and that scheme never materialised either.

Quite often the D.A. arranged the onward transmission of

a load of bags (books and diplomatic material) to Canada and the U.S.A. An officer courier locked securely in a railway compartment brought them from Admiralty. Lieut. Commander R. or one of the other officers should have dealt with it, but, once or twice he bent the rules a little and sent me with a naval working party to meet the train. As the sailors loaded the bags onto a lorry they'd wisecrack that an Admiral must be sending antiques out of the country. The bags, all sealed with a special leaded seal, were heavy and often queerly shaped.

We had absolute priority to requisition space in one of the ship's holds. I can now imagine the chagrin of the Chief Officer of a ship like the Queen Mary, or the Ile de France, when a young girl like me arrived waving this all-powerful scrap of paper. One Mate I remember grumbled "What the hell is in these bags anyway?" Once on the Queen Mary, coming back with the receipt I got lost! Coming down in a different lift, I must have turned to port instead of starboard. To my shame I had to ask for directions to the gangway – a proper sailor like me!

By 2nd May 1945 things were beginning to look much brighter, and we listened eagerly to radio news bulletins. It was reported that Hitler had committed suicide, and Admiral Doenitz was in charge. Italian partisans had shot Mussolini and his mistress. We each harboured the secret hope that the end of the War in Europe was very close, but daren't voice the thought. During the afternoon of 7th May a signal arrived at the office divulging the wonderful news that the War was over. Churchill was to make the official announcement on the radio the following afternoon at 3.00 p.m. This time was carefully chosen to suit all the other countries involved. Wildly excited we rushed back to quarters to tell the others. Those who hadn't seen the signal were still a bit sceptical. I can't remember when the BBC News Bulletin announced it to the general public. Most of us sat that evening in stunned disbelief in the recreation room, having heard of wild parties and dancing in the street at the end of the 1st World War it all seemed a tremendous anti-climax. The initial feeling of great relief and excitement had fizzled out like a burst bubble. Suddenly we felt old and tired.

Although the War in Europe was over, it was hard to see how we could expect a quick end to hostilities in the Far East. Had we the courage and strength to carry on? Whereas before we didn't think of the future we now viewed it with uncertainty. A great deal had happened and our lives had been turned upside down. Mixed with all the heartbreak, danger and harrowing experiences, there was great comradeship, loyalty, pride, fun and laughter.

With the office locked at lunchtime on the 8th May, we all went to the Guildhall to hear Winston Churchill. Amazingly, although the Bargate had been almost obliterated the Guildhall stood unharmed by enemy bombs. It was no longer a rumour – we had heard for ourselves that the War really was over! At last there was a party-atmosphere, with crowds singing, dancing, cheering and hugging perfect strangers. Four uniformed sailors splashed around the specially turned on fountains.

We joined a group of Americans dancing a snake-like conga down the Bargate with some foolhardy ones climbing in and out of the bomb craters. It was all more like I had expected it would be. In London there was a tremendous celebration with the singing, cheering crowd in Piccadilly, Trafalgar Square, pushing down the Mall to Buckingham Palace. When Churchill appeared on the Palace Balcony with the Royal Family a tremendous roar arose from the hysterically happy people. The atmosphere was electric. Later we saw it all on the cinema newsreel and envied those who had been part of such a memorable scene. "Now", we thought "there's only the Japanese to beat."

R. the boss, worked like a Trojan in a crisis but now that things had quietened down, had a habit of disappearing around noon vaguely muttering something about the Dolphin Hotel. I had to wait in the office until he returned, and in Quarters they always kept a meal aside for me. One day, even later than usual, I went straight to the Mess before going up to my cabin. The Wren Steward had long since cleared away the evidence of a meal. As she was taking the rather dried-up plate of unappetising looking meat and potatoes out of the oven a messenger came to say that Chief Officer wanted to see me immediately. I wondered what was wrong but I couldn't think of any crime I'd committed – Perhaps I'd absentmindedly passed an Officer in the street without saluting? Smiling broadly Chief Officer said "Do sit down P.O. I have some good news. Your promotion to Chief Wren has just come through." I was absolutely stunned. It was the last thing I expected. Unable to believe I'd heard correctly I immediately said:-
"There's been a mistake Ma'am. I haven't been a P.O. long enough

to be even at the bottom of the promotion roster." "Yes," she replied, "I know. There has been no mistake. C.-in-C. has sent this signal and you've been advanced for the splendid work you did over the D-day period."

I was so amazed that afterwards I never could remember whether I had been advanced fifteen, fifty or five hundred places! "Is he allowed to do that?" I asked. "Oh yes," she laughed, "The Commander-in-Chief has power to do all those type of things." She went on about official recommendation for devotion to duty, but I was too dazed to take in all she said. Seeing the expression of my face she queried "What's the matter, aren't you happy? "I thought you'd be delighted. I'm very pleased and proud of you."

I blurted out "No, I don't like Chiefs", and, silly ass that I was, "I don't know what the others will say as I never did anything special." All my life I've worried about what "they" think and been inhibited because of what I thought their reactions would be. It has taken me a long long time to realise that people are too busy with their own affairs to give me more than a passing thought.

Still hardly believing this incredible news I went down to the Mess and said to the Steward "I'm sorry I can't eat that. I've just been made a Chief." As she removed the offending plate she drew me a dirty look. I feared that she had got the impression that now I held the exalted rank of Chief Wren I wouldn't eat the Petty Officer's meal – not that they got anything different to eat! There were only four Chiefs in the Unit, all old in my eyes, (probably even in their thirties!), and always seemed to be grumbling about the noise from the Record Player, the cigarette ash, or the untidy pile of newspapers left by the Petty Officers. Accused of "pulling rank" they weren't very popular. I wasn't often in the Recreation Room so they didn't bother me too much but now I was to be one of them – horrors!

On August 1, 1945 I was sent on a residential course on Economics which was being run by a Naval Commander, under the auspices of Southampton University. I was unsure if I'd been selected because I was so dumb that I needed instruction, or because I was so bright that it wouldn't be too much of a challenge. Most likely it was because as a newly appointed Chief they didn't know what to do with me! Astute planning resulted in three different types of lecturers, presenting the subject from entirely different view points. One was a quietly spoken soberly dressed gentleman very much a Conservative, and another a rather scruffy-looking Communist with a long unkempt red beard. The third gave no indication of his political leanings. He certainly wasn't a "don't know" type – had a more middle-of-the-road approach, and entreated us to think things out for ourselves.

I found it tremendously interesting. Throughout all the years two things from the course still stand our very clearly. One, stuck in my mind, was that the word Dishcup was an easy way to remember the attributes of money. Money must be – Divisible, Indestructible, Stable, Homogeneous, Cognizable, Universally Acceptable and Portable.

The other thing, much more important, was that THE WAR ENDED while we were there.

After the atom bomb had been dropped on Hiroshima, and then one at Nagasaki, the Japanese surrendered and V.J. day (Victory in Japan) came quickly. Suddenly at midnight on 14/15 August we heard an American voice over the tannoy from a nearby P.O.W. Camp reporting THE WAR IS OVER THAT IS ALL - THE WAR IS OVER.

Joan, my room mate and I had been lying in our beds chatting when we heard this incredible wonderful news. "The War is over" we echoed. There were only four girls on the course and we were accommodated in two Nissan huts behind the main building. We leapt up dressed quickly and rushed out. The back door was locked and we ran through a little passageway to the front of the house.

Someone opened a window in the Recreation Room and we fell into the middle of a madly noisy excited group. Ted, a red-haired Subby, was shouting "Who has the keys of the Bar?" Someone was strumming at the piano and a sing-song was developing. We were stopped abruptly by the grim dressing-gowned Royal Naval Commander in charge sternly demanding "What is going on here?"

"The War is over, sir" we chorused. "Yes, so I hear. I'm not deaf. There is no need to go mad. Get back to your rooms at once, and remember lectures will proceed as usual at 9.00 a.m. in the morning."

"But sir......." we protested. He interrupted;

"Now that the War is over it all the more important that the course carries on as usual. You will be given a few days leave once you return to your units and can celebrate then. Go back to bed at once. Good night."

Incredibly we turned and went to our rooms. I can't think why we didn't defy him openly, but we were so stunned that we acted like a flock of sheep. I remember thinking "You've got little beady eyes, and a horrid grey dressing gown. Pig! I'll never forgive you." I don't think I ever did. I certainly never forget him.

In the morning the boys told us they had opened an upstairs window, climbed out, slid down the drainpipe and went off to join in the celebrations. It turned out to be a bit of washout even for them. By the time they had walked down town the initial street parties had fizzled out. One small group were singing round a bonfire still blazing
away on a bombed-out site but nothing much was happening. The fun had been in the spontaneity of the moment and in joint celebration with strangers. The Commander had stolen all that from us, and nothing could ever compensate. We felt horribly cheated. Down in the South Western Hotel where we lived, the girls had all rushed out into the street without waiting for permission. Some went to parties on ships in the nearby docks, and in general, although the Pubs were shut, there had been much singing and laughter.

I felt swindled out of it all. For me it was a damp squib with grey almost black thread twisting back to D. Day. I couldn't imagine myself some months later whooping round Guildford Square while home on leave, and shouting "The War is over" to the startled passers-by. When I phoned Mum she told me that on the island they had celebrated in style. Most people walked into town and a tremendous crowd gathered on the front, singing, laughing and crying too with all the excitement and released tension. Hearing the broadcast on the midnight news some people had just thrown coats over their night-clothes. With lights all switched on, and the Entertainers in the Winter Garden giving an impromptu show a party atmosphere quickly developed. At last the ghastly War was over.

Time has blotted many incidents from my mind, but not my first sight of Prisoners of War. Smart in their uniforms, and carrying good leather suitcases, the Germans arriving directly from the recaptured Channel Islands, looked about them interestedly.
As they were marched from the docks to the P.O.W. Camp, the scars of War all round must have given them a feeling of satisfaction. They could see that the German air attacks had very nearly immobilised the port. These well fed, well groomed smug looking – men didn't look

as if they had been involved in a War at all.

In contrast, it was a very moving scene when eventually the first batch of British boys, ex-Prisoners of War in the Far East, arrived by sea. Despite all the weeks on passage they were bone thin men still bearing evidence of years of malnutrition and ill treatment. The troopship pulled in alongside the quay at Southampton, seething with cheering men. Returning from hell they were about to land back into the word held dear in their dreams over the long years of waiting. The sunburn and the yellowing of their skins, caused by the anti-malaria drugs would fade, but the memory of all the horrors would endure perhaps forever. Who knows what thoughts they have, more than fifty years on, as an increasingly small number attend Burma Star Reunions throughout the country.

My draft came through and for the last few months in the Service I was stationed at Greenock. There was a very restless unsettled feeling in the air with ships paying-off and people being demobbed. Few stopped to think how difficult it would be to settle down and sadly many never did. Most of the girls in the C.B. Office at that time came from the Glasgow area and often went home in the evenings, for a few hours. I went back to the island as often as I could. There was no opportunity to stay on in the Service as a Chief in Confidential Books as the category was more or less abolished in peace time. As I didn't particularly want to transfer to an Administrative Post, I just took my discharge in May 1946. I hadn't made many close friends in Greenock, so didn't have a big farewell party, but just slipped quietly back to Civvie Street.

The Careers Officer suggested all kinds of jobs and given me leaflets on every subject from Architecture to Zoo Keeper, but few seemed suitable. I had, while in Southampton, been offered a job in the Purser's Office on a Cunard ship and had been sorely tempted to accept, but unfortunately Mum had had a recurrence of rheumatic fever, and I felt I had to refuse. Sailing out of Southampton meant I'd probably just get home on annual leave, and for a while at least it seemed wise to be nearer home. I never mentioned this matter to Mum, as being far from the clinging type of Mother, she would have hated to think I'd turned down an opportunity on her account. I was lucky to have a job waiting for me, and went back to the Kyles of Bute Hydro, this time as book-keeper receptionist. I was a civilian again.

Chapter Six
Behind the scenes at Kyles Hydro

The Navy left the Hydro in good order, but a tremendous amount of work was required before it could reopen. The smooth running of a good hotel, depends on the calibre of its staff so recruitment was an early priority. There was redecorating throughout, then furniture was brought out of storage, upholstery and carpets cleaned, bed-linen and curtains laundered. Finally stores had to be bought, - all manner of things from soap and boot polish to food. With gleaming silver on the dining room tables, furniture polished, banks of fresh flowers and coal fires crackling a welcome eventually all was ready.

Unfortunately the Directors lacked the foresight to grasp the opportunity of modernising the place. Although once one of the top hotels in the country, it now badly lacked facilities like en-suite rooms. Even the car park was totally inadequate. Despite these drawbacks a surprisingly large percentage of the old clientele came back to sample the good food, enjoy excellent service, the beautiful spacious rooms, the wonderful view and best of all the friendly atmosphere.

My hours were anti-social. As I didn't want a special boy friend, when asked out by one of the locals, I was glad to have the genuine excuse "Sorry I'm working." I worked five evenings per week, and in the summer was on duty every weekend – so that narrowed the field a lot! Apart from anything else I no longer seemed to meet anyone who set the blood racing in my veins.

Nowadays I'm often asked why I have never married. Short of telling my whole life story it is hard to explain, but looking at other people's husbands I'm often glad I didn't. For me there would have had to be the near certainty that it would be a lasting relationship. I've been surprised by the number of girls who, mesmerized by the idea of a big showy wedding, accepted the first proposal they had, without appreciating the tremendous commitment involved. I probably could have had a happy life with several of the boys I met, but my years in the Wrens made me independent and critical of those who later crossed my path. The older I grew the fussier I became, and stupidly made comparisons with the past.

My greatest regret is in not having any children of my own as I have a highly developed maternal instinct. At an early age most of my friends thought young babies were crying, smelly and spoilt nuisances, whereas to me they were adorable little bundles. I was always the one happy to stay back and play with friends' younger brothers and sisters or take a baby out in a pram – best of all to help at bathing time. It so happened later that most of my life was involved in looking after other peoples' children. That's another story . . . .

I did, of course, go out from time to time. If any yachtsman was looking for someone to crew I was there like a flash. In the winter I always tried to be free on a Tuesday evening and went to the Country Dancing. There was still a submarine depot ship in the bay and sometimes I'd be invited to a cocktail party or out to dinner.

A much coveted invitation came for the Summer Ball – a really posh affair. As I, in full evening dress, was helped out of the boat by the stern-sheetsman,and greeted on the quarter-deck with all the other lady guests, the shy young Wren inside me gave a secretive smile and with difficulty resisted the impulse to salute! The men were very impressive in full dress uniform and wore medals not just ribbons! The upper deck was transformed with bunting, fairy lights etc., and the buffet even complete with a boar's head. As I toyed with the smoked salmon, and made the usual small talk, my thoughts drifted back to Jimmie, the Jaunty's Messman and the good plain food he brought us! I thoroughly enjoyed the evening but was bemused by all the comparison with wartime experience. Tangled threads twisted back to the hours I spent cooped up in that little office beneath the sea.

Back at the Hydro the Assistant Manageress left early in 1948 to be married, and I stepped into her shoes, relieving in all departments as I had done as a junior fresh from school. Although I had taken a correspondence course in Hotel Management, it was of little value compared with practical experience. Almost three years later when the Manageress retired I allowed the Directors to persuade me to take her job and be in full charge. At the time of my appointment there had been a loss of £400, while at the end of my first year of management the Balance Sheet showed a profit of £800 – peanuts in today's money! The Accountant was delighted when he told me, but I was close to tears as it seemed such a paltry little sum to show for all the hard work.

Although it carried a great deal of responsibility I enjoyed the challenge, and was glad that I wasn't stuck in a dreary nine to five job. It certainly was never boring. I was extremely fortunate in having good supportive staff. Young girls who came from the Outer Hebrides were soon transformed into efficient waitresses or house-maids. They had lovely soft Highland voices and when off duty lapsed into Gaelic and fits of giggles. We were still able to maintain pre-war standards. Morning tea was served in each room, beds were turned down, evening clothes laid out, shoes cleaned etc. Glad of the extra money to supplement their grants, students helped in all departments. We couldn't have functioned without them. It wasn't easy to teach a young six-footer, who excelled in the rugby field to manoeuvre serving spoons without dropping vegetables on the table cloth, or worse, on a guest's lap, but we managed. Built behind the Hydro, the staff quarters had accommodation for about twenty – the boys on the ground floor and the girls upstairs. The rooms were small, mostly for two people, but all had coal fires and the corridors and bathrooms centrally heated. I knew there were parties and all kinds of capers, but as long as the staff appeared for work in the morning I turned a blind eye and concentrated on "the front of the house."

One Housekeeper, a very refined lady, said "Bay, bay" instead of "Bye, bye". Proud of her appearance she always sported a lace-trimmed handkerchief to match the snowy white collar on her dress. I was surprised, in fact startled, when she announced that an English gentleman friend was taking her on a cruise to the Far East and she was leaving five days later. Somehow I hadn't imagined that anyone in their fifties could have an obviously affluent gentlemen friend! It wasn't the most convenient of times for her to leave, but she wasn't really the best of Housekeepers.

For a while Alec, a little bespectacled Glaswegian, was in charge of the stillroom. He kept the Dining Room Staff at bay constantly saying "Keep the heid, keep the heid." As the calls came for "Two single teapots," "One Bovril", "Toast for three", "A dish of ginger marmalade", "A glass of hot milk" and "Coffee Pot for two" he coped with them swiftly, all the time saying "Keep the heid. Don't panic." Usually things went smoothly with clockwork service, however, beyond sight of the Public, small dramas occurred. A Kitchen Porter with a cut thumb, a waiter dropping a pile of plates, or the milk urn running dry – these little incidents were dealt with quickly and quietly.

At times someone had to be rushed to hospital – an elderly gentleman who had had a heart attack, a housemaid with a ruptured appendix, or a young tree climber with a broken arm. I became used to dealing with those emergencies, and the complications which arose when anyone had to be taken to a Glasgow hospital. In those days the ambulance did not leave the island, and the stretcher was laid on the back seat in the steamer lounge, with a curtain drawn across to keep the patient discreetly hidden from public gaze. Incredible as it now seems, the ambulance was crewed by one of the local garages! Whoever accompanied the patient on the long uncomfortable journey to Glasgow had to organise the transportation of the stretcher from steamer to train, and be responsible until the St John's Ambulance men took over at Glasgow Central.

One stormy Sunday I had a horrendous journey with an elderly lady who had a fractured femur and was going to the MacAlpine Nursing Home. Unfortunately we had to change trains at Port Glasgow, and I was most grateful when a young man came forward and helped me with the stretcher into the relief train. All the time I muttered to myself Alec's advice "Keep the heid, keep the heid."

Varbel's bell stood in the entrance hall beside a wooden plaque commemorating the years that the Twelfth Submarine Flotilla had been in occupancy. It was disappointing that so few people remarked on it. Sometimes a pipe-chewing man would read the inscription and mutter "Brave chaps, brave chaps," or a teenager would say "Gee Dad, look at this." Mostly it went unnoticed and became part of the furnishings. If anyone asked about it, I had to resist the impulse to talk at length about midget submarines and submarines in general.

In May 1950 a retired Engineer Admiral and his wife came to stay for a couple of weeks. Having a glorious view of hills and sea from their bedroom, they had no complaint about the lack of ensuite facilities. Admiral Dunlop had designed the prototype floating dock and was thrilled to find one still serving a useful purpose, anchored in Port Bannatyne Bay. Unfortunately he collapsed suddenly and was dead within three days. His last wish, to be buried at sea, wasn't too difficult to carry out as his eldest son, a high-ranking official in the Admiralty, made all the necessary arrangements. The coffin borne on a gun carriage to the jetty was then transferred to the destroyer

Tenacious. Accompanied by the submarines Ambush and Anchorite they went out beyond the three mile limit for the burial at sea. As this all took place discreetly at lunchtime, most of the guests were greatly surprised to read of it in the next day's newspapers.

Again the shuttle moved in the intricate pattern of my life. The threads twisted back, and I imagined a ghost from the Twelfth Submarine Flotilla lurking in a corner of the hall watching it all. There were of course other deaths and disasters. In 1952 the Gaelic Mod was held in Rothesay. All the hotels on the island were crowded, but we had been able to squeeze in the London Gaelic and the Greenock Choirs. There wasn't even a little attic room left unoccupied. Lieutenant Dumfries, who had been Cypher Officer on board the Cyclops was by that time the Fifth Marquess of Bute. His Aunt Lady Margaret McRae and her husband Sir Colin were staying at the Hydro. for an indefinite period, with a lady's maid and a chauffeur in attendance. Lady Margaret ate all meals in her room but Sir Colin sat at a small single window table in the Dining Room. One evening, at dinner, just as the waiter placed the tomato soup in front of him, Sir Colin fell off his seat and hit the floor with an ominous thud. He'd had a cerebral haemorrhage and died instantly.

I was supervising the service at the hot plate, when a waitress rushed out to tell me what had happened. Before I went into the Dining Room I phoned and asked the Porter to bring up a stretcher. The Head Waitress hurried forward with a Doctor. As she said "Stand back please and let a Doctor in" four heads turned from the group round the body and four voices in unison said "I am a Doctor." Later it transpired that two of them were Harley Street specialists. As I went out with the stretcher party, one of the Doctors said "He's dead, you know" as he so very obviously was. I wondered what to do with the body, and was reluctant to give up my own bedroom, yet felt it would be impossible to have him carried in beside his wife! Suddenly I thought of the Chauffeur's room, and as a temporary measure, had him taken there.

The Lady's maid was coming along the corridor and I asked her to break the news gently to Lady Margaret. To my horror she flung open the bedroom door and in a loud voice announced "Oh my Lady, Sir Colin has just dropped dead." There isn't an easy way to break bad news but that was just too abrupt.

Connected to the Bute family through marriage, Sir Colin was quite a personage in his own right. He was one of the select band of the specially appointed Royal Company of Archers, the Queen's Bodyguard in Scotland. When I phoned Mount Stuart the butler fobbed me off saying "His Lordship is at dinner." I explained that I was the Manageress of the Kyles of Bute Hydro and had an urgent message for the Marquess about his uncle, Sir Colin MacRae. The butler persisted "His Lordship is at dinner" so I was forced to say, "Well, when he has finished please ask him to telephone me as Sir Colin has just died." He must have interrupted the meal because Lord Bute phoned back almost immediately and from then on the arrangements were in his hands.

When I returned to the Hot Plate it gave me quite a turn to hear the orders being called out fast and furious "Three Chicken, Veg. Dish for three" "Two Soups" etc. Most of the guests didn't know Sir Colin and were unaware that anything untoward had taken place. It reminded me of the lost submarines and how I'd once thought the submariners from other boats callous in their reaction to death. The words "life goes on" echoed through my mind.

A sudden death has to be reported to the Police, this I did. The previous week when a guest collapsed and died in the main hall I'd immediately had him moved to his room. Sergeant Duguid in the local police force had rightly demanded "Why did you move the body?" and naturally I replied "I didn't know he was dead." This time he grunted:- "I'm going to ask you the usual question, and I suppose you will give me the same answer" – as indeed I was. He quite despaired of me. I assured him that if anyone was found dead in bed or in a bath I wouldn't dream of touching the body! We parted on this understanding. Strangely, I never did find a body in either a bed or a bath.

Life at the Hydro was like a theatre, where the show must go on. We tried to control things behind scenes, and deal with incidents at the front of the house as unobtrusively as possible. Mrs Haddley frequently mistook her room and wandered into Mr Brown's next door. He didn't complain until one day she walked in just as he was about to put on his pyjamas. His grievance was "I know she is 85, and short-sighted,
but why did she need to scream like that?" Tony was only six but managed to create havoc by muddling up all the shoes left outside bedroom doors for the night-porter to clean. The seventeen year old MacPhersons twins set off one day at 11.00 a.m. for a cycle ride, taking

picnic lunches with them. When they hadn't returned by 8.00 p.m. their father drove round the island looking for them. He wasn't too pleased when he found them drinking in the Pub at Kingarth.

There was a very eccentric resident in Room 76. A retired stockbroker, he was very wealthy but sadly didn't know how to make proper use of his money. In moments of bravado he had been known to light his cigar using a rolled-up ten shilling note as a spill. He hoarded all manner of things in his room - sweet papers, teaspoons, toast racks, silver-plated cream jugs, and even teapots and hot water jugs. Wrapped up in tissue paper they'd be stuffed in a drawer with his socks, or hidden on the top of his wardrobe. When we started to get short of some items I broached the matter tactfully. He wasn't at all pleased when I insisted we had to get into his room for stock-taking purposes. As well as the collection on top of the wardrobe I found two large entrée dish covers behind his bed. He always had breakfast served in his room, and sometimes lunch too and consequently his collection had grown rapidly. Threatening the housemaid that she must bring everything back to the silver room or there would be trouble had little effect. She afterwards admitted that he was in the habit of slipping her a pound note to leave the tray and overlook any missing items. He said he was saving up things in case there was another War and a scarcity of essentials.

The resident of Room 74 was a totally different type of man. He originally came from Orkney, but had lived most of his life in Glasgow where he had been a senior partner in a Law firm. He loved walking and often took a packed lunch with him and rambled all over the island. He wouldn't have a radio, - not even to listen to the news.
"The world is such a mess", he said "it is bad enough reading about all the trouble in the newspapers, without hearing it the night before."

Then there was Miss Taylor. Her great aunt, Mary Taylor, had been a close friend of Charlotte Bronte, and she had inherited a pile of letters exchanged between them. After her death her niece donated the letters to the Bronte Museum. Miss Taylor in her late eighties, still had a sharp memory, and was a fascinating story teller. She always went to bed about 6.00 p.m. and had dinner served in her room. If I could leave the lounge while the military whist was in progress I loved to go and chat to her.

Some time after she died I was in London on holiday and her niece took me to the Dorchester for afternoon tea. She'd had a nightmare time trying to clear out Miss Taylor's house in Yorkshire which had been crammed with furniture, books spilling out of bookcases, things hanging out of drawers. Worst of all had been the wardrobes, - great old fashioned things bulging with clothes belonging to her parents and grandparents too! It took many months to sift through it all. Like a scene from Great Expectations the dining room table had been left set for six people. The house had been left unoccupied for six years with at first an old couple as caretakers living nearby. On their deaths their cottage was found to be in an equally over crowded state.

The most memorable guests were Sir William and Lady Burrell who came to stay for a month from their home at Chirnside, Berwickshire. It was at the time of the Coronation, and Sir William was so fascinated with the television I suspected that he hadn't seen one before. When Sothebys or Christies had a big auction in London, he'd usually ask me to phone his agent. One day, particularly anxious to get a jet necklace he kept saying "Tell him, bid another hundred." Before Direct Dialling, it was quite nerve-racking, holding on for Trunks with Sir William impatiently talking at my elbow. His bid was successful, and when I said that I hoped he'd let us see it, he replied "I'll probably never see it myself, I buy these things to stop them falling into the hands of Americans or wealthy Arabs. I made my money in Scotland, and I'm leaving everything for the people of Scotland to see, especially the people of Glasgow." Amazingly in 1953 few people had heard of him and of the wonderful collection which is now one of Scotland's great treasures. I don't think that the local newspaper even reported that he was staying on the island.

The Burrells were a very unassuming couple. She referred to him as Willie – never Sir William, or my husband, and he always spoke of her as Connie. When they were invited to Mount Stuart for lunch, Lady Burrell asked me to telephone Lord Bute, thank him, but make some excuse and refuse. "Willie has a bit of a cold" she said, "but between ourselves the real reason he doesn't want to go is that he hasn't a decent shirt to wear." That was true. She had made a brave attempt at cobbling together the
holes made by the points of his collar, but it couldn't have been called darning, and actually drew attention to the holes. I suggested that the Head Porter went into town and bought a new shirt for Sir William. "Oh no," she said, "it isn't worth it at his age."

His 93rd birthday was approaching and she asked if I could think of a suitable present. I daren't say a shirt, and didn't know what to suggest for a millionaire. Next day she told me she had had a brainwave. "I'll give Willie an elevator for his birthday" she said. "An elevator?" I queried. "Yes", she said, pointing to the lift. "One of those things except a little smaller." I was sure she pictured it being delivered the following week wrapped in birthday paper and tied up with huge red ribbon bows. I tried to explain that it was quite complicated – plans had to be made, and maybe even alterations. She was quite adamant that there was plenty of room in the hall and on the landing in Hutton Castle. Finally I persuaded her to let me telephone and arrange for the Manager of Waygood Otis to go to Chirnside for discussion with the factor. Recently I heard that the lift had indeed been installed, and was glad that Sir William lived for a few more years to benefit from his present. He was a private man and shunned publicity. I think of him fondly.

The Hogmanay Fancy Dress Ball was one of the high spots of the Festive Season. Some of the costumes had been planned months ahead but many ingenious creations were thought up on the spur of the moment. The poor judges had an almost impossible task. One year it coincided with Emma's twenty-first birthday party. Her father, a Glasgow business man, spared no expense. On the stroke of midnight a jeroboam of champagne was wheeled into the ballroom on a little trolley designed for the purpose. Chef proudly carried aloft a giant cake in the shape of a key. The ballroom was crowded and cries of "Happy Birthday" mingled with "A Happy New Year.

The following week one of the permanent residents invited sixty people to her 90th birthday party. Her hair had been tinted a bright shade of purple. As she queened it over her guests I wondered if she had planned it as an effective foil for her emerald green diamante-crusted evening gown. Her long ivory cigarette-holder got in the way when she tried to balance a glass of sherry and a piece of cake. Her theatrical performance deserved applause – quite a show for a ninety year old.

Chapter Seven

Escape to sea

Memory is like an inexplicable curve, and things don't always come back in order. Many people are not here, but I may remember them to-morrow. Many incidents that moved me to tears, filled me with joy, or made me laugh are not foremost in my mind today.

Originally when the Hydro. opened there had been a strict rule that no intoxicating liquor would be allowed on the premises. Change had come. It was sheer hypocrisy to pretend it was a temperance hotel, as many of the guests had a bottle or two secreted in their wardrobes; A flourishing off-licence shop, almost at the main gate, simplified the buying of liquor. Pre-dinner sherry parties were common and I suspected that the cigar-smoking gentlemen strolling on the lawn after dinner, or snoozing in the comfort of the billiard room chairs had just enjoyed a stiff brandy. The Directors wouldn't consider applying for a licence. The guests were all known by name, not just room number, and those who returned year after year became firm friends. Summers were hectic with few vacancies, while there was a waiting list for accommodation at Easter, Christmas and New Year. Alas, it wasn't enough. The remainder of the year was sinisterly quiet with often only the ten elderly residents creeping about the long corridors.

It wasn't financially viable to keep such a big building fully heated and staffed all year. Small economies were made – the West Wing was closed down, and staff hours reduced. Being a Limited Company no one had more than one hundred pounds invested. Many shareholders had inherited from parents or grandparents, and kept the shares for sentimental reasons. They didn't expect a dividend, and were content to benefit from reduced terms wherever they came to stay. Had a keen business brain been involved and more capital invested to thoroughly modernise the place it would have been a very different story. It was a difficult task trying to keep the standard of service while operating on a shoe-string budget. I struggled on, often in despair.

We became renowned as the ideal venue for children's parties. The spacious ballroom was ideal for games, and sufficiently far from the main lounge for all the excited shrieks not to disturb the residents. With the buffet set up in the table- tennis room, there was no problem if ice-cream or trifle was spilled on the terrazzo floor. Chef's speciality was making and decorating unusual birthday cakes – a railway engine, a little house and once a swimming pool. The masterpiece was a three funnelled boat for young Keith. His face lit up, as he spluttered excitedly "I knew I'd get a cake but not one like that. – gee, three red chimmleys." Little did I know how often through the years I'd think back on those wonderful "three red chimmleys."

After the closing muster of the Clyde Cruising Club the annual dinner-dance was held at the Hydro. It was a question of "all hands on deck" decorating the dining room and ballroom in nautical fashion, but worth all the hassle to hear all the complimentary remarks. The Royal Hotel in the Port paid us a nominal sum as rental, applied for a special licence and did a roaring trade. It was galling to think that all the profit from the thirsty dancers was trickling down the hill; and seemed financially crazy to me when more and more dances were held there, more drink consumed, and more money made by other people!

It was a marvellous spot for a wedding and the first young couple married in Croc-an-Raar for decades set the fashion. All these years later I can still recall how beautiful Margaret, the young bride looked as she came down the marble staircase on the arm of her kilted groom. The seating arrangements for one wedding caused a terrible dilemma with twin sisters as the brides. It wasn't easy to work out who-was-to-sit-where at the top table with only one set of bride's parents and two lots of groom's parents. All went well and no offence caused. Unfortunately, an elderly great aunt of the girls took a mild stroke and slightly dampened the proceedings. A group of country dance enthusiasts and a badminton club met weekly, bringing chatter and laughter into the building and breathing life into the place again.

From Easter until October I stupidly seldom had a day off but usually tried to go home for a couple of hours after lunch. Even sitting quietly in the garden I was unable to relax. Problems, some real, some imagined, always popped into my mind – I'd wonder –

"Will Miss Hodge make a scene when she discovers she can't get her usual little window table in the dining room, because Mrs Park has extended her stay?"

"Will the chickens come up from town in time for Chef?"

"I wonder if the new apprentice gardener will fit into the team – he seemed so sulky this morning?"

"What will I do if John the kitchen porter, is drunk again? He has already had a couple of warnings, I should sack him, but will I be able to find a replacement quickly?"

"Will the Wilsons make sarcastic remarks if they can't get a suitable parking space for their Rover?"

Endless petty things grew to assume gigantic proportions. Nothing in my personal life mattered. Mum said I was a bore with my sole topic of conversation being Hydro related. I lived, breathed, ate and thought of the Hydro all the time, and lay awake for hours unable to sleep. I couldn't get lost in a book or enjoy music – without the faces of the elderly residents swimming before me.

Change came one spring morning. Wakened by the dawn chorus of birds I stopped and looked out of the window. For the first time in months I seemed to see the magnificent view properly. It was really breath-taking with the hills, pink and amber in the early morning light standing like sentinels guarding Loch Striven, I thought how lucky I was to have that glorious scenery spread out before me all the time. The sheer beauty of the place clutched at my heart and overwhelmed me. All day as I went about my work the words of W.H. Davies echoed in my mind. "What is this life, if, full of care, we have no time to stand and stare?"

It was true, so true. Surely there was more to life than work? The next day a beautiful rainbow shone above the Cowal hills. More vivid than any other I'd ever seen with its reflection lingering over the calm sea it appeared like an omen. For a day or two while I was doing and saying other things a little voice inside me kept on and on telling me to stop and think seriously about my own life.

No one on the Board of Directors appreciated how difficult it was to run things on a low budget in the effort to make even a few hundred pounds. We weren't alone in having financial problems. With the advent of package holidays, most British hoteliers were altering their image - promoting special golf, fishing or painting holidays, or catering for coach parties. It became cheaper for people to tour abroad than to have a holiday in Scotland, with the added bonus of sunshine outwith the U.K. None of the Directors had a sufficiently dynamic personality to market the Hydro properly. The little voice persisted and I discussed with my Mother the idea that I should change from the Hydro and do something else. Mum's health had greatly improved, and, wanting me to be happy, she encouraged me to think of leaving the island.

The Directors were most surprised and somewhat alarmed one May day when I announced that I wanted to leave at the end of the season. I wasn't persuaded by the offer of an increased salary. Money really didn't come into it. The only thing I was certain about was that I wanted to leave and try another kind of job. In the autumn as a suitable replacement still hadn't been found I agreed to wait until the beginning of January. Unable to bear the thought of lots of farewells and fuss I insisted that my imminent departure wasn't divulged to the guests.

I warned the Board that while still at Kyles I was going to apply for other jobs. In those days there were more opportunities for work, but it was with some trepidation that I sent off applications. At the end of the War I had drifted back to the Hydro, without giving serious thought to a career for life. Apart from my service days, all my work experience had been at the Hydro. Wanting to work with people, I applied for jobs in personnel management etc. The one that really appealed to me was for a Welfare Officer with Barnados Children's Homes. Interviewed by a very charming lady in the Edinburgh office, I was intrigued to see that her office walls were covered with photographs of happy smiling children. She said that although they didn't usually employ unqualified people, she'd strongly recommend me but it would be between four and six weeks before I was called in London for a second interview. The vacancy was in Sussex and I would have to learn to drive a car.

The last Christmas and New Year at the Hydro proved a terrible emotional strain. While I was discussing the menu with Chef, the household stores with the Housekeeper, or just sitting in the ballroom talking to a guest, that little voice insisted "Smile, it will all be over soon." As I waved the guests goodbye at the front door, most of them cried "Thanks for a wonderful time. See you at Easter," and I thought "I'll probably never see you again." I tried not to panic at the thought of the uncertainty of my future. All I wanted to do was escape.

One cold January day with the books and pictures from my sitting room packed into a tea chest, I went home by taxi. After a good sleep I felt more confident that I would be able to obey the Doctor's orders. He had said firmly "You are suffering from severe nervous depression. Don't think about looking for any kind of work for a couple of months. Don't let yourself get overtired, but go out in the fresh air for long walks. Go out to parties too and enjoy yourself." I took the pills he prescribed with little confidence.

It was a strange in-between time. I felt tired, dead tired, but couldn't sleep. The hollow-eyed solemn-faced person who looked back at me from the mirror was a zombie-like stranger – it didn't seem to be me. It was like delayed shock, as is if all the traumatic wartime experiences crowded round me, although I hadn't consciously thought back to them. I'd never been off sick or out of work before and didn't think I'd enjoy the experience.

The days in the Hydro, had been busy happy ones but I'd foolishly worked until everything got on top of me and was for ever apologising for things over which I had no control. After I left they did get a licence the following year and transformed a corner of the Billiard Room into a Bar but there still wasn't enough spare cash to modernise the bedrooms. Anyone could see the writing on the wall. The Hydro was sold a few years after that and eventually fell into disrepair. Sadly, 50 years on it has all been demolished and not a stone remains to show where that magnificent building stood.

Jenny had a brilliant idea. "Why don't you try to go to sea, in the Purser's office? Even one voyage should do the trick," she said. I was so apathetic I didn't even bother to look for the address of the Cunard people I'd met in Southampton. By chance a retired Sea Captain turned up to visit Jenny. He suggested that I wrote to the Captain of the Glasgow Shipping Federation. It seemed to be a very forlorn hope that I would be able to go off for one voyage, just as my Grandfather had done when I was five years old. Mum brushed aside my excuse of "I'll think about it, and perhaps write tomorrow." She bullied me in to writing and posted the letter herself. "What harm can it do?" she queried.

In a few days back came a reply saying that female Purser staff were employed directly by the various companies – P.& O., Canadian Pacific, and of course Cunard. The qualifications were:- "Age over 26, good health, bright outgoing personality, proficient in office procedure, and preferably with the ability to speak a foreign language." My heart sank. The age qualification was the only one I could confidently meet. I had a very poor self image with nerves jangling like broken wires. Although I had a Pitman's Certificate for shorthand 120 w.p.m. I hadn't used it for years. I had a first class credit in book-keeping, and my typing was reasonable. No one looking at my solemn face could say I was bright and outgoing, and I was sure my rusty school French and hastily learnt German wouldn't be adequate.

Mum tried to coax me into writing applications "If you could run a big place like the Hydro, so well" she said, "Working in a ship's office would be a piece of cake." I didn't feel at all confident and refused to be further bullied. "I'll think about it" I said. Jenny and she were worried and puzzled at my apathy.

The most incredible thing happened two days later. A telegram came, saying "Temporary vacancy stewardess Anchor Line. Report 9.00 a.m. Monday – Shipping Federation 200 Broomielaw,Glasgow." I was speechless but unsure. A stewardess? What would I have to do? Visions of mopping up sick and serving meals didn't have instant appeal. "What's the matter?" Mum queried. "It is a marvellous chance. The Anchor Line go to New York. Anyway it is only temporary. Of course you'll go – I just wish I'd been given a chance like that!"

On the Monday Mum more or less pushed me out of the door, in time for the early steamer. "Tell them," she said, "About the Wrens, being in the Guides, and, as well as dealing with all those people in the Hydro, you have a St John's Ambulance Certificate and have been taught to sail properly by a Naval Commander." As I wasn't applying for a job on a yacht I didn't think that would impress them greatly! Off I went to Glasgow.

Terrified of being late, I hurried down the Broomielaw. The further I went the less I was inclined to go near the place. Groups of men were loitering about smoking or talking in doorways. Some stared at me, some whistled, and at that early hour I was shocked to see a man swigging beer from a bottle. I felt just as confused and nervous as I had been when as a raw schoolgirl I stepped into the Hydro's hall for the first time, or when I first saluted the Cyclops quarter deck. The threads in the pattern of my life were twisting back.

I nervously waited in a noisy smoky room full of men without another female in sight. The Captain put me at ease, asked a few questions and said I appeared to be very suitable. "It is," he said "Only temporary and only out to Singapore." I was amazed and wondered if I had heard correctly. How could anyone use the word "only" when speaking of Singapore – half across the world? He explained that the ship – the Empire Clyde, normally carried troops, but this time she was taking service families out to the Far East. Thereafter the ship would go on to Beira with the regular crew, and the forty-eight extra personnel would be flown home.

Still dazed I went up to the Anchor Line Office in St. Vincent Street for a further interview. I was startled when the Superintendent told me I had to join the ship the next morning in Yorkhill Quay. He brushed aside my query re uniform, and said I'd find out all details once I was on board. I didn't think of asking about pay or anything else. Still unable to believe it I went out into the street and found a Public Telephone Box. Mum was delighted when my excited voice proclaimed "I've got the job I'm not going to New York, but to Singapore." She said I sounded animated for the first time in months. She rushed round to tell Jenny that I sounded like a different person. I certainly felt different. In a few hours my life had changed completely.

Back at the Shipping Federation there was some form filling and a Medical Exam to be passed. Then I had to find my way to the Seamen's Union, and pay several pounds for the privilege of joining. I indignantly submitted to have my fingerprints taken for an Identity Card. All kinds of surprising things were happening. Overhearing a remark one of the Union Officials made about first trippers I realised how fortune had come my way. Seemingly it was difficult to join the Union until you had a ship, and normally you couldn't get a ship until you were a Union Member! I guessed it was what was called "a closed shop". Still bemused I travelled home not at all certain what the job entailed. "You will be attending to the care and comfort of the women and children" was all the Superintendent had told me.

When I reached the island it was a mad rush. First I went to tell the Doctor that I'd got a job and furthermore passed a medical. He said I had been snatched from the brink of a severe breakdown, and wished me good luck. I found time to say goodbye to a few friends who were all thrilled at my news.

Mum was really pleased at this unexpected turn of events. We stayed up late talking and hardly slept in case I missed the early steamer. The Union Man had said he thought she wasn't sailing for a few days but nothing seemed certain. On the train from Weymss

Bay to Glasgow I wanted to speak to the snooty looking girl sitting opposite. Smart in her city suit, she filed one of her broken red painted nails. I wanted to ask her "Do you work in an office?" and boast "I'm going to Singapore. I am joining my ship this morning!" "Joining my ship" – that had a romantic ring to it! I took a taxi down to the ship in Yorkhill Quay. Until the day before I'd never heard of her, but there she was lying in the quay looking huge and foreboding

Although I'd served on Cyclops and Forth the Merchant Navy was a totally different scene. I'd been told to report to the Chief Steward in the Main Square. Main Square? I hadn't a clue what that meant – it turned out to be a kind of foyer. I was very fortunate in meeting Nancy, crossing the gangway just behind me, she immediately took me under her wing. A qualified hair-dresser, she normally sailed on the Canadian run, but had grasped this chance to go to the Far East and signing on as a stewardess. "Are you a first tripper?" she asked, "Don't tell the others, I'll help you."

Round the corner I bumped into Helen. She had been a housemaid in the Hydro the previous year, but was sailing as a Bath Stewardess under another surname. She begged me not to mention knowing her and I was only too glad of her assurance that, in return, she wouldn't disclose that she knew me under very different circumstances.

It was strange for me to work physically with no mental strain and no responsibility. As I washed drawers, put clean paper in them, cleaned mirrors, polished tumblers and thermos flasks, I smothered the thought "How the mighty have fallen!" If anyone questioned me I planned to tell them the half truth "I've been on a ship before but have been working in a hotel for the past few years." No one bothered about me, or where I'd been."They" were all too busy with their own lives – (would I never learn that?)

There was more form filling for passports and visas, and we had several inoculations. I was sent to Paisleys to buy my uniform. As we were not sailing immediately I travelled from Rothesay daily. The ship moved to a dock in Govan and we had to report by 8.00 p.m. on the Saturday as she was due to sail very early on the Sunday morning.

Looking at the ship towering above me, threads twisted back over the years to Cyclops in dock, and how excited I'd been when we sailed from Rothesay to Glasgow, now here I was joining another ship and going to sail thousands of miles. Previously when postcards used to arrive from friends, holidaying on the continent, Mum was upset and would say, "If you didn't give me so much of your pay, you'd be able to go to all these places too." I'd always tried to pretend that I wasn't interested in travel, but here I was going – not just to Europe but to Singapore.

When I phoned Irene she too had been delighted to hear my news. She had been teaching Domestic Science in London, and was thinking of swapping career for marriage. After all the games we'd played of ships and shipwrecks, and all the stories I'd read of foreign travel, it had all surprisingly come true for me. I wasn't exactly running away to sea in the traditional manner but was certainly escaping to sea.

The voyage down to Birkenhead was uneventful, and we were working all the time, not gazing at the scenery as I had foolishly hoped. My early training at home and in the Guides came in useful but making up all the bunks was quite a task. I could easily turn hospital corners, but found great emphasis was placed on the importance of the anchor on the top bed mat being exactly in the centre. The Chief Steward was so meticulous he must have had an inbuilt tape measure in his head. Alas it was before duvets, or life would have been much simpler. They were very particular about everything not just the bunks. The expression "ship-shape and Bristol fashion" took on a new meaning. I absolutely had no time to stand far less to stare!

We docked in Seaforth, on the Birkenhead side of the Mersey and after a couple of days crossed over to the Liverpool Landing Stage for passenger embarkation. The majority of the passengers were unaccompanied Naval families. In total there were three hundred children! Soon the tannoy was blaring forth "All visitors ashore, the vessel is preparing for sea. All visitors ashore." There didn't seem to be many visitors on board. Nancy and I sneaked up on deck just as the ship started to move away. It wasn't at all like the departure of a cruise liner as glamorised by cinema and T.V. Disappointingly there was no band and no crowds excitedly waving and hurling streamers. It was a non-event.

The dark oil-stained water between the grim grey buildings ashore and the ship widened. The throbbing and thudding of the ship's engine grew louder. Soon the few people on the Landing Stage became little dots and the lights on the Liver Building grew smaller and smaller. The passengers huddling round the rails turned up their coat collars against the cold February wind. Most of them looked solemn and apprehensive and none of them appeared thrilled to death like me! I was going to Singapore! I was going to the sunshine!

So off I went to sea! Another adventure! A new life.

Chapter Eight

'Only' to Singapore

I was allocated a section of cabins on E deck with Sam, a steward to help me – or, to be exact, I was to help him! He made the top bunks, mopped the decks etc. As an old hand he knew all the dodges. He was seldom seen without a cigarette hanging on his lower lip and frequently disappeared for half an hour or so. The smell of beer betrayed where he had been, but he was a cheerful soul and didn't complain about me being a first tripper.

It was quite rough. For the first two days most green-faced sick passengers lay on their bunks, refusing to believe that they would feel better in the fresh air up top. Sam suggested I went around sucking peppermints, and I managed to overcome the feeling of nausea caused by the revolting smell and the stuffy heat in the cabin.

The stewards scattered sawdust along the alleyways to prevent anyone from slipping into the nauseating mess of sickness. It was all quite disgusting and I prayed that the ship would soon reach a calmer patch. In any case no one could run away and the saying "We are all in the same boat" was certainly true. The passengers were warned not to be sick in the wash-hand basins as they were easily choked but told to use the cuspidors provided. Cuspidor was a new word for me, and I found it was a rather dreary looking cardboard spittoon. There was a very strict rule that no food was to be served in the cabins except dry biscuits and apples. After the first thirty hours the angry seas subsided and more normal routine resumed. It was a mad rush trying to be ready for the Daily Inspection, with so many people still in the cabins, but I did my best – hastily even dusting the little mirror hinges and polishing the wash-basin taps. It couldn't have been a greater contrast to my life at the Hydro, but it didn't involve much thought and I had no responsibility.

Before long I started asking the girls for advice about obtaining a permanent job. The prospect seemed remote. Apparently if there wasn't a vacancy on the Pool (Shipping Federation) the procedure was to write directly to the various shipping companies and ask to be placed on their waiting list. The application had to be accompanied by the seaman's book, showing the record of voyages. I intended to try at the end of the trip, but didn't think I had much chance with only one voyage in my book.

The Royal Naval Commander in charge of all the passengers constantly reminded the Service wives that they had to obey the rules laid down by the Navy. Every time I saw him I thought back to that horrid grey dressing-gowned Commander on V.J. Day. I don't think I'll ever forget him!

All the children between the age of one and five had to be left in the nurseries from 9.00 a.m. until noon and again from 2.00 – 4.00 p.m., while the older children went to the schoolroom at those hours. The Service wives were expected to vacate their cabins by 10.00 a.m. and had to stay on deck or in one of the public rooms. Babies under a year old could stay with their mothers. There were frequent compulsory lectures on hygiene and tropical diseases or the geographical and political aspects of the country of their new posting. In First Class most of the officers were travelling with their families but the passengers in my section were all unaccompanied.

Commander D. R.N. and his wife were sitting at the Captain's table. Although we weren't close friends, I'd met them several times socially when they had been stationed in Rothesay and lived at Kames Castle. Mary questioned her stewardess about my whereabouts and came to my lowly quarters to invite me up for drinks one evening. Next evening as soon as we were off duty Nancy and I ventured up to the First Class. It was a long way, up a few decks, and along seemingly endless alleyways. Outwardly confident looking, but quivering inside, we made our way without being challenged. Amongst the guests already assembled was Gabby, a Sub-Lieutenant whom I knew from country dancing days. He'd never been amongst my Top Ten people and I felt that night he was more than a little condescending towards us – two lowly Merchant Navy crew members. We had a couple of drinks, ate some crisps and nuts, and tried to join in the usual meaningless party talk. Although it was kind of Mary to have invited us we were both self-conscious and ill at ease. It was a great change from our usual routine. Most of our free time seemed to be spent showering and getting our uniform ready for the next day.

Lying in my bunk that night, I thought seriously that the Royal

Navy hadn't given proper credit to all that the Merchant Navy had done, and all the losses and deprivation they had suffered during the War. The War wouldn't have been won without the vital part played by the Merchant Seamen. I was ashamed to admit to myself that I too had been guilty and hadn't given them much thought either. After that evening Nancy and I grew bolder. We sometimes changed into civvies and slipped quietly into the cinema – creeping out just before the lights went on. The films weren't always good, but it made us feel slightly wicked to pretend we were passengers.

We arrived at Gibraltar at 6.30 a.m. but were sailing at 9.30 a.m. there was no shore leave. As soon as I could escape from the section I sneaked up on deck to have my first glimpse of a foreign port. There was a lot of activity on the quay and it was hard to make out what was going on but I wasn't disappointed with what I saw. We had come through the Bay of Biscay, sailed past Spain, and here we were at Gibraltar, with the Mediterranean ahead of us. We were soon on our way again.

I was surprised at the nearness of the African coast. The sea changed from steely grey to blue, pale at first, then a darker almost navy blue. On bright sunny days the ship seemed to be cutting through a path of sparkling sunbeams dancing on the calm sea. A day of heavy rain and squally showers heralded the approach to Malta. There were lots of fishing boats around and a couple of coastal steamers, but most of the time we seemed to be alone on the sea. The boys explained it was because we all kept to our own shipping lanes, but I was never very sure if what they said was true or if they were pulling my leg.

The ship wasn't air-conditioned and the substance that came through the blowers didn't merit the term "air", it was more like warm cotton wool. Horrid! Despite constant showers and baths we still felt hot and perspired a lot. We had all been warned about "prickly heat" and faithfully took the salt tablets provided. The temperature rose daily.

As soon as we were off duty in the evenings we escaped to the after deck and fresh air. Two of the quarter-masters – Donald and Alasdair – from Harris and Lewis respectively provided music with bagpipe and fiddle. A couple of sailors played mouth organs and the Third Engineer was a wizard with the spoons. In no time an impromptu Ceilidh developed. Any one hearing the laughter and the singing of nostalgic songs about dear old Scotland would think we had all been away from home for years and years. The days passed quickly and soon we were approaching Port Said. Most surprisingly there was a huge sign in the sky above the harbour visible for miles it entreated "Don't be vague. Ask for Haig." Advertising slogans like that didn't fit in at all with my preconceived picture of the Middle East. The harbour was crowded. Ships of all sizes and nationalities were squeezed into every available berth. The confusion and the colour on the quay was fascinating.

The famous bum boats laden with leather goods and toys were soon buzzing round the ship. The Empire Clyde with so many women and children looking eagerly down from the rails must have seemed a golden opportunity for lots of sales. Surprisingly the boatmen all had broad Glasgow accents and called up declaring they had names like Jock MacGregor and Angus MacPherson. One even kept chanting "It's a braw bricht moonlicht nicht" trying to give proof that he was a real Scot. I wondered if they'd greet American ships in voices from the Bronx and proclaim their names were Hank or Bud. One thing is certain they were astute salesmen and their patter a delight. The regular crew members were all adept at bartering and able to buy goods at half the price the passengers paid. We hadn't time to venture far from the ship, but it was good to step on dry land again. The biggest store seemed to be Simon Artz, and there was also a large Woolworth, although the prices were high and certainly not at all in keeping with the U.K. stores.

I was delighted to get a bundle of letters from home, including one from Barnados which had arrived in Rothesay the day after I sailed. It was actually offering me a position without a second interview. For a moment I wondered if I had been foolish to take a temporary job instead of waiting for a permanent one, but carefree and happy, I was glad I had grasped the rare opportunity of seeing other parts of the world and being paid for it too.

Before we sailed the "Gully-gully man" came on board. This Arab skilled in conjuring tricks and all kinds of magic was a tremendous attraction. His voluminous robe was a perfect guise for concealing things. Moving swiftly, he appeared to bring a string of live chickens out of an unsuspecting bystander's mouth. It was a talking point for days and even the greatest sceptic had to admit that he was jolly smart. The Empire Clyde prepared to sail again and after some manoeuvring took her place in the line of ships ready for the southbound convoy through the Canal. It was very narrow in parts with miles of desert on each bank. I was surprised to see the height of some of the sand hills and thrilled to see a couple of camels. The few people seen walking along the canal banks appeared like characters from a Bible story. We had stepped back in time. Huge cactus grotesquely silhouetted against the sky line and feathery palm trees were everywhere.

The ship was held up on "the cuts" and the Bitter Lakes for a short time. Pinching myself to make sure that I wasn't dreaming, I was actually passing places like Ismalia, Suez and Port Taufig. There were several large oil tankers around, and a couple of Jedda bound ships dangerously laden with pilgrims for Mecca. I was quite excited and surprised, almost annoyed at Jean's attitude. A stewardess in her fifties, she declared "When you've been at sea as long as I have, you won't bother to look out. All that really matters is that the next port brings the end of the voyage and the pay-off nearer." I couldn't imagine that I'd ever be so cynical and lose the sense of wonder, but, of course I have always been interested in people and places. I was sure I'd store in my memory for ever all that was happening.

A cold wind had been blowing when we left the Mersey but as we sailed down the canal the air was heavy and stifling. As it grew hotter wind chutes were put out of the port holes to try and catch some air. The Red Sea narrowed a little as we passed two huge rocks. "We are going through the gates of Hell", they told us. It was an apt name.

Aden was another remarkable place. As there had been a recent uprising ashore the passengers were not allowed off the ship. They had to be content with buying from the bum boat boys and admiring their skill as they swam and dived around the ship. The ship's crew went off ashore regardless of any trouble, searching for bargains in this Duty Free Port.

Odd little images remain in my mind – not just the heat, dust, beggars and the strange smell, but the astonishing variety of clothing – particularly the headgear worn. Most of the men wore little skull caps or a fez, and one or two even sported woolly hats (in that heat!). Some wore long white Arab robes, others seemed to be out in their pyjama trousers, or long knee length shirts. It was all like a picture in a story book, or a film.

One cheeky barefooted urchin wearing very ragged khaki shorts grinned cheerfully, and we were unable to resist his plea "Missie, please me clean shoes good for you." We sat on a very rickety bench in the street in full view of a curious crowd, while he made a splendid job of whitening our dusty shoes. We probably paid him twice the regular price. His huge brown eyes brightened and his smile widened as he said "May Allah be with you." The crowd continued to follow us, no doubt imagining that we were rich tourists.

Dark flashing-eyed men called out and tried to entice us into sinister looking shops. In Port Said I had brought a "genuine leather pouffe" and in Aden I restricted my purchases to some postcards, a couple of scarves and a most unusual basket bought from an old man with a very wrinkled walnut face. It had a glorious picture of a dhow sailing into a vivid red sunset on one side, while on the other a bright moon shone on a dark sea. Alas, the handle broke before I was back on board. Later I found the lining had been nailed to broken bits of basket and it very soon disintegrated. Through time I learned to be suspicious of goods so eagerly offered for sale, although the Port Said pouffe survives to this day.

We hadn't a lot of money with us, but most of the crew were loaded with radios, tape recorders, cameras, Japanese tea sets etc. Sam told me it was one of the best ports on "the run" for shopping. Many of them had a sideline reselling the goods at a handsome profit. I'd never dreamt of that part of the business, and was disillusioned when he said "Goodness that's what most of us sign on for." Like Jean he wasn't interested in seeing new places – acquiring money was his priority.

As we sailed on through the Indian Ocean a welcome breeze was with us for a couple of days but almost overnight it became hotter. Only half of the crew was granted shore leave at Trincomalee. I tossed with Sam and lost, but was happy enough to sit on the deck and look across at Ceylon (Sri Lanka). I imagined I could smell the bougainvillea, frangipani and hibiscus ashore, and thought it was sad that many of the crew wouldn't even notice all the exotic flowers. An old woman paddling a canoe laden with fruit called up to me. I bargained for a while and finally paid 1/6d. for a huge pineapple. It turned out to taste like a turnip but I didn't care. It was the first pineapple that I had eaten straight off the bush; it hadn't been in a shop or market stall.

After Trincomalee we were told that those who so desired could sleep out on deck for the rest of the voyage. Nancy and I were happy to do this, in preference to the stuffy cabin. The sunsets were truly spectacular. Night came swiftly in the East, and the darkness fell around 7 p.m. bringing welcome cooler air. The Southern Cross and many other strange groups of stars tumbled down from the dark velvet sky. I wished I'd taken a keener interest in Astronomy – these unknown stars appeared larger and brighter than ours, but I was totally ignorant of their names. It didn't seem possible that that queer top part of the moon was a bit of the moon that would shine over the hills at home in a few hours. Although there had been many grey and black patches in my life, now suddenly lots of blue and golden threads were being woven.

We finally approached Singapore. The harbour was busy and the passengers in a flurry of excitement disembarked onto the crowded quay. Little cameo pictures stay with me – huge modern skyscrapers, the brightly dressed dainty little women, the smiling children, the white washing strung up across many of the streets, the small houseboats crowded with people – and the particularly pungent smell of fish. The Empire Clyde went off to Beira with the regular crew and we were left behind in Conell House (The Merchant Navy Officers' Club) to await the plane to take us home.

We were told we'd likely be there for two days, as the plane, an old York chartered by the Ministry of Transport, had broken down at Beirut and a replacement was being flown out. Friends from submarine days were based in Singapore, and were astonished to hear me on the 'phone. I'd last seen them dancing the "Duke of Perth" in the Hydro ballroom. Owing to the uncertainty of our departure I wasn't allowed to accept the invitation to stay at their flat, but they arranged to collect Nancy and me early in the morning.

That first evening about ten of us went out to explore the town. We were indignant when refused admission to the NAAFI. A very supercilious looking female said, "It is strictly for Service people. We don't admit civilians." The boys told us that some places bent the rules on seeing their identity cards, but they had become resigned to being regarded as second-class citizens. The older men had had a very tough time during the War, serving in icy Arctic water or in the U-Boat infested Atlantic. Several of them had been torpedoed and spent days in an open boat. They never spoke about these incidents unless pressed to do so.

Spurning the snooty woman's suggestion that we look for the Seaman's Mission, we went into Raffles Hotel – right into the pages of a Somerset Maughan novel. The Ladies Room was impressive with an old Chinese woman in attendance. She was able to supply everything from elastoplasts to safety pins and shoe laces. There was a super floor show – acrobats on bicycles etc. Suddenly subtle lighting changed the scene and an agile Egyptian belly dancer took centre stage to loud applause and wolf whistles.

In the morning Olive and Jimmy came and took Nancy and me on a sightseeing tour. We pushed our way with the bargain-seeking crowds through Change Alley – a colourful version of Petticoat Lane. After a brief glance at the Tiger Balm gardens we went across the peninsula to Johor Baharu in Malaysia. We passed Changi Prison and reflected on all the horrors that had taken place there. As instructed we reported back to Conell House at 7 p.m. but there was still no definite word of our departure. We had crammed a lot into the day, and were grateful to Olive and Jimmy for sparing the time to show us around.

Refreshed by a shower and a change of clothing we were ready to go out again. Coming downstairs Nancy literally bumped into two boys who'd sailed on the Canadian run with her. They were with another Glasgow boy and he too came over to talk. Soon the five of us decided to go out for a meal. They took us to the real Chinese heart of the town. Through the restaurant's open window I watched the colourful crowds in the streets below. The street scene held my attention much more than the meal, or my companions. I vaguely remember struggling with chopsticks and how the Restaurant Manager presented me with them at the end of the meal, but much clearer I recall my surprise at seeing so many small children still out at what I considered to be long past bedtime.

Before we left Douglas asked me for my home address and 'phone number. He was an engineer and had been "standing by" a Shell Tanker in dock for several months. He expected to be flown home shortly on leave. As he scribbled my 'phone number and address on a cigarette packet I never really thought I'd hear from him again. "Besides," I told him casually, "If I get another ship soon I might be in any part of the world when you come home."

The plane taking us back to Britain an old York, was so noisy that normal conversation was impossible. Nancy and I filled a notebook with scribbled scraps of chatter, and played word games to help pass the time. As the plane only had one crew, we had overnight stops. We flew all night and came down at Dum Dum Airport Calcutta, for breakfast and a brief rest for the crew. We were surprised to find that the First Class Ladies Toilet was no more than a hole in the ground and wondered if the Third Class Passengers had to dig their own holes!

All day we flew across the Indian continent. Below us hour after hour we saw cracked dried yellow-brown earth, with hardly a glimpse of greenery anywhere. Karachi Airport was right out in the desert, and the glare of the sun on the white sand forced us to stop and put on sun-glasses as we left the plane. The heat was ferocious. We had to turn our watches back a couple of hours, and I always felt somehow cheated of that time. Having already spent these hours in a hot noisy plane we didn't want to relive them again. A taxi fare to town would have swallowed up the little money we had, and the rate of exchange wasn't favourable, so we stayed all evening in the airport hotel, grateful for a little cooler air when the sun went down.

For most of the next day we flew over the Persian Gulf. There were a great many ships around and umpteen islands. A ramshackle coach took us from Baghdad Airport to the Regent Palace Hotel, on the banks of the Tigris. It seemed bitterly cold after Karachi, and we dressed for dinner in suits, coats, scarves – the lot. We did, however, remove our gloves when we reached the dining room. In the morning we startled the locals by going for a short walk in the street outside the hotel. They weren't used to seeing unescorted women walking about, and Kate, a brassy blonde, was a particular attraction.

In the late afternoon we landed at Malta. A long dusty drive from the airport led us to our hotel at Valetta Harbour. I was delighted by this overnight stop as Jill and David, great friends of mine were with the Navy there. I had their address but not their 'phone number. Bravely I set out in a taxi. The driver spoke in Maltese and went through so many long narrow twisting streets that I feared I was being led into the Casbah! It seemed a very long way to their house in Slima. I rang the bell on the gate and David came out looked over the terrace wall, and couldn't believe his eyes when he saw me. As far as he knew I was still in Rothesay. There was tremendous amazement at my unexpected appearance and there was much chatter and laughter well into the night. They had lived for a while in a furnished house in Ardmory Road, and I was able to bring them up to date with all the local news. In the morning we were off on the final leg of the flight home.

We flew into Stanstead Airport and were sent up to Scotland by train. The Easter holidaymakers were delighted at the appearance of a rather watery sun, but after our brief sojourn in the Tropics we felt it was distinctly chilly. It was quite strange to be home again. Mum was eager to hear about the voyage and the glimpse I had had of all those foreign parts and of course, the long flight home. In the short time that I had been away the years, the cares and some excess pounds had slipped away. According to my friends, I was more animated looked younger and slimmer. Certainly I was a much happier person than the one who had sailed away.

At first I enjoyed the holiday at home with lots of time to "stand and stare" but gradually little niggling doubts crept back. In the sleepless dark I realised that my problems hadn't gone away and were beginning to push their way through from the back of my mind. I had no job and no clear idea of what career I should pursue. As soon as I could I had written off to several shipping companies. The replies were prompt but curt, and informed me that although there were no vacancies my name would go on a fairly lengthy waiting list. Some time had passed since I'd been in touch with Barnardos but I decided to write and ask if I could be considered for the next vacancy.

The letter was written but lying unposted on the hall table, when the doorbell went and a boy handed in a telegram. I blinked in surprise as I read "Report 200 Broomielaw Tuesday 9.00 a.m. I phoned Nancy and learned the reason for the change of plans. The Empire Clyde had been ordered to Singapore from Beira and bringing back Service families to the U.K. on completion of their overseas posting. A crew with all the necessary inoculations was required to fly out. "It seems I'm not meant to work for Barnardos," I thought. I could almost hear my Granny say "What's for ye will not gang bye ye".

I didn't need to be coaxed or bullied I went off quite happily to catch the early steamer, and made my way down the Broomielaw. Strangely I didn't notice anyone lurking in a doorway and it almost seemed a friendly place! I was told that as this time the stopovers were to be Beirut, Rangoon and Bangkok additional visas were required. I was about to complete a form when Captain Clark sent for me and suggested that instead of this half trip I went on the Bombay run. "The Cilicia is a first class ship and it would be a permanent job" he said.

I only hesitated for a moment. In this present time of high unemployment it seems incredible that I was given the choice of two attractive sounding jobs. I really wasn't sure that I wanted to go to sea permanently but I thought that it was a good chance to go and see India. Not only had I been brought up on Kipling but I had just finished reading John Master's novels and E.M. Forster's "Passage to India". Now I could see it for myself.

Amazingly Douglas didn't lose my address and a letter had arrived from Singapore a few days after I was back at home. He said he was impatient to see me again and hoped to be back in Scotland in a few weeks. Fate intervened once again. About an hour before we sailed from Liverpool Landing Stage Mum managed to get through on the 'phone and told me that Douglas had sent a cable announcing his arrival at Heathrow that very evening.

It was too late. I was off to India.

Chapter Nine

India via Africa

The Cilicia with her sister ships Circassia and Caledonia maintained a regular passenger service to Karachi and Bombay; and also carried the mail and some cargo. There were several noticeable differences between a troop-ship like the Empire Clyde and first class passenger ships. With no Naval Commander to order them about, the passengers were free to do as they pleased. Many of them had meals in their cabins, especially breakfast, and could stay there all day if they so desired, although the cabin staff tried to persuade them to go out on deck before the Captain's Inspection.

I was one of nine female members of the crew, and pleased to be no longer a first tripper. Two of the stewardesses had been at sea for over twenty years and between them seemed to have been everywhere – U.S.A. Canada, Australia, New Zealand and even up the Amazon. I listened with awe to some of their stories. My one trip was rather tame in comparison, although I could boast about staying in the Regent Palace Hotel in Baghdad.

A few extra words were added to my vocabulary. A rosy was a wastepaper basket. Anything extra or superfluous was gash. A fiddle was the name of the narrow edge round the dining room tables, fixed in position in rough weather to prevent dishes and cutlery sliding off. The wooden shutter on the porthole was called the jalousie and there were also heavy metal deadlights for extra protection in a gale. When "Close all deadlights" was ordered from the Bridge it meant that a storm was expected. The portholes on the Promenade Deck were called windows, as indeed they were. The Captain's Tiger, his personal steward, was like a Batman in the Army. Mindful of Cyclops days I shuddered when I heard "Upstairs and Downstairs" being freely used but supposed it would not be easy to train the fare-paying passengers to use the traditional Naval terms.

Four young Egyptian Army Officers, fresh from Sandhurst, travelled back from the U.K. to Port Said that trip. There had been media rumblings about trouble brewing in the Canal Zone, and the passengers regarded these polite, quiet young men with great interest; especially when they discovered that one of them was Colonel Nasser's brother. He assured our Captain that despite all the tales of impending trouble he would ask his brother to facilitate the Cilicia's safe passage through the Canal. We did, in fact sail to India and back without any unusual incident occurring.

To my disappointment we went through the first part of the Canal during the night and so missed most of the scenery. We stopped unexpectedly at Port Sudan to discharge cargo. Under the blazing sun the temperature soared to the upper nineties. As soon as we could we went ashore and out on a glass bottomed boat to a sunken reef which lay almost a mile away. As we looked through the clear water an amazingly beautiful sight of coral and underwater life appeared beneath us. Strange fish swam around, some a deep deep blue and several wearing look-a-like football jerseys with stripes green and white or red and black. Beds of vivid sea anemones and other wonderful bright flowers embedded in a riot of coloured coral branches.

The cheerful smiling natives had a terrific amount of hair standing straight up like a Guardsman's busby, plastered with ochre-coloured mud or, some said, it was cow dung. They had a unique system of counting and only accepted two shilling pieces.

A couple of intending passengers offering two half crowns, would be turned back unless they could produce two florins. All coins except florins were regarded as being worthless. Since decimalisation they doubtless have altered their ideas! It was never a regular port of call for passenger liners but Port Sudan was so close to Khartoum that the reefs could have been a great tourist attraction. One of the passengers said that, in his opinion, although much smaller it was just as spectacular as the Great Barrier Reef. It was an extra bonus to have seen it all.

After Aden, we turned into the Indian Ocean and encountered quite a swell. It often seemed rougher there than in the dreaded Bay of Biscay. The ship rose and fell like a bucking horse, but next day as if by magic we were sailing on a smooth sapphire-like sea. Schools of dolphins turned somersaults and performed all kinds of gymnastics. Crowds clambered round the ship's rails with cameras clicking. Sometimes we saw basking sharks, and once a water spout.

Shimmering in the sunlight just above the waves were tiny

flying fish. A shoal doesn't seem the correct collective name, and flock isn't right either, although they appeared to me more as tiny birds than as fish. One minute they would rush along just under the clear water, then in a fascinating glittering cloud jump from one wave's crest to the next. I never found out how deep they could swim or how far they could fly.

Memories blur with time. I had a hazy recollection of having had a camel ride in Edinburgh Zoo when I was very young and yet perhaps it was an elephant. I do, however, most clearly remember my ride on a camel in Karachi. It was just outside the busy dock gates and we only went a short distance along the road. A camel isn't the most comfortable of steeds and that one was very old. It wasn't as stubborn as a donkey, but wasn't as docile as it looked.

This isn't meant to be a travelogue, but more a kaleidoscope of impressions. The term "culture shock" is freely bandied about these days and I was certainly shocked but fascinated too at what I saw, heard and smelt in Bombay. I had a preconceived idea that India was a vast jumble of palaces, rajahs, sahibs, polo players, dust, heat, beggars and dire poverty. Throughout my travels I never came across an elephant, but I did see snakes and wild monkeys and a crocodile half asleep in a swamp. I never met a polo player or a rajah although I visited the next door flat to a Rajah's town house!

If I shake the kaleidoscope I see the crowd – mostly white robes and dhotis (*a kind of loincloth worn by Indian men*) mingled with the rainbow colours of saris, jostling along the pavements and spilling out onto the road like a mob at a Football Cup Final; Crawford Market, the Gold Market, the Victorian-style Taj Mahal Hotel beside the Gates of India – and the beggars. Another shake reveals the vultures at the Towers of Silence waiting to pick the bones of dead Parsees, the crows that seemed to be everywhere, the crafty carpet salesmen, the skirl of the bagpipes at a Hindu wedding and the beggars again. The next twirl shows the worried little policeman stepping off his box and disappearing into the crowd, and leaving the chaotic traffic to sort itself out. Chaotic is certainly the correct description of traffic – tramcars, carts, lorries, bicycles and cars all perpetually hooted their way through a muddle of pedestrians, barrows, bullock carts, and often a holy cow. Another good shake reveals the beggars again with one legless man hurtling along the pavement on a type of skate-board, small grubby children all beseeching "Bucksheesh, give me busksheesh". Outside

Crawford Market there were usually two lepers sticking skinny diseased arms imploringly through taxi windows.

Books and films about India had left me unprepared for the ghastly poverty or for the colour and bustle in the Bombay streets. My attention momentarily taken up with the amazing combination of colour in piles of saris on a market stall, would then switch to the flies on a baby's face and the terrible ulcers on an old man's leg. At first I thought the gutters were running with blood, and then realised that it was caused by old men squatting on the pavement, spitting out the betel nut they constantly chewed. It was quite revolting.

I'd heard about people sleeping in the streets but the full horror didn't hit me until coming out of a cinema and stepping over bundles of rags I realised with dismay that they were actually human beings. These people were truly homeless, they hadn't left home because of a family dispute or been lured to the city by the prospect of work, most of them had never had a home. They lived and died in the street. The more fortunate ones found overnight shelter in a doorway. Early every morning the Sanitary Squad patrolled in a lorry and removed the bodies of the dead. I was haunted for a long time by the sight of these pathetic souls. Many things surprised me, horrified me, and will stay in my mind forever.

There didn't seem to be a typical Indian. There were Hindus, Parsees, Muslims, Brahmins, with a visible distinction between them and Sikhs and Buddhists. It surprised and upset me that flagrant examples of man's inhumanity to man was still rooted in the Hindu caste system, in the way that they treated the sweeper class – the Untouchables. I was woefully ignorant about the Hindu faith and was glad to hear that Ken the Radio Officer was quite an authority on gods and lesser gods. He was happy to explain things to any one, like me, willing to listen.

A group of us, five boys and three girls, exploring the little back streets behind the market, were once lured by the sound of bagpipes into a hall. Although we really were gatecrashers, we were told that a Hindu wedding was in progress and they'd be honoured if we attended. The Bride looked very young and more frightened than happy. At one part of the ceremony the couple were united by a piece of twine binding their foreheads together. At that time our knowledge of Hindi was confined to useful phrases that would tell the taxi driver not to take us a tour of the city when we just wanted to go a short distance, and the shop-keepers not to swindle us too much. This being so we were grateful when an Anglo-Indian called William volunteered to translate for us. I was so impressed with the Bridegroom's declaration that I asked for it to be written down. It went like this:-

"I take thy hand in mine, yearning for happiness. I ask you to live with me thy husband, till both of us, with time, grow old. I am the words, you are the melody. I am the melody, you are the words." Although it was an arranged marriage I thought it was romantic.

After the ceremony the guests queued up to give their gifts to the happy couple. Our boys all gave money, but I wanted to give something personal so fished in my handbag and found a solid perfume stick which the Bride received with a look more puzzled than grateful. Afterwards I wondered if she knew what it was and the boys thought she'd eat it. I hoped that a man who could say these words with such feeling would be kind and faithful to his wife. William the Anglo-Indian asked if he could join us and was delighted when told "Sure, the more the merrier." Betrayed by their colour, the palms of their hands and sing-song voices, Anglo-Indians are an unhappy race. At that time neither the British or the Indians readily accepted them as half-brothers but now, decades later, I'm sure feelings won't run so high and surely they must have been accepted by one culture or another.

On board the Cilicia we had a real hotch-potch of nationalities. All the officers, petty officers and female crew were Scots, but the waiters, stewards, pantry and most of the kitchen staff were Goanese. These poor men were in a very awkward position as India was in dispute with Portugal over their little country. Feeling more Portuguese than Indian, they were very sensitive about it. Some of them hadn't seen their wives and families for years, but were able to send money home from the U.K. through the Bank of Portugal. They were gentle, softly spoken men and splendid workers. In particular I still remember Quadros, DelMelo, Santos, Lorenzo and De Souza and how sympathetic I felt towards them. They were all devout Roman Catholics and that further distanced them from the Indian stokers and deck hands who were Muslims.

Although I knew that all the followers of Mohammed said their prayers five times daily, I marvelled that they instinctively seemed to know in which direction Mecca lay and turned to face it, no matter where they were. Then of course there was Ramadan, the Holy month when they kept a strict fast from sunrise to sunset. We Scots were lucky as on the ship Christmas, Hogmanay, Easter, St. Andrew's Night, Halloween and Burns Night – as well as all the Muslim and Hindu festivals were celebrated. We had the best of all worlds. Amongst all the mixture of cultures we managed to strike a reasonable balance of tolerance.

Daily I realised how little I knew of other countries and other creeds. I was telling a story one night to one of my five year old passengers, a little Indian girl determined to stay awake until her parents came back from dinner. Puzzled she asked "What do you mean? What is Christmas?" I shouldn't have been surprised as I knew nothing about Diwali, Idman or any of their Festivals.

On the homeward trip there was no shore leave at all at Port Said. It was obvious that the situation in the Middle East had rapidly deteriorated. Port Officials appeared to be sullen and unhelpful. Even the bum-boat men weren't cheerful and appeared almost resentful. Fighting soon broke out between Israel and Egypt. On 6th November Britain and France landed troops at Suez and as the Canal was closed all ships bound for India and the Far East had to go "the long way round" – via the Cape of Good Hope. We were told that on the next voyage the ship would probably be calling at Las Palmas and Durban – New Places!

The voyage wasn't officially over until the ship returned to Glasgow, her home port. We left her in Liverpool for cargo discharge and came home by train. We'd been told to 'phone the office after three or four days. When I did I was told "She'll dock tomorrow so report on Wednesday." Although the sea had always been in the background, and always part of my life, I didn't make a conscious decision to keep on working on the ship, somehow it just happened. At the pay off I followed the others "signed off articles" at one table, and walked to the adjoining table and "signed on" again for the next voyage. The thought flashed through my mind "I'll just do one more trip". Little did I realise that most seamen who are doing this one more trip are hardened old sea dogs before they realise it! It gets in their blood – something lures them back again and again.

Douglas was on the scene again and apart from wanting to see these new places, I subconsciously chose this as an escape route – a kind of bolt hole – from him. Our first meeting had been in March and although we had exchanged several letters and 'phone calls, our second meeting wasn't until November. He had several months leave due. I should have been flattered that he had waited at home while I went out to India and back but somehow he rushed me too much, and panic arose within me. I was quite out of practice at refusing proposals and thought "Help! We'll be married before I know him properly."

The main stumbling block was that he was six years younger that I was. He swore it didn't matter in the least, but I was paranoid about it. Having a lot of premature grey hairs didn't help my ego, and he looked incredibly young. He hadn't seemed so out in Singapore, but then everything under that moon out there had seemed quite different. At home in Scotland our relationship seemed fraught with obstacles most of them I now admit of my own making. We had a few more days leave after the sign-on and even when we were "standing by" the ship, only worked a few hours. Our friendship developed. We liked the same things and laughed at the same things. Mum and he got on well together, but I wasn't too sure that his mother approved of me. I was quite nervous when he took me home to meet his family. He even came down to Birkenhead by train and stayed in a hotel in Seaforth for four days just to have extra time with me when I was off duty. It hardly seems credible in this permissive age, but it never occurred to us to have sex before marriage. It just wasn't done.

My heart beat a little faster when we were together, but I was terribly afraid that the feeling between us wouldn't stand the test of time, and separation. I remember sitting at dinner in a Chester hotel thinking "Will this last? Will he still feel the same about me when I am wrinkled and white-haired?" Looking back I realise I was a fool. I was super-sensitive about my age, and raked the matter up at every opportunity. I'd say "Oh, you wouldn't remember – you would still be a little schoolboy then". In my mind I compared him with the others I had known before – all still young and dashing and some glamorised by death. I'd long since stopped dreaming of what-might-have-been but somehow wasn't prepared to take the step that would lead to what-could-be.

In role reversal I sailed away to India and left Douglas standing forlorn on the quay. I'll admit now that almost as soon as the Pilot left the ship at Holyhead I began to have regrets. It was as if something deep inside had driven me to destroy the happiness that could have lain ahead, just as it had been snatched away from me before. When

I came back to the U.K. he had sailed for Japan. After that we exchanged letters and phone calls, but weren't often in the same country at the same time.

Once, however, we spent almost a week with his aunt and uncle in Rannoch. We helped build a rockery, fished for salmon, climbed a mountain, walked the dogs, and in general had a great time. I can't imagine why I never thought of disguising my grey hairs or trying to improve my self-image, instead of eternally pointing out the faults.

During a long weekend we had together at home in Rothesay the following year, he was suddenly recalled and had to fly immediately out to the U.S.A. That day, I felt, not surprisingly I suppose, that he was beginning to be a little indifferent towards me. I missed him a lot, and had we been able to spend more time together then, things might have altered. In any event it wasn't easy with both of us away from home and usually sailing in opposite directions. After about four years we finally drifted apart.

When we sailed from the U.K. the regulation uniform was "blues". For the female crew this originally meant wearing a blue uniform dress with stiff collar, starched cap, big aprons – the lot! Fortunately it was soon decreed that we could dispense with the cap and apron. It was certainly more attractive and practical. When the temperature rose the order for "Whites" would come from the Bridge. The girls happily exchanged their blue dresses for white ones and hard black shoes for comfortable white sandals. The glamour of the men's navy uniforms greatly diminished as white shorts revealed hairy legs or thin stick-like ones! Disillusionment set in!

We were in tropical gear as we approached the Canaries. I hadn't expected to see so many volcanic islands in the group. History and geography had always been favourite subjects of mine – here it was all around me, but the further I went the more ignorant I realised I was! The ship's swimming pool was busy and the passengers settled down to enjoy the sunshine. At Las Palmas, after my first run ashore I returned to the ship bereft of pesetas, but had acquired a Spanish doll, a bottle of sherry, a newspaper, and a huge bunch of incredibly cheap flowers.

Shortly after we sailed the weather changed and a cold wind seemed to be blowing right up from the Arctic. The sea was vast and empty, and unlike the Mediterranean there was no land in sight. Indeed there were no other ships around. It proved to be cold enough for the Captain to order the return to blues for a few days. We asked the boys on the Bridge if they were sure we were going in the right direction. "Hope so" said Iain the second mate, "but of course we haven't been this way before and neither has the ship!" He came from Barra and was often at loggerheads with Kenny the quartermaster who was an Islay man. They were a couple of real Teuchters!

All was well, however, and we soon came round the Cape of Good Hope. It was tantalising to see the outline of Table Mountain on the skyline and buildings in Capetown shimmering in the sunlight and sail past it, but our next scheduled port of call was Durban. The highlight of that trip was the Crossing the Line Ceremony. I believe that on some ships crossing the Line Certificates are actually sold in the ship's shop but it certainly wasn't so on the Cicilia. Every member of the Ancient Order of Globetrotters who gained a certificate earned it, and had been through the initiation ceremony. The ceremony varies from ship to ship but generally Neptune holds court, and the unfortunate victims are covered in soap suds or shaving cream, and eventually thrown in the swimming pool. The Chief Steward made an excellent Father Neptune, with the Nursing Sister as his chief attendant. I was duly grabbed while I was spectating, and chucked into the pool, in full uniform. The Ceremony was greatly enjoyed by the passengers and certainly broke the tedium of the day for the Assistant Pursers frolicking in the pool instead of working in a stuffy office. The camera enthusiasts got lots of good shots.

The homeward trip was even more eventful. Early one morning we had just passed Madagascar when a shudder went through the ship. Afterwards we heard that at that precise moment the Mate was showing two giggly girl passengers over the Bridge. When they said, "Gosh, was that a bump?" He replied "Oh no, we have just crossed the Equator". One protested "I thought it was an imaginary line," but he went on at great length about troughs in the ocean comparing them to geological faults, like the Great Glen in Scotland. The girls weren't fully convinced, but later discovered, as we all did, that a propeller had fallen off. This meant that we had to reduce speed and make for dry dock to get the spare fitted. There was a P. & O. ship in Durban Dry Dock, which meant we had to go on to Capetown and lie off shore for twenty-four hours before we could dock there.

We were told that all passengers and female staff would be

accommodated in hotels ashore at the Anchor Line's expense. It caused a headache for the Purser's office as several passengers who appeared to be British were travelling on Indian passports. It took tactful arranging to obey the laws of South Africa. The Captain spoke to all the crew about apartheid. Coming from India where there was virtually no colour bar we were quite appalled when we were told that if we met any of the Indian passengers or crew or any Goanese crew in the street we were not to speak to them. Although we knew that South Africa had this policy towards coloured people the full implication didn't dawn on us until we saw it in practice. Even on the buses there were only about five seats at the back reserved for coloured people and they were not allowed to sit anywhere else, even if the bus was half empty, or if a white person was sitting on their seats. That seemed quite iniquitous to us, as did the separate queues in the Post Office for stamps etc.

We were all pleased to have a few days holiday in Cape Town and enjoyed the comfort of the Avalon Hotel. The only drawback was that we hadn't enough money to act like real tourists. I don't think Visa cards existed in those days. We did, however, take a cable car up Table Mountain. The descent was steeper than it looked, but the view was even more spectacular than imagined. A carpet of Alpine flowers nestled in the rocks too far below for us to identify.

We enjoyed the unexpected time in Cape Town although that particular voyage seemed endless – it was almost four months from "sign on" to "sign off". As we approached the UK a strange but common malady known as the Channels affected most of the crew – a feeling of anticipation, and an air of excitement. We were returning to the world of houses, super-markets, cars and trains, woods and gardens. An odd group of people had been banded together and we'd all go off on our separate ways when the ship docked.

The arrival of the Pilot at port was quite an event. Although it was often in the early hours of the morning I usually helped the Pursers sort the mail, and thus could get my own letters quicker. I was lucky and usually received several, but in turn I wrote quite a lot too. Letters are very important to those at sea without a handy telephone or a daily newspaper. Unfortunately after the first few voyages I stopped keeping a diary. There wasn't a lot of spare time, and I didn't realise that even mundane daily routine matters would be of interest in the years ahead.

I found it maddening on leave when people greeted me with "On holiday again? Aren't you lucky having such a good job, with so much free time?" They didn't seem to understand that we worked ten hours daily. There are no days off at sea. Saturdays, Sundays, Christmas Day and New Year – are all the same. I was often taken aback by the questions "Was it stormy?" Never "Were you very busy?" or "Were you involved in that riot?" or even "Was it terribly hot?" We were much too busy to pay attention to the weather and if we had been off duty because of sea-sickness (or sunburn, which is self-inflicted) we wouldn't have been signed on again for the next voyage.

I went back for "just one more trip" – and it proved to be for years and years!

Chapter Ten

Three Arab kings

S ometimes we were fortunate enough to be in Bombay when a Hindu feast day was being celebrated. Diwali, the Festival of Lights was intriguing. Twinkling lights outlining many of the buildings momentarily hide the misery and squalor in the dark shadows they cast. It was all reminiscent of the Fireworks Display and Illuminations at home in Rothesay – especially pre-war when crowded chartered steamers cruised round the Bay. Hundreds of padella lights brightened the town and sparkled on the sea wall, the window ledges and doorsteps of the houses. Padella lights obtained from the Gas Works were curious saucer-shaped tins filled with a thick type of candle wax with a sturdy wick that burned for hours, the Bombay lights were very similar. During Diwali there seemed to be an even greater seething mass of humanity milling around the streets all chattering excitedly.

One September Mrs Kildon took us to see a Gunpati procession in honour of a much revered God with an elephant head and a man's body. Even the poorest Hindus tried to have an image, bedecked with flowers and surrounded by offerings of food. People moved from house to house bearing a gift in homage to Ganesh. The wealthier a household was, the larger was the Ganesh. We watched the long straggly procession winding its way through the streets and on to Chappati beach. Each group carried its Ganesh, some in their hands, some on trays but many were displayed proudly, on elaborate litters. The bearers waded out waist high and then, to our astonishment, cast their images into the sea. Mrs Kildon, a Roman Catholic, dismissed it all as heathenish nonsense. Throwing away Ganesh was an act of sacrifice but puzzled our
Western minds especially as so many people had not enough food for themselves. Mrs Kildon an ex-passenger, was Anglo-Indian but unusually didn't try to conceal her true origin. Small and dark, she always wore Western clothes. Her grandfather had come from

Essex but her other forbearers were all Indian. Her husband had an administrative post on the railways. With Irish blood in his veins as well as Indian he was only very slightly coloured. We enjoyed visiting them and eating their delicious spicy meals.

Mrs Kildon was secretary at Walsingham High school (formerly one of the Rajah of Kutch's Palaces). A wealthy Arab living in Bombay had negotiated with her for the lease of the school grounds to hold a series of receptions in honour of King Saud of Saudi Arabia who was visiting him privately. Mohammed Ali Sheka's wife had left him, and his sister acted as chaperone to his three young daughters. They spoke fluent Arabic and Hindustani and had a smattering of French, English and Russian. Mrs. Kildon had been asked to give them weekly English lessons and suggested we went for afternoon tea and helped with the conversation. Eager to savour every new experience Betty and I gladly accepted the invitation. We went to everything that came our way - from the Baptist Church Sunday School Party to a visit to a Leper Colony. This visit to an Arab household would certainly be different. Although a millionaire, Mohammed Ali Sheka's lifestyle was very different from that of Sir William Burrell, my other millionaire, a world away.

Memory is strange and only the eldest girl's name remains – Amna. Almost sixteen when we first met her she was honoured and excited that she was shortly going into the harem of the King's eldest son. We were a trifle shocked and grateful to be able to make such important decisions ourselves.

All their customs were alien to us. We were forewarned that at a meal we were expected to take two helpings of everything to signify our appreciation. One helping would be impolite and give the impression that we didn't like it, whilst to take three would be greedy. I struggled with the second little green marzipan cake, and washed it down with a second cup of tea sickly sweet with goat's milk feeling very noble as normally I don't take either milk or sugar.

Once a month the girls were allowed to choose which concert, art show or cinema they wanted to attend. One evening Betty and I went with them to the cinema. I hoped none of the boys from the ship would see us stepping from the chauffeur-driven lemon coloured Cadillac with Auntie and the three girls all in purdah veils, and a bearer in attendance. The boys would probably have imagined we had been kidnapped and staged a rescue.

By Western standards the house wasn't especially grand or well furnished but we were greatly honoured to be asked to dinner one evening. When the main dish arrived I had a nasty shock, as several pairs of eyes were staring up at me from the steaming hot brown mess. I never found out if they were the eyes of a goat, a camel, a dog, or some other animal. Betty muttered to me "I'm not putting my hands into that muck" and sure enough when I looked round the table there was no cutlery. Auntie must have noticed my anxious glance, and a servant standing behind my chair was duly despatched to the kitchen for a couple of spoons. It tasted much better than it looked and fortunately we managed to avoid the eyes. We were uncertain if we could eat it all, far less a second helping but were "saved by the bell." If ever an expression was apt, it was at that moment – the call to prayers sent everyone out to the verandah. Left alone in the room, we lined my big white drawstring handbag with paper tissues and transferred the contents of our plates. I had to hold the bag most gingerly thereafter. Alas, it never recovered. Scrubbing vigorously and leaving it to dry in the sun, removed most of the stains, but not the smell or the memory!

Normally a couple of scruffily dressed guards loitered unobtrusively by the main door, but one evening a splendid fellow with a red fez and a broad red sash over his sparkling white uniform stood on the pavement. After scrutinising us carefully he let us pass. A similarly dressed guard was positioned upstairs at the door of the flat beside the row of shoes. Amna was greatly excited "Three Kings have come to visit my father" she said. Indeed her father was cloistered in a room with three wealthy Arab sheiks. Being in purdah there was no chance of the girls meeting them, but at their suggestion and stifling our giggles we peeped at the Arabs through the slats in the louvered doors. When her father came through to greet us, Amna begged him to ask if we could be presented. The Sheiks, likely under the impression that we were high-born ladies touring India, agreed to receive us, never imagining that we were two Scots girls working jolly hard on a ship.

On entering the room we exchanged bows and said "Salaam, Salaam, Namaste Namaste" which we hoped was an appropriate greeting. Our acquaintance was brief, very brief, as only one of them spoke English and that was rather basic. Flashing very white teeth he bent close to my face and said "You like India?" "Yes, lovely country", I replied. His face almost touched mine and he gazed into my eyes saying "Ah my country is much much better, you must come and see." A vision swam before me of being lured away to an Arab oil state and I wondered how many camels he'd offer my mother in exchange for me! I simply couldn't imagine any camel settling down happily in Ardbeg Road! The other two Sheiks were smiling at Betty but didn't speak. Later she said they had sly leering smiles and gave her the creeps. We bowed again, exchanged Salaams and Namastes and backed out of the room, stifling a desire to giggle.

The Dock Police were often difficult when we arrived in a gurri (a grotty looking type of cab) or even a chota (small) taxi, but they waved us through in the air-conditioned Cadillac – a blue one this time. No one on board seemed particularly impressed with our story, so waited until we returned to Scotland before we could boast about it! Telling the story in Rothesay it all seemed unreal and I felt like phoning Betty to get confirmation that it really happened.

Eventually the Cilicia went into Yorkhill Dock for a refit, and we were given "harbour wages" – a kind of retainer. It pleased the Glasgow members of the crew to have lots of time at home, but it didn't work out so well for me. From Monday to Friday we had to report on board at 9.00 a.m. and although we had two and a half hours for lunch, we had to report back to the ship and weren't free to leave until 3.00 p.m. This meant I had to travel from Rothesay by the first steamer and wasn't home until after 7.00 p.m. It was a long boring day. We were given a few tapes to sew on pillowcases and towels, but frittered most of the time away in idle chatter and in drinking cups of coffee. I told the office that I much preferred to be at sea and that I intended applying to other companies.

Still anxious to go to South America, I wrote to Royal Mail and they replied that they would offer me a position in the near future, and presumed I spoke Spanish. In a panic I swotted basic phrases beginning with "Habla usted Inglis?" (can you speak English?) I carried scraps of paper with me bearing the words for meal, deck, port-hole etc. Threads twisted back to the days I'd lain in the bath in Southampton muttering irregular German verbs. As often as possible I now mumbled Spanish words under my breath. On the Weymss Bay train I'd try to avoid talking to fellow travellers, but frequently someone would spot me and demand to hear about the places I had visited. It is just as well that the job didn't materialise as I couldn't have claimed honestly that I was a fluent Spanish speaker.

Hindustani was a different matter, with little grammar to worry about. Most of us picked up enough to be useful while dealing with taxi drivers, stall holders and beggars, the Dock Police and the Customs Officials. Some of the words were a delight – In particular I liked the sound of ooltah pooltah which meant topsy-turvey or mixter-maxter. While we were in Bombay we helped Johnny, the Head Linen-Keeper, at least one morning per voyage when mountains of linen came back from the Indian Laundry. It usually was an extremely hot forenoon when the linen was spread out on the Promenade Deck and we each paired with an Indian checker. On they droned "iggara, barra, tierra" etc. in monotonous tones, until we were all almost asleep. The numbers in Spanish were fairly easy to master, and I wondered if I'd ever have a chance to use them.

After we had been "standing by" for a couple of weeks the Superintendent sent for me one morning at 9.30 a.m. He explained that owing to a sudden bereavement one of the girls on the Circassia was unable to sail, and a replacement was urgently required. "Here is your chance to get back to sea. You'll be able to catch the ship at the Landing Stage" he said. I was speechless, certainly I wanted to go back to sea, but not just on the sister ship. I had little option but to agree, rush back to Rothesay, pack and catch the last steamer. I travelled overnight, and, in a breathless whirl, joined the ship a couple of hours before passenger embarkation. There were a few familiar faces amongst the crew as the Third Mate and the Second Sparks (Radio Officer) had also transferred from the Cilicia. As the Suez Canal had reopened, we went through the Mediterranean and down the Red Sea once again. Old Jean's prediction hadn't come true and I still enjoyed all there was to see.

On docking day in Bombay I was pleased when Pat and Milly came on board to welcome new arrivals. They were Australian and had travelled out on the Cilicia a few months previously, with Pete the dearest little smiling baby. I was delighted when they asked me to go to dinner the following evening at their flat on Malabar Hill. An old Chinese servant who had travelled half round the world with them did all the housework and the shopping, while Milly attended to most of the cooking. "It stops all that ghastly nonsense with the caste system" she said "The flat is fully air-conditioned and I don't find it too difficult." It was refreshing to hear this viewpoint and I was keen to see it in operation.

Most households had a great range of Indian servants, each with a specially allotted task. If anything was accidentally spilt on the table or floor, it was impossible for the bearer to wipe it up, as all dirty jobs were allotted to the sweeper. If this ritual wasn't observed it meant "loss of face" for everyone. It was hard at first for Westerners to understand the system, but they soon caught on. I often wondered how some of the expatriates would settle down in Durham or Dundee without a servant in sight.

The first Sunday we were in Bombay, Jim one of the Assistant Pursers organised an outing to Ooran. Bearing a large picnic basket we set off for the steamer. We were a mixed bunch – two from the Purser's office, a Cadet, a Quarter-Master, the Third Mate, the Second Cook, the Baker and three girls. Ashore we found a shady spot near a well. Like a scene from another age, graceful dusky women, bright in their cotton saris, passed on their way to and from the village, with huge water pots on their heads. Although they couldn't speak English and didn't understand our Hindi, we somehow managed to exchange friendly greetings. The pots were so heavy our boys could hardly lift them, and certainly couldn't balance them on their heads. Despite the suffocating heat, we spent a pleasant afternoon in Ooran and returned on the crowded steamer feeling that we had been away from the Circassia for ages.

Next day Ann Moore telephoned to see if I would be allowed to stay at her flat for two or three nights while her husband was up in Delhi in business. The set procedure was to write the host's name, address and phone number in a book in the Purser's office and report back to the ship before 8.30 a.m. daily. As their car was in the garage for a service, I had to go by taxi to the Marine Drive flat.

It was very hot indeed and it was a long walk from the ship's berth to the Red Gate. We had learned that it was prudent to select one small boy from the eager mob of youngsters milling round the gate. He not only carried parcels but, keen to earn a rupee or so, acted as a kind of protector and chased all the other boys and beggars away. We found which ones were trustworthy and I was greatly relieved when Ali sprang to attention and quickly found me a chota taxi. By the time I reached the flat I was extremely hot and had a thumping headache.

Even after a shower and a meal I still felt weary, so we shelved the plan to go to the Metro cinema. We lounged about in the welcome coolness of the air conditioning and Ann showed me a cine film of their honeymoon in Kashmir. It was a pleasant change for me not to go to the cinema. Bombay was dry at the time and, with no Pubs to frequent, the boys usually haunted the Chinese restaurants and the surprisingly large number of modern cinemas. Somehow we always seemed to end up at a Wild West film. The Cilicia girls had issued the ultimatum "If you don't take us to a film we want to see, you can go yourselves!" We had warned them that if we saw one more band of brave cowboys rounding up cattle and moving them to the next valley, we'd scream! I supposed it would be the same on the Circassia and it suited my mood to watch the quiet beauty of Kashmir.

In the morning the driver took me back to the ship. Still feeling tired, I was glad I hadn't had to hunt for a taxi or walk through the noisy dockyard. While the ship was in Glasgow a start had been made on installing the air-conditioning system, but the Dining Saloon was the only place that had been completed. I forgot to put on a cardigan when I went down for lunch, and found it distinctly chilly. I wasn't at all hungry, but there was a strict rule that everyone had to appear at meal times. At sea we were forbidden to talk about passengers during a meal, and if someone did default there would be cries of "No shop talk here." It wasn't easy while we were sailing, as we hadn't been out anywhere or even watching T.V. the previous evening, but it certainly sharpened our conversational skills.

Margaret, the Nursing Sister, described a visit she'd paid to a Shell compound, and how she'd been driven through a huge horrendous refugee camp. Hundreds of little tattered tents crowded together provided the only fragile security these unfortunate people had had for years. The actual experience of seeing it had left her quite shaken. I strained to catch what she was saying but her words got blurred and fainter. The portion of fish that the steward was about to serve grew larger and loomed above me. The room whirled round. Apparently there was an almighty crash and I fell to the deck. The next thing I knew I was lying on the settee on B deck square with the Ship's Doctor bending over me. I never dared ask how many people had carried me away from the debris of broken china and scattered cutlery!

After a cursory examination the Doctor ordered me to rest in my cabin for the remainder of the day brushing aside my protests

"It was just the air-conditioning, and I'll be better off staying in my friend's flat ashore. I'm alright now." He promised to phone Ann and explain matters, saying my temperature was abnormally high he escorted me to my cabin on the Boat Deck. I was still feverish in the late afternoon when the Doctor came to see me before going ashore. I didn't want any dinner, but later in the evening felt much better and went to Nan's cabin across the alleyway.

The two young cadets were passing by, so she sent them to the deck pantry to ask the duty Goanese Steward for a tray of tea and sandwiches. The boys gobbled them up, but I only toyed with mine. Suddenly I felt terribly hot and got the others to confirm that it wasn't just imagination. "Hot?" said Hugh "It feels as if you are on fire." Back I went to the airless cabin, but even after a shower didn't feel any cooler. I couldn't sleep and about 3.00 a.m. went and sat at the edge of the empty swimming pool, hoping that it might be a little cooler up there. As soon as the Lascar seamen arrived to holystone (clean) the deck, I moved down below again and chased a mosquito in a half-hearted fashion before I fell asleep.

I woke with a start at 8.10 a.m. and felt better. I was half-dressed when the Doctor appeared "Where do you think you are going?" he queried. Before I could answer Nan came in to see if I wanted Lorenzo, our steward, to bring in a breakfast tray. Simultaneously John the hairdresser tapped on the outside jalousie.
"Have you got my Sunday Post?" he queried.
"This place is like Sauchiehall Street" grumbled the Doctor and shouted at them "Get away from here at once but stay in your cabins until I see you."

I seldom look in a mirror – the reflected image never comes up to expectations, but as I put on my lipstick that morning I'd noticed a couple of spots on my face. "These wretched mosquitoes," I thought. The Doctor's thoughts lay in other directions.
"What's this?" he said poking at some spots on my neck. Then he said "Now don't panic, you'll be alright, but when were you last vaccinated?" Panic! I was horrified. Surely, surely, he couldn't mean smallpox? Muttering something about notifying the Port Health he made me promise not to let anyone into the cabin.

"I'll be back soon" he said, closing the door firmly behind him. Later he revealed that he'd gone to check the amount of vaccine in stock.

I don't remember getting undressed and going back to bed, but I do remember looking in the mirror. Great juicy spots seemed to be popping out even as I looked. The vague headache I'd had developed into a real thumping one. Numb with shock I lay on top of the bed. Later I heard that the Doctor had immediately vaccinated Nan, John, the Hairdresser, Margaret the Nursing Sister, and the two cadets. The Captain was breakfasting on one of the Company's cargo ships a few berths away. The newly vaccinated deck apprentice was sent to ask him to come back urgently. The Purser cadet was sent for the Port Health Authorities and the Quarter-Master instructed to put up notices closing the gangway.

When the Captain returned to the ship, he kicked the blackboard notice aside saying "I'm the Master here, and shall put up any notice required." He was wrong; in such a serious matter the Doctor's word was law. Most of the Goanese crew had been going to Mass and gathered on deck chattering excitedly. On hearing the Quarter-Master prophesy "Go off now, for as sure as eggs is eggs it'll be closed again," they scuttled ashore. Jean, the shop girl, invited to Bombay races, a posh affair, turned back for her gloves just as the gangway was re-opened. When she saw that our cabin section on Boat Deck was roped off with huge "Quarantine. Keep Out" notices at each end of the alleyway she thought it wiser not to approach and hurried gloveless off the ship again.

Meantime the Doctor had returned to my cabin and demanded to know the name of everyone with whom I had been out since the ship's docking. Counting the group who'd gone on the Sunday picnic and the two cadets who had actually touched my neck the previous evening there weren't many Europeans who hadn't had contact with me. As a precaution he re-vaccinated all the European crew. A young sari-clad Indian doctor came from the Port Health. After examining me thoroughly she asked if I had been ashore in either Aden or Karachi. She admitted being puzzled but said she was the most junior member of the Port Health and would have to go back and report to her senior colleagues. The Ship's doctor had a degree in tropical medicine, but admitted that he had never actually seen an active case. "If she has to go to hospital" she said "I'll do my best to provide a bed," explaining that Europeans were usually nursed at home. In the General Hospital no beds were provided. It sounded far from hygienic – all cases lie on the floor together – typhoid, smallpox, syphilis, malaria etc. Hordes of relatives squat round the patient with cooking pots, prayer mats and often Ju Ju (black magic) paraphernalia. The Doctor and I were shocked and he said "I'm sure the Master of the ship will not let a member of the crew, far less a female be treated like that." The Doctor smiled "I'll be back soon, but in the meantime keep up the quarantine of the ship." Back went the notice at the gangway. She did come back quite quickly with two male senior officials. I was never fully assured, but it was concluded that I had a particularly virulent type of chicken pox. On condition that I was kept very strictly isolated they agreed to let the ship sail as scheduled. The Company would have incurred a severe financial loss had the ship been forced to lie outside the harbour for three weeks.

The Isolation Hospital right at the stern was no more than a cubby hole with a toilet and a washbasin. It had been used on the previous voyage to house a stowaway. The ship sailed on time, but at first I felt too wretched to care about anything. Once at sea I greatly appreciated a little breeze that blew in now and then. I was allowed to sit on the outer deck if no one else was around, but was honour bound not to go outside if the wind was blowing for'ard. Soon the little breeze disappeared and the relentless sun beat down from a sky more yellow than blue. There didn't seem to be any dolphins around and the hours ticked slowly by in a nightmare haze of heat. These twisting threads formed a grey patch beside the measles of D Day.

Daily Margaret came up before breakfast to take my temperature, which apparently had been alarmingly high for a few days. The Doctor visited each evening before dinner. Stan the hospital attendant brought my meals up on a tray which he laid down on the deck some distance away, and then phoned to tell me where to locate it. I'd been instructed to wash the dishes in dettol and put the tray back outside. I once caught a glimpse of Stan who rushed off as if I had the plague. It broke the monotony when the Muslims came aft to pray five times daily, and I sat on the edge of my bed and watched them. First they washed their feet, unrolled their prayer mats and then turned to face Mecca. Greatly impressed with their devotion if I'd been able to study the Koran I might have adopted their religion!

I had plenty of time to stand and stare, as I'd longed to do in the days when I wasted hours worrying over petty details in the Hydro's daily life. Devouring every book brought to me I scribbled some short stories and poems myself. When I was eventually released from quarantine they were all put over the side. A clear picture flashes back of seeing the books dropping down under the waves and of my cotton dress, housecoat and nightdresses all floating away. I thought "What a waste. The Doctor is really a bit of a fusspot." One of the so-called poems I wrote was by way of thanks to him. Once I started I got carried away with words like dedication, appreciation, consternation, desperation and of course isolation. It had umpteen verses, and the more I thought about it, the more words came tumbling out – realisation, trepidation and many more. I don't suppose he took a copy before he chucked it over the side – vexation! A master piece was lost! although I tried to rewrite it later. I wasn't allowed to send any letters but the Doctor wrote to Mum and told her not worry as I was well but infectious. She regarded it like the telegram that she had been sent on D.Day – one of the hazards of the job.

Hour after hour I used to watch the log line trailing behind the ship's stern and wondered if I could cut it and cause a slight diversion! Sometimes in the night one of the deck officers would ring up from the Bridge. The sound of another human voice was welcome, but of course I had to thoroughly disinfect the 'phone after I had used it.

At each port of call the Port Health Doctor came to see me. These doctors lurk in the corner of my mind as beady-eyed little men, fat and perspiring in grubby white shorts. Subconsciously I resented them, fearing I might catch another awful disease when they touched me!

Ashore I'd been accustomed to clouds of flying ants attracted by the lights, and to amazingly agile lizards darting about, even up the inside walls of a house during dinner. I had seen regiments of ants marching along to the scene of a spilled drink or a mere drop of sugar left in the bottom of a coffee cup, but at sea, apart from the odd cockroach there didn't seem to be any insects, or so I thought. How wrong I was!

One very hot afternoon as we sailed up the Red Sea, the heat haze blotted out the horizon. Suddenly there was a dark cloud, and then a swarm of insects descended on the ship. Some of these creatures fastened on my dress and were even in my hair. I was almost hysterical, and rushed out unthinkingly almost falling over the little men chanting their prayers. I wasn't too sure what kind of insects they were but the Serang (Lascar bo'sun) tried to reassure me "Don't worry memsahib, locusts don't bite." Locusts! I'd imagined they belonged to Bible stories, and certainly never thought they could be blown off course and land on a ship. I demanded that the Serang sent for the Doctor and refused to go back into the hospital until every last one had been despatched. That was the only time I broke the rule about going out on deck, but I felt it was excusable. The Doctor tried to convince me that they were just a kind of harmless grasshopper, but I reckoned they were more sinister than all the other creepy-crawlies I'd ever encountered.

Seeing how upset I was the Doctor stayed for quite a while chatting, and later sent Stan up with a drink for me from the Bar. The Port Health Doctor at Port Said released me from quarantine and I happily went back to my cabin, although I wasn't allowed to go on duty. I counted the days until we reached Liverpool reckoning I'd probably just have about four days leave at home before I rejoined the Cilicia and set off to India again, I knew I'd savour every moment of my leave. The next morning Ann, one of the stewardesses, while serving early teas (chota harzy as the passengers called it) found time to rush in and give me a cup of coffee. She paused long enough to say "I think that Doctor is nuts – and has smallpox on the brain. Now he is saying that one of the Indian crew has it". Previously Margaret had told me that one of the stokers was ill with a very high temperature. Suspecting pneumonia the Doctor was moving him up to isolation once I was discharged. That little room would be a big improvement on sharing a deck space with about fifteen others. Surely this couldn't be the man Ann was talking about?

Margaret came along from Sick Bay to tell me what had happened. Apparently the Doctor concerned about his new patient had gone back to pay him another visit after dinner. To his horror large pox had come out on the man's face, neck and hands. Not wanting to cross swords with the Captain again, he asked three passenger Doctors to confirm his diagnosis. The verdict was haemorrhagic smallpox. He told the Captain and World Health Organisation were then notified. All during the night he physically examined and vaccinated every coloured member of the crew. Two passenger Doctors took over the routine hospital matters and our Doctor isolated himself with the patient. Big canvas screens soaked with disinfectant were put up behind the hospital. His nightmare had materialised.

Before long over the Tannoy came the solemn words, "There is no cause for alarm, but here is an important announcement. Owing to a suspected case of smallpox on board, it is essential that everyone be re-vaccinated immediately regardless of the date of the last vaccination. All passengers who joined the ship at Bombay please report at once to the First Class lounge, all passengers from Karachi please report to the First Class Smoke Room, and all European Crew members report to the hospital".

As we sailed on under the blue Mediterranean sky everyone from the Captain to the youngest baby was re-vaccinated. All those involved at the time of the scare over me were given yet another jab. Life on board went on as usual with concerts, deck tournaments, bingo, horse racing, daily cinema shows and dances. As the pilot came on at Holyhead and the voyage was drawing to a close we were all a little apprehensive.

Flying the yellow quarantine flag, we lay in the Mersey some distance off shore, and watched a fire boat bringing out a team of Port Health Officials. Soon the orders were blaring forth – passengers and crew alike all had to be seen officially. We, the European crew lined up outside the hospital. No one came back – each person who went into the hospital disappeared – (presumably leaving by the port side door and along another alleyway). One of the boys was due to be married a week later and his pals joked about it being an omen and a lucky escape. The Second Steward appeared with a crew list in his hand. When we asked what was happening he said "Oh the reason for the delay is they have had to send ashore for more bells." "Bells?" we echoed stupidly. "Yes", he said, "We'll each get one to ring and shout "unclean, unclean". We were sure he must be joking and yet were a trifled worried. All being virtually in quarantine on the ship since Port Said, we had hoped that would have been the end of the matter.

They subjected me to a proper examination, and then to my relief let me go. There weren't any bells but all passengers and crew were given a card saying "This person is a direct smallpox contact, if he or she collapses in the street do not touch the body. Phone the Medical Officer of Health or call the Police. Penalty for not carrying the card at all times £100". I couldn't imagine how anyone would find the card without touching the body! I carried it faithfully and threw it away after the final period of quarantine was over. We were told that we were not to leave the country for twenty-one days. Provided all members of the household had been re-vaccinated in the previous twenty-four hours we would be allowed to go home. Surprisingly the Doctor was allowed out of his self-imposed quarantine and able to go on leave like the rest of us. A small isolation hospital in Rockferry on the Wirral, was reopened specially to accommodate the smallpox case.

No visitors were allowed on board and only the few office staff who had been re-vaccinated came down to the ship. I'm not sure if the Liverpool dockers were re-vaccinated or not, but they refused to discharge the cargo. On receipt of extra payment they unloaded the passengers' baggage. We had to sail back to Glasgow with the ship, and not go on ahead by train as usual. With the twenty-one day ban on leaving the country, I realised that I would miss the sailing of the Cilicia.

As soon as we reached the Tail of the Bank, the Glasgow Port Health came on board with a Decontamination Squad. They went all round the ship freely dousing every corner with the strong smelling disinfectant formaldehyde. The news of the ship's arrival was broadcast, featured on T.V., and in the newspapers. When I got permission I 'phoned Mum to reassure her that I was alright and not the crew member mentioned. I told her that she would have to be vaccinated before I would be able to go home. We were allowed to leave the ship at Yorkhill, and use public transport, but had to report back on board every morning for two weeks for examination by the Health Authorities. The usual taxi firm was reluctant to come down to the ship, so off I went by bus to the Central Station and caught the train for Weymss Bay.

I was conscious of still smelling strongly of formaldehyde as my baggage had been scooted with the wretched stuff when I crossed the Circassia's gangway. Two retired teachers sat opposite me in the train. One looked up from the Evening Times and remarked "Fancy bringing that ship into Glasgow. I believe smallpox spreads like wildfire". For a moment I wickedly wondered what their reaction would be if I produced my card and said I didn't feel well. I thought perhaps they'd pull the emergency cord or else collapse in a state of shock.

I resisted the impulse, and buried my head in a book. The reason that they used such stringent measures in Glasgow was that there had been a smallpox epidemic there in 1950. The case of an Asian seaman who was alleged to have chickenpox had been demonstrated to a class of medical students illustrating the slight difference between it and smallpox. Alas, even the Professor had been wrong. The man had smallpox and several other cases resulted. All medical students who graduated after that date had an extra awareness of the difficulty of accurate diagnosis. Now, eight years later they were still doubly vigilant – this was why the Glasgow M.O.H. had sent a team down to the ship, and didn't just leave it to the authorities in Greenock. They insisted that everyone should show evidence of a positive reaction. Our Captain in particular was most indignant. He swore – really swore loudly and long that he had had more inoculations than he could count, and now never had had any reaction, but regardless of this he was given yet another jab! I trailed up to Glasgow daily to show the minute scab on my arm.

In the meantime the sick man was being nursed in the little hospital in Rockferry but despite every precaution, some other cases developed on the Wirral. An elderly woman living nearby caught smallpox, and, we were told, had died. Apparently her young grandson had been ill first, but, fairly recently vaccinated, had a mild attack and recovered. Several other contacts with that particular house became victims of smallpox and the authorities were very perplexed about the source of the leakage. Eventually it was presumed that the family cat must have strayed into the hospital grounds and transmitted the virus. I felt that our Doctor should have been greatly complimented on the way he managed to contain the disease and that there was only the one case on the ship. No further cases were reported amongst the passengers or crew – all scattered throughout the U.K. once the ship docked.

The Cilicia was well on her way back to Bombay by the time that I was signed off from the Circassia. I didn't want to stay there in what really was another girl's place, but was financially unable to wait for my own ship. Once again I was at a crossroads. Nightly I thought "What shall I do? Wait hopefully for another ship? or do something else?" The twisting threads seemed to have become knotted.

Chapter Eleven

Sailing down 'The Coast'

While I was away our friend Jenny had had an operation for cancer and radium treatment to which she reacted very badly. A smaller much older looking Jenny than the Jenny I had known all my life managed a weak smile when I returned from that ill-fated voyage on the Circassia. She had always appeared to have excellent health, but now was frequently sick, and always tired. The doctor must have realised that it was unlikely that she'd live very long, because although he had vaccinated Mum he said it didn't matter if Jenny wasn't done. After a couple of weeks she seemed to have lost the will to live. She slept a great deal. I was glad that I was at home when she died.

Although Jenny's death made a great gap in Mum's life she fortunately had a wide circle of supportive friends. She was most insistent that I didn't consider staying at home on her account. There were few full time jobs in Rothesay and almost all my peers had left the island to find work or by this time were married. There were no vacancies on the Glasgow Pool and I was beginning to have little confidence in Royal Mail's assurance that they would shortly send for me. What should I do? The question of the future loomed large in my mind and the problem grew greater each night as I tried to sleep.

A temporary answer to my problem came when my Aunt in London called for help. She had angina and was unable to cope with the family while my cousin had a minor operation. Off I went to London. I felt quite competent as I made beds, cleaned the house, washed and ironed, but I wasn't so confident about the cooking. My practical experience in that line was extremely limited. Surprisingly I had no complaints and they all survived! I enjoyed exploring London with the three children and took them to the Tower, The Maze at Hampton Court and Madam Tussaud's.

Well versed in the procedure I registered at the London Pool and wrote applications to a few shipping companies, hoping to get on a shorter run and be home more frequently. I still had my Spanish notebook and went around mumbling phrases while I hovered and dusted. Union Castle and Elder Dempster both interviewed me, and I waited impatiently for a definite appointment. In response to a telegram from Elder Dempster, I went off to Tilbury and joined the Calabar. Within three days I sailed for West Africa. The Calabar and her sister ship Winnebah were the smallest and oldest of Elder Dempster's passenger ships. She turned out to be an extremely hot but a very happy ship.

Dorothy and I, the only female members of the crew, were expected to attend to the cabins, and also look after the children in the Nursery. She regarded the latter duty with horror, while I was delighted to be there all day. We worked it out that she did all the cabins while I looked after the children. It wasn't a proper nursery but an improvised deck space with the minimum of play equipment. I enjoyed making up stories and inventing games and competitions. The hours passed swiftly. I liked to think that the children were having as good a time as I was.

Our first port of call, Madeira, loomed out of the sea early one morning. In order to allow the passengers the maximum time ashore breakfast was served at 7.00 a.m. and I helped Dorothy with the cabins so that we too could get ashore early. My particular memories are of flowers everywhere with a surprise profusion of geraniums white, pale pink and crimson growing wild by the roadside; the women patiently working at marvellous embroidery, and the taste of local wine in a cool dark cellar. A little bus chugged uphill with us and a magnificent view spread out below with the ship looking much too small to have braved the stormy seas.

We went into the famous Reids Hotel for afternoon tea. Although it was a trifle expensive we relished the quiet Victorian atmosphere. The elderly frock-coated waiters served us most courteously as if we were rich and famous like so many of the guests. For once I was leading the life as other people imagined it would be! I'd stayed in the Regent Palace Bagdhad, been to Raffles in Singapore, Shepherds in Cairo, the Taj Mahal in Bombay and was now in Reids for tea. Somehow "being at sea" had an undeserved ring of glamour about it with no one appreciating the difficulties of working long hours in tremendous heat with little time to relax. We didn't get ashore at every port, and often when we did, found scenes of incredible poverty and unimaginable smells. When home in Bute it all seemed blurred and unreal and I never emphasised the negative aspect.

Almost overnight as we approached Sierra Leone the temperature changed from temperate to tropical. Used to the Mediterranean and the more gradual build up to the heat. I wasn't prepared for the overnight jump of about 18 F in the thermometer reading. A blanket of heat lay on the horizon as Mount Aureol appeared through the mist with Freetown sprawling below. Palm trees like huge crooked feather dusters fringed the coast line.

With a couple of tugs fussing round we drew alongside the wharf. The docks were smaller than those at Karachi or Bombay but the scene of hustle and bustle was familiar. My first impression of West Africans was that they were bigger, noisier and darker-skinned than the Arabs or Indians. As soon as the gangway was lowered crowds of people pushed their way on board. As well as the shipping office staff there were others on legitimate business – dockers, Port officials, customs and police. Then too there were people to welcome new arrivals or to greet friends returning from leave. One of the Deck Officers and a Quarter Master stood at the head of the gangway, checking identification and boarding passes and trying to prevent stowaways slipping past.

On the crowded quay a motley group stood aimlessly staring at the ship. Ever the romantic, I thought they were marvelling at where we'd been or dreaming that some day they'd be able to buy a ticket and come with us. The more experienced and more sceptical members of the crew warned "Make sure your porthole is tightly shut, in fact put down the deadlight, or that lot will steal everything within reach." Once, I think it was in Aden, I left the porthole swinging on one of the lugs and discovered my face cloth, toothbrush, tube of toothpaste had somehow been snatched from outside!

Unlike Port Said or Aden there weren't any bum boats but a group of youths swam round the ship like fish. They dived deeply and flashed white teeth in appreciative smiles when they surfaced with coins thrown by the passengers. The traders on the quay seemed to have only cheap plastic goods for sale, but several large African women offered slices of melon and paw-paw, mostly covered with flies. Flies crawled everywhere even on the faces of sleeping children tucked cosily onto their mothers' backs. They didn't seem to notice.

As we were only in port for a short time we didn't get shore leave. There were lots of taxis outside the quay but I looked in vain for a camel, a bullock cart or even a donkey.

Soon the engines started up, the alleyways throbbed with life again and we were on our way to Takordi. Tema Harbour the port for Accra was yet to be built. My old school atlas showed the Gold Coast plainly but at Independence in 1957 it had been renamed Ghana. It was all part of the notorious "White Man's Grave." All over West Africa the mosquitoes were carriers of malaria. It certainly wasn't the healthiest part of the world. There were frequent outbreaks of dysentery, typhoid, yellow fever, dengue fever and other troubles caused by the bite of the tsetse fly. Fearful of catching malaria as well as developing prickly heat, we took paludrine and salt tablets daily. The mosquitoes chewing round my ankles and taking lumps out of my neck were larger and fiercer than any I'd experienced before. I vowed that I would never complain about midges at home again.

Apart from what I knew of David Livingston and Mungo Park's explorations and half-remembered tales of missionaries, I was woefully ignorant about West Africa. The number of different countries was quite bewildering, and the size of them reduced Britain to a mere dot on the map.

There are hundreds of different languages and dialects in Africa but in Nigeria English was probably the most commonly spoken. The Yoruba and Ibo tribes all jealously guarded their native tongues and were reluctant to teach us a word. Pidgin English was often confusing but widely used on the Coast (as the whole of British West Africa was called.) "He no be done gone in time" simply meant "he's late" and "Massa, he say, he-no for-be" could mean the Master isn't coming or even that he's just been. I never understood why they had superfluous words like make-you go instead of go and one-time instead of merely once. Although it interested me, like my smattering of German and Spanish it isn't now so easily recalled. We adopted many words subconsciously and lapsed into the habit of saying "chop" instead of food, and "plenty palaver" seemed an apt description for a heated discussion. Nigeria was less than a day's sailing from Ghana, and the voyage quite suddenly came to an abrupt end. Passengers feverishly packing transformed their cabins into incredibly untidy rooms.

A few miles off shore the pilot boat came alongside and several small coasting vessels, fishing boats and even canoes appeared on the scene as if to escort us into Lagos. At the rough stone breakwater (the Bar) a group of Europeans stood waving a welcome. "There's the Yacht Club it hasn't changed" said one of the old Coasters. We could see plainly the small tables and the sun umbrellas set out, then we passed close to Government House, a big white mansion with a well manicured lawn and a private jetty. Lagos with unexpected modern multi-storeyed buildings and broad Marine promenade lay on an island across the harbour from Apapa docks. Judging by the crowd on the quay the arrival of the mail boat was obviously a very important event. Those who had boarding-passes soon came up the gangway. There were more visitors than passengers. Probably some were just sight-seeing and had bribed their way on board. The African crew were given a few days leave and a spare crew came to take their places.

The funnels of the other ships in dock, and their registration ports betrayed the country of origin. There were ships of Palm Line, Blue Funnel, John Holt, Holland America, Black Star, a Japanese ship, Panamanian and Monrovia ships also a couple of Elder Dempster cargo boats. There was, of course no familiar black funnel of the Anchor Line, and no City Line ships either. The passengers had a long tiring wait in the airless customs shed. The heat was really fierce, the sun relentless, and the docks shade less. The dazzle on the water hurt our eyes and we were grateful when darkness fell and a cool breeze blew across the narrow breakwater from the sea.

Next day Dorothy and I went across to Lagos in one of the company's boats, not by the long road and Carter Bridge. A few years later a modern causeway was built and despite frequent traffic jams the journey time was almost halved. Taxis and bicycles weaved dangerously in and out of the line of cars, lorries and mammy wagons. Crossing the lagoon by boat was much more peaceful.

We didn't venture far from the jetty on our initial expedition ashore. Dorothy was appalled by her first glimpse of the place as previously her only foreign port had been New York. We were assailed by a curious mixture of odours which wasn't surprising as the back streets were bordered by frightful open drains. The smell of fish mingled with that of petrol, palm kernels and wood smoke. We made our way to Kingsway the biggest shop in town. I was disappointed as it was just a replica of a U.K. store. "This modern place can't be Africa", I thought. The crowds in the streets were a mixed bunch – predominantly Yoruba, but there were Ibos, Fulani and Housamen too. The Yoruba women wore an overtop and a skirt wrap (a lappa) of distinctive blue. Just in the same way as European women couldn't wear a sari with the same grace as Indians, the Yorubas had a specially skilful way of tying their headgear, that didn't come easily to other nationalities.

The street traders sold everything from sunglasses, gaudy plastic handbags, cheap French perfume to photos of Hollywood stars. If one gave them more than a brief glance they grew more and more persistent, and a second's hesitation could mean the purchase of a useless article. Many of the African women carried most amazingly heavy things on their heads with apparent ease. There were beggars too, but fewer were so pathetically defeated looking or so grotesquely deformed as the Indian ones. These ones seemed much fitter and certainly bolder. There were no tramcars or holy cows wandering around as in Bombay, but there were lots of barrow pushers and bicycle riders obstructing the cars and crowded buses.

There had been a threat of rain in the grey skies all morning and it quickly turned to a heavy downpour. We splashed back through the mud and puddles to the waiting launch for Apapa. Just as I was stepping into the boat I met a Port Bannatyne man. It was incredible. In Takoradi I had discovered that the Pilot's parents lived in Wyndham Road, and here was someone else from home. The rest of the crew couldn't believe in two such meetings in one short voyage. "This Bute must be a really ghastly place, when people leave it and come to West Africa", teased the Purser. "I've been at sea for ten years and have never met anyone from Blackpool, my home town, far less anyone I actually knew". It was hard to explain that island dwellers were a close community and we all knew several hundred people by name. "Scotland", said the Africans "that must be England's Bushland? Not so? Why you no go for independence like us?" I told them that we were supposed to be equal partners with England and not some inferior dependency, and tried to impress them by rattling off some Scottish inventors – Bell, Baird, Murdoch, Fleming etc.. They were thoroughly confused and scornful of the fact that English was the language spoken and very few Scots could speak Gaelic. They pointed out to me that even the BBC constantly refers to the Queen of England, and almost never the Queen of Great Britain.

Some Africans seriously said "You Scottish people are to blame for all our troubles. If you hadn't sent explorers and missionaries to the villages we would all still have been happy living there instead of coming to Lagos and learning all the bad habits of the white man." It was hard to answer that without raking up the fact that in the past – the days of the all powerful Chief he, as well as the white man, had sold many of their forbearers into slavery. On the whole the Scotsman is highly respected abroad, but alas sometimes thought of as an escapee from the Bush! I was a good Publicity Officer for Bute and frequently boasted about its beauty, lack of snow, and the palm trees flourishing right on the sea front.

One day I sat on the afterdeck in my off duty time reading an old Buteman. Alex. The 2nd Mate sunbathing nearby said "Can I borrow your newspaper?" I handed it over and he glanced briefly at the headlines, and then turned to the back, "Is this the sports page?" he asked puzzled. "Shinty, what on earth is that? Indoor Football, Rugby, Indoor Bowls? Pub Darts, but where's the soccer?" He was quite speechless when I admitted we didn't really have a football team. "No football? – that's incredible." I explained that there were quite a few Rangers and Celtic supporters on the island and that some of them went to Glasgow to see a match, or just to Greenock if they followed Morton. "Good grief," he said, "Talk about the Bush. That place must be the end of the earth. You really mean that they have to go by steamer and train to see a decent match?" He couldn't believe that there wasn't a mass exodus of the male population every Saturday, and wasn't impressed when I explained lots of men spent their leisure hours playing golf, or went out sailing, or fishing. "It is better", I said proudly "to take part in sport instead of just being a spectator."

After two trips on the Calabar I made a decision about my future. Having enjoyed working with the children enormously and feeling satisfied that I had really achieved something worthwhile, I decided that I'd stop sailing about aimlessly but get a job in a nursery ashore and study for my N.N.E.B. Then if I wanted to continue travelling I'd be properly qualified, and I might even become in charge of a ship's nursery.

I was only at home for a few days, and had written off a couple of applications for a nursery placement, when a phone call from Elder Dempster's Head Office in Liverpool changed the pattern of my life again. It transpired that the Captain of the Calabar had spoken in glowing terms about me to the Passenger Manager and a couple of parents had actually taken the trouble to write in, in similar vein.

An unexpected vacancy cropped up on the Apapa and, as my name was known, I was offered the position. I didn't hesitate to grasp the opportunity, packed my case again, and set off this time for Liverpool.

The Elder Dempster Shipping Company (founded by two Scotsmen) had for many years traded along the Coast – that is all along the old slave routes from Senegal to the Cameroons. In addition to the two London based ships the main link to the Coast was from Liverpool. The fleet of yellow funnelled cargo boats took machinery and general cargo out, and returned with timber, copra, groundnut oil, palm kernels and precious metals. The Apapa, her sistership Accra and the flagship Aureol maintained a regular service to Lagos carrying passengers, mail and cargo too. The expatriates on the Coast measured the length of their tours by the fortnightly arrival of one or other of the mail boats.

Once in Liverpool I took a taxi from Lime Street Station down to Canada Dock where my new ship, the Apapa, awaited me. My friends were beginning to complain that they needed more pages in their address books to accommodate me. I no longer wondered what the Square was, eventually my cabin was on the main square just beside the pilot door and very near the Purser's Office. As well as the normal ports of Las Palmas, Freetown, Takoradi and Lagos, serviced by the mail boats, the Apapa called at Bathurst in the Gambia. She was the only passenger ship ever to call there on a regular basis – another new place for me to see!

I was delighted when at last I started working in the nursery, even more so when it was modernised and upgraded. Another girl was recruited to help – there was certainly plenty to do. We worked daily from 7.30 a.m. until 6.00 p.m. and had an African steward to do the cleaning and odd jobs. It was exhausting but we loved it. There was a separate sitting for childrens' meals, before the adults, and accordingly the Nursery was especially crowded at breakfast and lunch time. Most children enjoyed themselves so much that they stayed with us all day. At times the noise was reminiscent of a rowdy childrens' party mingled with shouts from a busy school playground. Passengers used to look in and exclaim "Heavens, what terrible crime did you commit to have been put in there? It must be sheer purgatory." On hearing that we actually enjoyed the work they shook their heads in disbelief. No longer did I think "Just one more trip" I was settled, and delighted to be working with children.

With a different group of children each voyage it was like constantly starting a new job, and we had quickly to memorise their names and cabin number. That was easy enough with fair-haired Peter and freckled red-headed David but it was much harder to distinguish Addie from Allum; both aged two with black curly hair, white, white teeth, bewitching smiles, huge twinkling eyes and smooth brown velvet skins. The African babies were adorable. Eve, one of the other girls had great trouble in remembering names, but thought she had the answer when she wrote on her passenger list "Femi - Cabin A 5 6 – green jersey." She was nonplussed the next day when he appeared in a red track suit.

The southbound passengers were going to Africa to work, or were returning from university courses in the U.K. By 1958 there weren't many "pukka sahibs" travelling. The days of the sun helmeted European were long gone and the old school tie brigade was gradually being superseded by a new type of passenger. With the introduction of anti-malaria drugs and the advent of air-conditioning many more women and children were venturing out to the Coast. Bringing technical and artisan skills with them, the passengers came from all walks of life – road builders, telephone engineers, agents for commercial firms, hoteliers, medical staff, university lecturers and diplomats. Pre-decolonisation there were still quite a few British service men seconded to those West African countries.

Frequently Africans who had been studying or working in the U.K. were returning with families who had never seen their homeland. This presented quite a problem as children born and brought up in Bradford or Birmingham hadn't been prepared for the cultural shock. The adults too had become Westernised and their apprehension increased after they'd been ashore at the first African port of call. My thoughts twisted back to the wartime evacuees transferred from busy Glasgow to sleepy Bute, another culture.

One Nigerian doctor travelling back to his home in Enugu with his wife, a qualified dentist, and two charming children, confided in me that he was very worried. "I'm a fool," he said "It has only dawned on me now that it is most unlikely that my parents will have changed at all in the ten years that I've been away. I could see how shocked
the children were when we went ashore and saw and smelled Africa for

the first time. Frankly I'm not sure that Kara and I will be able to stand it either and we haven't prepared the children at all. Yet I want to help my country. I'm feeling very confused." I realised what he meant, and often wondered if they were able to settle down in Nigeria.

The children came in all sizes, ages and nationalities. The majority were British or African, but throughout the years there were children from every place imaginable. Joy a lovable three year old with a smile that lit up her whole face was a little Korean girl adopted by an American couple. Then there was Pip, a little boy from Finland whose divorced mother had remarried. He used to boast "I have two Daddies, one is English and lives in Finland and my new Daddy comes from Holland!" Talk about League of Nations!

The majority of children spoke English, but occasionally we were confronted with one who only spoke Polish, Hungarian or some language of which we were totally ignorant. It was vital to gain their confidence quickly and assure the bewildered youngsters that they hadn't been abandoned in an alien place. In a little notebook I wrote phonetically in various languages the phrase for "Don't cry, Mummy is coming back soon." My attempt at speaking Greek to two year old Demetrios was not a success and his sobs turned into loud screams! Goodness knows what I did say, it certainly hadn't the desired effect. It was no use – absolutely no use, and I quickly abandoned the idea and only spoke English. It is the tone of the voice as much as the actual words that gets results "No" said firmly is understood like"Non" or "Nein"

One voyage in particular we were almost in hysterics as there were even Bulgarian and Brazilian families travelling. Every second family seemed to have a very scanty knowledge of English. Homeward bound Onike, a seven year old Nigerian most unusually hadn't a word of English. I was really pleased with his progress during the trip, and often rewarded him with "You are a good boy, Onike". He had a disarming smile and greeted everyone with "Good morning, hullo." He was always reluctant to go back to his cabin in the evenings, and I had to say "Goodbye, Onike, see you tomorrow" in a very definite dismissive tone.

When he left the ship in Liverpool he gave me a big hug and an embroidered postcard he'd bought in Las Palmas. As he walked away along the quay he called up "Good boy, Nanny, good boy." I presumed he'd got mixed up and really meant goodbye, so I waved and called back "Goodbye Onike, goodbye. You are a good boy, goodbye." Where is he now? a businessman in London, a car salesman in Bradford, a shop owner in Benin? a hotel manager in Ibadan or a powerful army officer in Lagos? Does he have fond memories of his first trip to the U.K? I hope so.

I'm absolutely sure that Bob and Bill Turnbull will never forget their first glimpse of Liverpool. Their English father's firm had been building a road through the Bush. Most Europeans only did a fifteen or an eighteen month tour, but he hadn't taken leave for five years and travelling home with his young African wife and the four year old twin boys. They were wildly excited about everything, and were first at the nursery door every morning. They must really have lived deep in the Bush because electric light switches and the running water in the wash-hand basin held a special fascination for them. Early one November morning we drew in alongside the Liverpool Landing Stage with the brilliantly lit Liver Building towering in the background. They were enchanted. "Is that fairyland?" asked Bob, and their mother looked as if she wondered too. I hope their new country wasn't a disappointment.

Back to my first trip on the Apapa after Las Palmas our next port of call was Bathurst (now renamed Banjul). Our visits were important to the economy of the Gambia and were red-letter days in the social calendar of the two hundred or so expatriates. The pilot boarded at the river mouth as it was about thirty miles up to the port. Our arrival evoked special interest as for some passengers it was the first glimpse of Africa, the hot steamy country that was to be their new home. As the ship was several feet longer than the quay it had to be moored to buoys fore and aft. It was quite a task for the two Port Authority men who set out in a small boat to accomplish this. The wharf was crowded with people who soon swarmed onto the ship. The deck officer and quartermaster appointed to be on gangway duty were convinced they would easily get jobs ashore in crowd control. They had plenty of practice. It was a port they didn't enjoy at all.

On the southbound voyage at Bathurst we discharged general cargo, and only about ten passengers, but embarked almost fifty deck passengers, so called as they slept on deck. Most of them were traders and at each subsequent port they came and went although many sailed on to Lagos. The majority consisted of rather large women with huge bundles of their heads, a baby tucked in on their backs, and four or five small ones clinging onto their ample colourful skirts. Some children carried little bundles too or balanced a selection of enamel basins on their heads. There was always an opportunity for a stowaway to sneak on board, and I'm sure an extra child was sometimes smuggled onto the ship and could go off undetected in another country.

I didn't know how "the Deckers" coped on the deck in the rainy season but it must have been extremely unpleasant. A couple of security officers resplendent in khaki uniform travelled with them to keep order. Normally they were a happy bunch and gave little trouble. One of the female "deckers" had a heart attack and died an hour after she was admitted to the ship's hospital. Jim, the male nurse, told me she had £600 pinned under her skirt. Trading seemed a profitable business.

One southbound voyage a lady arrived in the Nursery with a clinging little boy of two and a half, saying "I'm afraid Michel has forgotten most of his English since he has been playing with his cousin in Paris, but he really is a bi-lingual child." I felt that although my school French was a bit rusty I might be able to communicate with him. At least it would be easier than trying to console a little Norwegian boy. At first Michel stood in a corner stamping his foot and in almost belligerent tone demanded to know why his parents were eating and he wasn't with them, "Papa mange la soupe, Mama mange la soupe et Michel est ici. Pour quoi? Pour quoi?" He was soon inveigled into a game and forgot his fears.

His English came back quite quickly, but stumped for a word, he'd use the French one. Conversely, if I couldn't remember the French I'd revert to English. His Parisian-born mother explained that from his birth she had only ever spoken to him in French, while his British father used English all the time. They had never broken this rule. I later learned that in their house in Bathurst there was a slight bias towards French as the steward came from Senegal and spoke no English. At the age of five Michel was sent to the British school and all his lessons were in English, but to balance things his best friends were French-speaking Lebanese children! Like his parents he became completely bilingual, and never had the least accent.

Our arrival in Bathurst was very often in the evening but I nevertheless always opened up the nursery again and entertained the visiting children while their parents were partying with friends going home. On the northbound trip Michel and his Mum came on board with the other Europeans. In his hot little hands he carried a bunch of wilting flowers for me. She said, "You are his first love. When we were at the beach yesterday someone mentioned the ship's arrival and he insisted on coming back to see you. You certainly made a hit!"

They visited faithfully after that, every time the Apapa docked. The crew would tease me "There's your French boyfriend again." If we weren't too busy or if it was too late in the evening for children to come aboard I'd go ashore for a quick visit. Their house was built on stilts on a sandy beach, with a pineapple bush and a lime tree in the shrub filled garden. Giant crabs scuttled along the beach. I imagined all kinds of animals lurked in the dark shadows of the mangrove swamp behind the house. It seemed like the Africa I'd imagined. I mention Michel and his Mum particularly because they came back into my life several years later.

Chapter Twelve

Strike of the African crew

Each voyage as soon as the Passenger List came up from the Printer's shop I scanned it anxiously. I foresaw a hectic trip ahead if there were lots of toddlers, or a predominance of six year old girls who would eternally try to lift the babies out of their cots. A number of seven year old boys who wanted to run about or climb around the place was another problem. We had to watch that crawling toddlers weren't stood on or knocked over, and didn't swallow bits of lego or jigsaw. Plasticine was another menace – it got entangled in hair, sat on, squashed or eaten. Baker's dough was much safer and almost as effective. Even transfers couldn't be distributed willy-nilly or some bright spark would stick them on his eyelids or on his tongue. It only took one child to do this and several others would copy him.

We became experts at on-the-spot First Aid and dealt swiftly with bumps and bruises or objects stuck up a nose or in an ear. Talk about eyes on the back of our heads, we needed several pairs! I was never in any doubt about my first request if a Good Fairy arrived to grant me three wishes. Extra eyes would have been paramount. It seems incredible now but we coped well with up to one hundred children and had more compliments than complaints.

We weren't forbidden to mix with the male crew, as we had been during the War on Cyclops and Forth, but while we were at sea we were much too tired to think of doing anything when off duty but have a shower, go down for dinner and attend to our uniform for the next day. Although I thoroughly enjoyed my job it was quite exhausting. The men, however, spent a lot of off duty time in the "Pig", the equivalent of their local Pub. They had sing-songs, played darts and sometimes had a Bingo session, or a cinema show. I'm sure that there wasn't a notice saying "Europeans only" but it didn't seem to attract the coloured crew members. They could collect drink from the bars if they so desired, but many of them were Muslims and didn't touch alcohol.

There never seemed to be any tension between the white and coloured crew members and they daily exchanged light-hearted banter. It was a complete surprise to me returning from leave in June 1959 to discover that the African crew had gone on strike. A few militant members having presented the company with a list of complaints were refusing to sail. Afterwards many of the men said that they had been intimidated with threats being made against their families in Nigeria, if they didn't participate. The Ibo majority of the catering staff were splendid workers. With hindsight, it was an early warning of what lay ahead.

We never found out properly what their grievances were but understood there was some complaint about overtime, and trifling little matters like only being allowed choice of four different brands of duty free cigarettes. Probably there was reference to the "Pig" too. They had tried to enlist the help of Bessie Braddock, then a Liverpool M.P., and organised a March from Water Street, up Church Street and through the town. Unfortunately, they failed to evoke sympathy from the Liverpudlians as the banners they carried faced inwards, and the message about alleged unfairness couldn't be read.

When I rejoined the ship on the day prior to the sailing date, plans were well underfoot for the ship to leave without the African crew. All the European crew agreed to help and different domestic duties were allocated. The passengers warned in advance of the situation, were delighted to receive a small daily allowance as housekeeping money. The majority of them had their fares paid by the Government or the employing Company, and this unexpected cash bonus was quickly spent in the Bars. Elder Dempster were able to take on some engineer apprentices to help with the work normally done by the African stokers, and also some deck cadet officers to release the quarter-masters for more menial tasks. The Company couldn't risk inflaming the delicate situation or of upsetting the British Union of Seaman so no extra members of the catering staff were signed on.

Prior to embarkation the passengers were all given a letter from the Head Office expressing the company's regret at any inconvenience caused, and giving assurance that everything was being done to minimise problems. From the moment they heard of a dispute, the Management had been in active discussion with senior officials of the British Seamens Union and the Nigerian Office and all agreed that there was no justification of any kind in allegations or complaints to warrant strike action. In general they had been very well served by the African Staff and felt the action was only a passing incident, the result of a small group of men misguided in their views and actions.

In addition the passengers were all given a notice "putting them in the picture." Briefly they were asked to make their own beds, and keep their cabins tidy. They also had to collect the dishes of their choice from the galley, as if in a self-service restaurant. The Purser's Office, the Nursery, the Shop, all Lounges and Bars would operate more or less as usual. There would be no laundry service, but several Washing Machines were specially installed for passengers use. The Ship's staff would serve morning teas, mid-morning refreshments, afternoon tea and late night snacks. The passengers were not expected to clear away used crockery or cutlery from the dining saloon, as this would be done by the ship's staff, who would also attend to the washing up and resetting of tables. It turned out to be an unusual but happy trip. Interesting situations developed with Miss X ironing Mr Y's shirts while he'd fetch her meals from the galley.

The nursery opening hour was officially changed to 8.30 a.m. and we were press-ganged into serving morning teas. Lying back like a Duchess in a rather scant frilly nightie and a face shining with cream, one English lady seemed determined to be awkward. One morning she wanted lemon tea, and the next day a pot of coffee "with cream, not milk." The following day it was "No, not coffee bring me two freshly squeezed oranges." I didn't mind the absence of "please" as much as I minded having to go down three decks to get the oranges! The Third Mate shared the side of the deck with me and declared that I should have accidentally spilt it as I handed it to her. He completed one side of A Deck in record time. The first morning he had demanded "Tea" or "Juice" in such an authoritative voice that his gentlemen passengers gave no trouble. He handed them a cup of tea already milked and sugared "It is an emergency" he said, "they are dammed lucky to get anything at all." Surprisingly his tactics worked and there were no complaints about his rough service. The Deck Steward was amazed that few people wanted lunch out on deck that voyage. All who normally ate on the Veranda Deck beside the swimming pool, announced that it was far too hot to eat outside, although they were there for afternoon tea or anything that was served to them!

For the first couple of days I found lunch- time quite frantic.

I tried to help some of the mothers by collecting meals from the galley, and raced around like a headless chicken. To obviate accidents children weren't encouraged in the galley, and it was easier to carry the meals myself rather than have a Mum leave restless toddlers. I overdid the rushing about and on the third day caused quite a sensation by fainting and sending two portions of mince and potatoes and a strained lamb's liver dinner flying over a couple of clean white tablecloths. The wretched stuff apparently went everywhere and cutlery from several tables had to be rewashed by the unfortunate "Peggy"(deck boy). As I fell I knocked over one of the large blackboards on which the menu was written. The Printer's shop was closed hence the blackboard. Sid, the usual printer divided his day between helping the Chief Linen-keeper and operating the cinema projector. The Pursers Office had a lot more typing to do, and many extra items to broadcast that voyage.

After my collapse the Powers-that-be sent a couple of stewardesses to help at the children's meal time. Another task that fell to us was to wash out the nursery in the evenings. Once when I was emptying the bucket of dirty water in the scupper *(a kind of gutter round the deck)* I noticed several empty cigarette packets and papers and instinctively collected them in the bucket. Head down, I started to move for'ard, and suddenly bumped into someone coming the other way. It was the Boson bent on the same task. "What the blazes are you doing?" he queried. I explained. We had a good laugh as that very morning I'd found him at the end of the Hot Plate trying to mix a very lumpy looking bowl of Farex. We agreed to try to keep to our allotted tasks. At both the Gala Dinner and Fancy Dress Dance I was asked to help in the smoke room for a couple of hours after dinner. My job was to collect the dirty glasses and give them to the shop's staff who were doing the washing up. I can still hear Bob, the ship's barber saying "It has put me off drink for life. I'll never touch another drop." He didn't keep his promise!

Like most strikes it fizzled out. Things hadn't turned out as the African crew expected. Not only had they broken their articles, but with no passports, and no means of support they had no legal right to stay in Britain. They were flown right back to Nigeria the day that the ship sailed. Most of them had never been on a plane before and were quite frightened. When the voyage was over they were all standing on Apapa quay to welcome the ship. They begged for their jobs back and were greatly surprised that we had managed without them. It had been particularly hard for the older Africans who had served in the company for decades. Several had been torpedoed during the War and had shared the awful experience of being adrift in a lifeboat for a week with the Chief Steward and other Europeans. They had a very special bond, and with divided loyalties had been very upset by the whole affair.

We were all given this Certificate.

ELDER DEMPSTER LINES LIMITED
R.M.V. "APAPA"
Voyage 98

Sailed from Liverpool, 25th June 1959

This is to certify that you were on the above voyage during which the following points of interest were noted:

1.　　The Boson has served approximately 11,700 single helpings of potatoes out of which one Deck Boy has removed 22,150 eyes.

2.　　Four Ordinary Seamen have washed 38,749 dishes in the course of which 17 were broken.

3.　　One Quartermaster, in addition to his normal duties on the 4 to 8 watch, and his helpers, have washed 70,400 knives, forks, spoons etc., which he can now see in his sleep. It has been reported that he has kept a complete set as a souvenir

4.　　It has been timed by stop watch that the average time spent in the queue for meals was 3 minutes per person, per meal per day.

5.　　The Chief Officer and his many Minions have been seen in the Laundry pressing the Cook's Whites and Aprons, to say nothing of Nappies and other unmentionables.

6.　　Mr and Mrs Mops have excelled themselves in keeping their cabin clean and tidy and no complaints were made by the Captain after his inspection.

7.　　The various members of the Crew appointed to clear the alleyways have christened them "The Burma Road Job."

8.　　The Third Engineer is now the world's best beer glass washer upper having washed uncountable numbers. We will not say how many he has emptied in the process.

9.　　The housekeeping money was well received and never was so much paid out to so many in so short a time.

10.　　Nanny and the "Girls" have qualified as Nippies.

11. The Doctor has had no complaints of indigestion.

12. The Bar and Shop have advertised business as usual during the crisis.

After four years on the Apapa I transferred to the Aureol, the flagship of the company. She carried even more children and we had more staff. The Aureol didn't call at Bathurst but between Freetown and Tema Harbour (Accra) went to Monrovia in Liberia. The nursery had been purpose build and occupied a half deck above the swimming pool. In addition to the well-equipped main nursery there was a teenage rumpus room with an exercise rowing machine, cassette player, table tennis table and even a machine to dispense coca-cola. I usually left the older ones to their own devices there. On the outside deck space there were slides, a see-saw, a swing and a paddling pool. There were three lavatories specially designed for little girls, and further down the alleyway three for boys, and a couple of miniature wash-hand basins in each area. The planners didn't get it quite right – as boiling water came out of the hot taps. I had to have it switched off altogether to avoid anyone being scalded.

Once in the middle of a rowdy game I glanced around and realised that one dear little chap had moved away from the castle of bricks he'd been quietly building in a corner and was missing. Found diligently using the lavatory brush with lots of soap and ducking a little African girl's head in the pan! he explained "I'm just washing it." There was a frenzied rush to remove the soapy evidence from the woolly head before an irate Mum came on the scene. Some voyages it became quite a favourite occupation and an eagle eye had to be kept to prevent determined spirits from wandering away. When Anne was found stark naked washing her knickers and T shirt not in the wash-basin but in the lavatory pan, my thoughts twisted back to the hours spent in childhood playing at the Ardbeg burn laundry. Our Mums really had nothing much to complain about!

Many children emerge from the far recesses of my mind and insist on a mention in this tale. They are grown-up now and scattered round the world. The quiet mouse-like ones were mostly soon forgotten, but I certainly will never forget the Pitters family. The six children who were travelling in Cabin Class with their Jamaican-born mother were going out to Freetown to join their father who had started a new job there some three months previously.

The first day out from Liverpool the Captain sent for me around 10.00 a.m. and asked if I would take on the additional task of looking after this family. He explained that the mother had gone into labour during the first night and a missionary midwife had assisted the hospital staff in the delivery of a six pound baby girl. Although there was a nursery in cabin class the Captain felt it was best that I took on full responsibility of attending to the children at meal times, bedtime etc. He suggested that I took the family into the First Class Dining Saloon and then up to the First Class Nursery and looked after them there with the rest of the children. As there were no empty cabins on the ship I had to sleep in the Cabin Class with the children. It was quite a problem as Astley (ten months) and Canute who was two, had a three year old asthmatic sister – Sonia, then there was Gladstone aged four and Winsome and Geraldo twins of five.

A whole book could be written about my experience during that voyage and I certainly earned the extra overtime I was given. The twins and Gladstone were in one cabin and I was directly opposite with the younger ones. I slept on a top bunk with Sonia underneath me. The mattresses had been removed from the single bunk under the porthole and two legless cots had been secured there for the babies. Astley and Canute both still in nappies (alas not the disposable kind commonly used now) and were still bottle fed. I quickly started to introduce more solid types of food. Astley was quite a problem and seemed to have been in the habit of sleeping most of the day and staying up half the night. My struggle to keep him awake during the day was not easy. The second day he fell asleep while I was bathing him. All was peaceful until about 1.00 a.m. when Sonia started to wheeze. I attended to her, and was just dropping off to sleep again about 2.00 a.m. when Astley woke – bright as a button, and prodded Canute until he was awake too.

They were all set to play – Canute was intrigued by the strap fixing his cot to the bulkhead, and Astley stuck his foot through the bars of his cot and chortled gleefully. For the merest second I thought of burying my head under the pillow and ignoring them, but instead I jumped up and changed them. As soon as I managed to quieten them, Gladstone in the next cabin, woke up in a fit of coughing. Looking after six children all under the age of six was certainly quite a task! Their mother developed phlebitis and was kept in hospital with the baby who was named Antionette-Aureol. I expect it was the first proper rest that Mrs Pitters had had in years. When we went to the hospital to visit, the children were all pleased to see her, but Winsome was the only one who showed the slightest interest in their tiny day old sister.

Apart from Antionette-Aureol they had all been born in London – and were little Cockney children with black faces. I soon grew fond of them all – especially Astley! I proudly cheered the older ones on at Sports Day, as if they were my own. Their mother hadn't been able to unpack, but she told me where to find their best clothes for the Children's Party. I still have a photograph showing them in all their finery.

Five years later they travelled back on the ship en route for the U.K. and were then going on to make their home in America. It was Antionette-Aureol's birthday, and, as was the custom, the ship provided a cake. I was invited down to Cabin Class as guest of honour. Mr Pitters made a speech saying how grateful they had all been to me, and presented me with a green leather drawstring bag. It is still to the fore, and now holds my dusters. The cake was a splendid one in the shape of a ship with a yellow funnel, and as the candles were blown out, little Keith's excited cry of "three red chimnleys" came back to me, across the years from the Hydro.

Four year old Frank comes to mind, not because he came from Greenock, but because at first he was very withdrawn and anti-social. At the end of the voyage he was totally changed. For the first couple of mornings he went straight into the wigwam and hid. If anyone looked in or tried to coax him out he'd retreat even further and shout "Big stinks to you." His Mum said these were his "worst swear words" and it showed how unhappy he was. On the second day I noticed he could sometimes be spotted lifting the canvas flap and peeping out to view the cause of all the hilarity. According to his Mum he only liked adults and never played with children. We had such fun that most of the children elected to stay in the nursery all day. I advised her on the third day not to rush up and collect Frank immediately after breakfast.

I had a brainwave and rummaged around in our big wardrobe-like cupboard until I found a feathered head-dress which I pushed in beside the little scowling boy. I set half a dozen children round a table to string beads, and some others to make feathers out of little scraps of cloth and with string, glue and some real feathers I got from Chef soon made a few more head-dresses. A coupe of older girls laboriously printed cardboard name tags – they decided on names like Burning Fire, Big Chief Red Deer and Chief Running Water. Soon everyone was involved. I made no comment when I noticed Frank had emerged from the tent, complete with head-dress and was standing on the fringe of a group making squaws' headbands.

It proved to be one of my best ideas. Frank was soon the leader of a band of whooping Indians, and when his Mum came he refused to leave and stayed until lunchtime. Old felt hats, kerchiefs and a couple of lengths of rope soon transformed another group into cowboys. It kept everyone happy for hours and we all had a great time. Frank's parents said I had achieved what they feared had been impossible. They had dreaded the thought of the tantrums he'd throw when he was due to go to school. After that he stayed with us all day, and like Onike, was reluctant to go back to his cabin in the evening.

Alas, I hadn't the same success with Hal, or rather with his Mum. In the Dining Saloon she used to pop a spoonful of food into his mouth and then run round the table barking like a dog, or mooing like a cow! She imitated whichever animal the five year old demanded to hear before he would deign to eat another spoonful. Needless to say it caused absolute havoc and soon a dozen or so children sitting nearby were meowing or growling! After a couple of chaotic meals I sought the Purser's advice. He tactfully asked her to let Hal either eat half an hour earlier or have his meals served in the cabin. To the chagrin of the stewardess she chose to have all her own meals served in the cabin, as well as Hal's. They were going out to Ghana for the first time, but she said that if Hal disliked it and didn't settle after three or four weeks they'd fly home leaving her husband to continue his tour of duty on his own. He had already been out in Sekondi for ten months. "Hal is such a sensitive child I don't suppose he'll like a strange place" she said. I never saw them again or heard any news of them, but could imagine the end of the story.

George aged six was also a problem in the Dining Saloon, but not a noisy disruptive one. "He only ever eats grapefruit and fried bacon" said his Mum. To our astonishment this he did at every meal. At the Children's Party he spurned the suggestion that he ate a sausage, a chocolate ice or a meringue and simply wouldn't try to eat anything else. His mother was surely to blame for having introduced him to such a strange combination of foods!

In the nursery the children all played happily together regardless of race or colour. I never knew if any of them became racist in adult life, or developed prejudices, but there was no evidence of it when they were young. It was wonderful too how they accepted disablement or deformities. In all the years that I worked with children only four who travelled were affected by Down's syndrome. They were all English boys, and I remember them as being extremely affectionate and lovable. Some of the parents had a strange attitude. Nigel played happily with the others for two days before his father mentioned casually that he was a haemophiliac. In their desperation to have him treated like the others they had put him in grave danger. Without any warning of his condition, we had no idea how careful we had to be and how important it was that he didn't get a knock or become involved in a skirmish.

Amy was a thalidomide victim – a lovely little girl with perfectly shaped hands growing out of her shoulders. She had ribbons on her toys and was expert at picking things up with her toes. At first none of the children remarked on it, but on the second day someone did say "Why has Amy got no arms?" Before I could answer seven year old Toby said "Don't be silly. It is just that they haven't grown properly yet, the same as my little baby brother can't walk and hasn't any teeth." That explanation seemed logical and the matter was never raised again. At meal times she held a spoon in her toes most naturally. It didn't evoke any comments or cause a disturbance like Hal and his mooing Mum.

Once seven year old Aruna was teaching some of her friends an Indian dance, when she suddenly had a fit. I wasn't alarmed, as when I was in the Hydro, fresh from school, the stillroom maid had epilepsy and I'd often seen her eyes rolling wildly seconds before she collapsed. Aruna's parents feigned surprise but when the Doctor spoke to them admitted that it wasn't a primary fit. She suffered from petit mal and was on medication. I felt we should have been warned about her condition so that we could have kept an extra watchful eye, although of course, we couldn't have prevented her from having a seizure. I was glad she hadn't taken a fit while on top of the slide, or the outcome could have been more serious.

Chapter Thirteen

Coping with a hundred children

There were usually about seventy children in the First Class, and once or twice we set out from the U.K. with a hundred, "How on earth could even three or four people cope with so many children?" you ask "It is utterly impossible." It took a great deal of imagination, ingenuity and patience for it to become possible, with sometimes only two of us on duty. It would have been bedlam, an absolute nightmare of confused noise if activities hadn't been planned in advance. If there wasn't order timid children would have been terrified by what sounded like an unruly mob.

My main objective was to quickly gain the children's confidence and keep them happily amused. The best plan seemed to be to immediately start to play an action game like the Hokey-Cokey, with about 30 children and then gradually another ten or twenty would join in, allowing the more timid ones to be onlookers. Before attention waned and the group splintered I'd switch to a game like Follow my Leader. Then, when we were all exhausted it would be story time – a time they all loved.

Sitting in a huge circle on the deck we would soon be lost in the fantasy world of castles, dragons, good fairies, lollipop tree, talking rabbits and dogs flying in outer space. I let my imagination rip and never had the foggiest idea of what would happen next. At times we had the old stories – the Gingerbread Man, Goldilocks and the Three Bears, or an elaborate version of the Three Pigs – Pinky, Perky and Peter; but the favourites were the improbable ones I invented.

Next day I'd be taken aback by the request "Tell us what happened after Charlie the crocodile went to his granny's house." Usually I'd completely forgotten about Charlie, but soon spun a yarn about his granny making his favourite fish cakes with chocolate sauce. It was easy for me to think up some nonsense but there was a problem with constant interruptions. I was always breaking in shouting "Put that baby down" or "Don't stand up on the slide." Strangely the children didn't seem to object to the confusion and soon picked up threads of the story. Unfortunately, it all has had a lasting effect on me and I have a grasshopper mind which in conversation darts from one subject to another. Even now, many years later, I often launch into an unconnected story and expect listeners to follow my reasoning!

There were plenty of things for the child who was wary of a large group to do. A specially designed shop had been installed, complete with scales and cash register fixed to a solid counter, and shelves displaying dummy boxes and tins. Often a gang of rowdy little boys would raid the shop and send the tins flying in the air. To avoid accidents I quickly removed all the dangerous goods and filled the shelves with light-weight plastic items. Crawling toddlers loved to munch any cardboard boxes that came their way, or put the tiny pieces of money in their mouths so they were all banished. Splendid ideas for about a dozen children were unsuitable when there were so many small ones around.

On the Apapa the ship's miniature bridge complete with steering wheel, voice pipe, compass and bell, was a great attraction, but also caused friction. Every little boy wanted to be the Captain and issue orders. The constant clanging of the ship's bell mingled with all the other noises would have driven us mad had I not swiftly removed the clapper each voyage after the first day at sea.

In the corner of Aureol's nursery there was a large blackboard and lots of little seats – ideal for playing school. At times I had to intervene when there were complaints of "She has been the teacher too long. It is my turn now." Playing hospitals was popular too although we only had three complete nurses' uniforms. The Administrator had to be persuaded to wear her own clothes while others had to make do with hastily made paper caps and aprons. One bossy child usually took over as Sister in charge and rounded up a few toddlers to be patients. "You must lie very still as you are very ill," she'd say or even "Lie down and be dead I said, be dead at once." After a while shouting would come from the irate Sister as some of the patients tired of being dead, or inoculated, as we all had been, against typhoid, yellow fever and smallpox, got up and wandered outside to the slides and see-saw. If a few boys joined in it became more confused as there might be four nurses, six doctors, three ambulance drivers, one stretcher bearer and one in the X-Ray Department, but only three patients!

In the midst of it often two little girls splendid in long flowing dresses dispensed tea to any one who cared to visit their house. They'd pounce on some quiet little boy whom they could order around and tell him "You are the Daddy." Trouble arose however, when they tried to lift a baby out of her cot to add to their household. I must have shouted "Put that baby down" so often, I'm sure I mumbled it in my sleep. There were two wooden cots and four small canvas cribs, all securely fastened to the bulkhead to prevent them moving in the rough weather. We had to be ever vigilant or someone would undo one of the straps and use the leather fastening for a gun holster.

Despite having a generous allowance to enable new games and toys to be ordered each voyage, I still became a terrible scrounger and went round the galley, bake-house, pursers office and even the hospital begging for wooden spoons, jam jars, old flags, scrap paper etc. Nancy, a stewardess, brought me several hats from a jumble sale and in the dressing up box we had a fireman's helmet, two sailors' hats, a hat for a policeman, a witch and a bus driver, as well as three super ones for Ascot or a garden party. Some days I organised a band with all kinds of things improvised as instruments – spoons, jam jars, combs, sticks, rubber bands, tumblers, toy banjos and drums. It couldn't have been called music by any stretch of imagination, at best it was a joyful noise, but it was great fun.

Tape recorders were still a novelty and most of the children loved talking into the microphone. If I left one of the older children acting as M.C. with a dozen eager performers pressing round the machine, I gained more time to be with the smaller fry. The few teenagers who travelled were usually left to their own devices in the Rumpus Room which was well equipped with table tennis, a music centre, a coke machine and an exercise bicycle. Twice a week we'd have a cinema show. I became as bored watching the antics of Tom and Jerry as I had been in Bombay with the Wild West.

The favourite game was a wedding with invitations written out and delivered in advance. We usually asked one of the teenagers to be the Bride – it avoided a lot of jealousy, and we drew for the other parts – parents, grandparents, bridesmaids, trainbearers, pages, ushers and guests galore. It was sometimes difficult to persuade one of the boys to be the Bridegroom but they all clamoured to be horses for the bridal carriage! The more we played it the more we thought of things to do, and it soon grew to be an elaborate affair lasting for ages. The dress rehearsal and the show of presents were held one day and the wedding the next. We even acquired an old wedding dress, and when it became too tattered we patched it with an old sheet. Good use was made of the sheets and curtains I had coaxed from the Chief Linen Keeper. The Deck Steward helped out with food for the wedding feast and brought up doughnuts, scones and tired looking sandwiches left-over from the afternoon teas. The cake was often a lump of dough decorated with smarties, and disguised with a large cake frill and a ribbon bow. It didn't look very appetising but no one cared. We half-filled cardboard tumblers with lemonade and the Bride and Groom were toasted with great enthusiasm. It wasn't much of a feast but the children pronounced it scrumptious.

We had to have several wedding services as some child would be determined to be a Hindu Priest, a Rabbi or a Vicar. The couple were well and truly married – and sometimes in the Muslim and Buddhist faiths too! The shop's counter decorated with paper flowers became the altar. It was a game that the children enjoyed enormously and except for the smallest babies all could participate.

Sometimes we had a Zoo with the counter brought into use as the ticket office. Growling, grunting or meowing animals encaged in the large playpen or an empty cot were fed by visitors. I had Hal's Mum to thank for this idea! A competition would be held for the best poster advertising elephant and camel rides. It usually developed into a circus with clowns and jugglers, and of course, a ring-master in charge of the Big Top. Great ideas often turn out to be dangerous and I banned acts like standing up on the rocking horse. Sounds of clapping, cheering, and shouting drifted down to the swimming pool below and caused the passengers to look up. They couldn't see what was happening and never knew what they would hear.

One voyage the air was filled with hallelujahs and gospel songs. A group of missionaries asked if they could bring their guitar and amuse the children between four and five p.m. As the children sat down on deck looking like a host of angels, it was hard to believe they were the very same ones who had tried to tie Sammy to the see-saw or brought water pistols into the nursery – (quickly confiscated). They joined in the singing with great enthusiasm. I feared we might get complaints about bias towards Christianity but none came.

Most voyages I wrote a play with two or three acts. It wasn't possible to rehearse it or even discuss it while the babies and toddlers were there, so I went back to the nursery with the older children at

6.30 p.m. for an hour or so. The actors took it all seriously and the stewardesses reported that they'd hear them muttering parts in the cabin, and find written scraps of paper under their pillows. Daily we'd rehearse an action song like "Ten in a bed", and ten children immediately had a part. Singing is not one of my strong points but I managed to write several parodies for songs, to suit the occasion. There had to be a King, Queen, Princess, Prince, Wicked Fairy, Fairy Godmother, Magician and Dragon or a Camel, sometimes both, and a company of soldiers. I tried to make all parts seem equally important; sometimes, however, the Wicked Fairy had more to say than the Fairy Godmother. The play was altered slightly each voyage, depending on the age and ability of the children.

Some of the more artistic children spent a lot of time in advance writing tickets and drawing handbills. There was always "standing room only" on the penultimate day of the trip when the play was performed. Excitement ran high, photographers were busy and proud parents were amazed at how much had been accomplished in a couple of weeks.

As in all shows there were a few mishaps. Once the curtain collapsed and revealed the Fairy Godmother in frilly pants, about to climb into her long dress. She was not amused. Another time the Princess's Crown slipped down over her ears and she said "Drat this thing" to which the King of Lollipop Land said "Amy, you aren't supposed to speak at all until the King sends for you." Then the camel's front and rear went their separate ways and split in the middle. The Sergeant Major bawled at a little soldier who panicked and turned right instead of left, causing confusion. Bursting into tears he rushed off stage to the comfort of his Mum's arms. There was never any need for a prompter as the older children knew the whole thing off by heart. If anyone hesitated for a second the others would chorus the words. I remember an indignant Duchess Delia Doughnut saying "Shut up you lot, I'm supposed to say that." Many of the things that came out impromptu were far better than the original script!

The parents were genuinely thrilled; especially on the northbound trip as those children had no experience of nursery schools or playing without adult supervision. As the applause rang out and the two boys who operated the curtain by an ingenious pulling of ropes, let it down after the final bows I was as pleased as if I'd been the Producer of a successful West End Show!

I was proud of the fact that I never heard complaints of boredom but prouder still after Mr Nicholson made a special trip up to the Nursery. Apparently he was a District Officer in Northern Nigeria and had been travelling backwards and forwards for twelve years. "There's usually unruly kids chasing each other up and down the alleyways and shrieking round the pool", he said. "This time there are none to be seen, and I couldn't believe it when the Purser told me there were eighty-four children in First Class this trip. He says they are all up here all day and are so happy they don't want to come out. Thanks to you I've had the best voyage I ever had. Congratulations. It must be dammed hard work. You deserve the O.B.E." I was really chuffed that he had taken the trouble to tell me this personally. It made me feel that all the energy I expended was worthwhile, when I had been complimented by an ordinary passenger.

I often suspected that some well-meaning mother of a couple of children (perhaps the Passenger Manager's wife?) was the originator of what was thought would be an improvement in the nursery facilities, but was quite unworkable with a crowd of children. Once at the end of the voyage, the Passenger Manager suggested that there was room on the outer deck for a sand pit. I objected loudly and vigorously and told him that it would be far too dangerous, visualising sand being thrown about, into eyes and certainly hair, and the young ones eating it. I won the day and there was no sand.

Thank goodness I was asked before it became a fait accompli!

Alas, I couldn't do much about the paddling pool, it had been there since the ship was built and caused many a nightmare. It would have been ideal for half a dozen children, but hopeless to supervise the number who travelled especially with such a variance in ages. The addition of sand would greatly increase our problems.

Longing for those extra eyes, I used every possible excuse to avoid having water put into the pool. Even as I wiped the perspiration from my face I'd declare "It is too cold. The water comes straight from the sea but perhaps tomorrow it will be warm enough." I cursed the Bridge when they started broadcasting the sea temperature as well as the air temperature thus invalidating my excuse. Knowing babies could drown in a few inches of water I feared for the safety of the little ones and wondered how to prevent an excited group from fooling around. Going down the coast the ship was frequently in port and then there was no opposition when I declared "The harbour water is filthy.

There's danger of typhoid and all kinds of trouble." Approaching the tropics it was too hot to go out in the blistering sun. I used to beg the Boson to delay putting up the awning on the outer deck even for twenty-four hours, and my excuse this time would be "It is far too hot to go out there." Thus I gained a little respite. In the rainy season torrents of water fell and it would be too wet even to stand on the outer deck so there was no question of the pool being used.

Some days of course there was nothing for it – we had to have water! I arranged with Adam (the sailor responsible for cleaning the outer deck) to fill the pool while we were at lunch. Yet another problem arose when I urgently wanted the pool emptied. The controlling valve was beside the main swimming pool and inaccessible to me. Adam, the envy of all the other sailors, had a plum job and was on duty at the swimming pool all day. I'd often see him on the deck below chatting to some bikini-clad sun bather, but he was quite deaf to my cries for help.

Water! It was everywhere – splashed all over the place. Soaking wet children discovered that they could hurtle down the big slide at twice the normal speed. Many a bruise and bumped forehead resulted – another danger! One of us had to paddle with the kids to try and keep order. It was equally difficult to be inside and to keep dry, pacified and amused those whose parents had decreed that on no account were they to go near the pool. Constant to-ing and fro-ing from the pool soon made the rubbery inside deck wet too and the hitherto dry, clean children would slip and get filthy. My cry changed from "Put that baby down" to "Shut that door" and "Wipe your feet before you come in here." There were more upsets over that wretched pool than over anything else. How I hated it!

The problem remained of how to get rid of the water quickly but ultimately we hit on the idea that the valve would be left open and the outlet drain covered with two heavy rubber mats, which in desperate situations one of us could pull aside to allow the water to trickle out. Bliss! It took ages to get all the children dried, dressed and order restored again. It was inevitable that someone's beloved Teddy would be thrown in the water, and he'd have to be the first patient in the hospital the next day.

I grew more cunning each voyage, and for example, if the wedding ceremony dragged on and wasn't finished by lunch time I'd say, "Well, it doesn't matter we can go on with it tomorrow because there will be water in the pool this afternoon." The children would plead, "Oh, can't we finish the wedding this afternoon? Please, please. We won't bother about the pool." I, of course, readily agreed, and none of them seemed to realise that I had deliberately delayed the start of the wedding game until late in the forenoon. Those who were keen swimmers could be taken by their parents to the main pool.

Having such busy working days it is small wonder that I was always taken aback when people at home stopped me in the street and asked "Was it stormy?" Never once did they ask if it had been a busy voyage, or wonder how on earth we kept our sanity with so few of us coping with so many children.

Stormy! Sometimes it was, but we were usually far too busy to bother and too many noteworthy things happened on a voyage for the weather to be of paramount importance. I have crossed the Bay of Biscay more than two hundred times but only remember about a dozen gales. More people felt ill on the outward voyage than on the north-bound one. Probably because they hadn't really become used to the ship's movements before we hit the Bay of Biscay; and also many of them were apprehensive about going off to new jobs in a strange country. Fortunately, few of the children were affected by sea-sickness. I never again witnessed the frightful scene of sawdust being put down on the slimy heaps of sick in the alleyways, as I'd seen on the Empire Clyde. Looking back – it was quite horrendous!

Off the coast of Liberia the problem was more with frequent electric storms than with rough seas. The sky would be an alarmingly blue or violently yellow with sheet lightning lasting for hours on end. It was very hot and eerie and seldom accompanied by crashing thunder, just a low far-off growl. At these times we were relieved to reach the safety of the harbour at Monrovia. Although I knew that Liberia had been established by freed slaves mostly from the southern states of the U.S.A., on my first visit I wasn't prepared to hear such strong native accents of the U.S.A. When I saw the armed white-helmeted police on the quay at Monrovia threads of memory twisted back to the American M. Ps. controlling the Southampton traffic around D.Day.

The order from the Bridge "Close all deadlights" warned of rough weather ahead and precautions were being taken to prevent the huge waves battering against the ship's side and smashing the portholes. When the ship's deck was on a permanent slope it felt as if we were climbing up and down mountains. It was quite exhausting and although I wasn't physically sick I'd often get a fierce headache. At these times I'd think "I'm mad, absolutely mad. Why did I deliberately choose to leave home and look after all these children in this foul weather?" Next day when the sea was calm and a watery sun struggled out from behind the grey clouds, a little black face would break into smiles and a tiny voice lisped "I love you, Miss" I felt the world wasn't such a bad place after all!

Our departure port was switched from Liverpool to Southampton. Most of the crew had homes in Liverpool and were not happy about this change. It suited me better as I could get a direct Southampton/Glasgow flight, thus gaining more time at home. One outward bound voyage less than twenty-four hours after we had passed the Isle of Wight it became stormy. A young man staggered across the swaying nursery deck, clutching his three month old daughter. "I think my wife and I are dying" he said, "It isn't just seasickness. Maybe food poisoning. We were very ill yesterday and both violently sick during the night. You seem a nice kind person. Please take care of Diana for us." He handed the baby over and bolted. Pinned to the baby's spare nappy was a note with his parents' address and phone number. When I took Diana back to their cabin at 6.00 p.m. they both just groaned. I bathed her and put her in her cot and tried to assure them they'd feel much better the next day. They didn't believe me, but a couple of days later emerged as one of the liveliest couples on board. They entered into all the deck sports, swam, sunbathed and forgot their initial misery. When they went ashore at Las Palmas they bought a tablecloth and napkins as a token of their appreciation for the help I'd given them. Almost two years later they returned from Ghana with Diana, a chubby little toddler, and weren't affected at all by the weather on the homeward trip.

One northbound voyage it was extremely rough and we were afterwards told it was reckoned to be Hurricane Force 14. I was surprised that families considered being parted at such a time, but several children were brought up to the Nursery. The Lounge Steward told me afterwards that most of the parents who'd left children with us, sat there for hours drinking brandy, with their own life jackets beside them.

In the nursery the tables were hooked permanently to the deck, and Adam had taken the precaution of lashing the smaller chairs to the horse, also a fixture. We had a king-size playpen with a solid base and I grumbled frequently about the space it occupied. It had room for about 8 children, but of course no more than 3 little ones could be there at the same time, or they'd stand on each other or fight! That stormy day it proved to be a blessing. Piling cot mattresses and pillows inside I squashed as many children as possible into it. The rest were secured on a built-in settee, behind a table. Some fool-hardy types sat on the deck squealing with delight as it tilted, and sent them crashing into the far bulkhead. When I managed to grab a couple of children rolling back I made them sit down with the rest of us. My eternal cry was "Sit down at once" was really superfluous as it was almost impossible to stand upright

We had a sing song and a competition for inventing tongue twisters. The best one was "Why would wobbly waves wash the woolly wamba, I wonder, Willie?" Next we acted a glorious muddle of fairy tales. We were in fits of laughter with Red Riding Hood huffing and puffing on the hot porridge. Grandmother and the Wolf slept in the beds in the brick house while Peter, Porky and Perky Pig tried to blow it down. We could see the stern rising out of the water but we were too happily occupied to think of the ship being in danger.

Suddenly a fire extinguisher broke loose from the bulkhead and hurtled across the room smashing into the outer door. Amazingly there was no shattered glass – only a tremendous cracking noise. The wretched thing rolled about on the deck in an alarming fashion until one of the older boys captured it and put in a cupboard behind the shop's counter. Away up on the nursery deck we had no idea what was happening in the rest of the ship. We discovered later that owing to the severity of the gale, and the danger with pots sliding about, all cooking was suspended in the galley. In the dining saloon every chair was hooked on to the deck, fiddles were fixed round the tables and water jugs emptied out to make the cutlery stick to the tablecloths. The pantry men made piles of sandwiches but the majority of passengers jammed themselves into their bunks and brushed aside all offers of food. During the night several large leather settees in the smoke-room had moved right against the doors leading to the Promenade Deck, and the room was out of bounds until the gale subsided.

When we eventually reached Liverpool the damage to the superstructure was evident. There were two large holes in the bow and shining white paint had flaked off leaving a rusty neglected looking area. We certainly hit the headlines in the Liverpool Echo, and probably the national press too. That, however, was an exceptional trip and usually we weren't at all affected by the ship's movement. Working long hours and sailing into countries with unhealthy climates we needed to keep really fit, and knew that seasick crew members wouldn't be signed on again for the next voyage. Crossing over from Weymss Bay to Rothesay, I always wanted it to be really rough, so that I could compare it with the storms we experienced while sailing "deep sea."

When I hear the word Africa, I usually think of the West African ports to which I sailed for many years, but other pictures jostle for a place in my mind:- my first glimpse of desert, the bustle of the Suez Canal, the blistering heat, the unexpected beauty of Port Sudan's coral reefs, rickshaws in Durban and Alpine flowers on Table Mountain. We spent more time in Nigeria than in any other country. Marie and I loved wandering in the Lagos cloth market. A hive of activity and colour, it was a wonderland for any clever dressmaker with lengths of yellow and fuchsia piled beside bales of garish green cotton often patterned with strange looking fish or red elephants. Tailors sat in little booths with ancient sewing machines whirring away and managed to transform gaudy cotton into shirts and dresses. The stallholders were usually large Yoruba women with cheerful chuckles and ready smiles. Gradually we became better at bargaining although it was tiresome having to haggle over the price of the smallest article. The taxi-drivers presuming we were rich tourists always declared "Meter he no work." We had to go down a whole row of taxis refusing to enter when quoted an exorbitant rate. Eventually it would take the threat of calling a policeman before a reasonable price was fixed.

We discovered the Bush wasn't a prairie or a jungle but merely a tangled wooded web of twisted long grass, thorns and stunted clumps of palm trees rib boning the tarmacadamed roads. At night frogs and crickets leapt about the Bush and the Apapa marshes with strange croaking and squeals filling the air. Many Africans still believe in Black Magic or Juju and in the Nursery we often found babies with bead-entwined leather bands round their tummies or ankles, like a St. Christopher to keep them safe while travelling. When changing a nappy we had to be very careful not to disturb the Juju.

Once, returning from Ibadan, with some friends we went off the main road to a place where they heard that fresh eggs were for sale. Only a huddle of huts in a swamp clearance, it hardly merited the name of a village. A group of children naked except for beaded necklaces, with matchstick legs and swollen tummies played half heartedly in the dust with a tired looking dog. A few adults sat aimlessly around in the doorways of their shacks. The heat was intense, the air was heavy and still. Peggy, an Irish Doctor who worked for the Public Health Department, told me that it wasn't just lethargy that had attacked them but severe anaemia. Unfortunately that problem exists all over Africa.

Every time I passed the white sky scrapers on Lagos Marine, I was conscious that it was just a facade screening the crowded part of the town. Many people from outlying villages had been lured to the capital imagining that the streets were paved, if not by gold, at least with golden opportunities. Sadly many of them had found they were soon living in abject poverty in slum conditions. On the crowded streets the contrasts were incredible. Outside Kingsway a single photograph could capture a coloured man sweltering in a pin-stripe suit walking beside a man in a towelling dressing-gown, a European woman in trim white shorts looking as if she had stepped off the Centre Court of Wimbledon and none of them glancing at the ragged beggar crawling in the dusty kerb. Traders swarmed everywhere pursuing every white face offering a strange selection of goods – everything from feather dusters and cheap sunglasses to unknown brands of cosmetics.

In Sierra Leone the deck passengers frequently tried to sell a "genuine diamond" and in Accra one would sometimes be offered a lump of gold. Apart from not having spare cash, I was always afraid they'd be fake, but quite a few of the crew were tempted. In those days ivory wasn't socially unacceptable, as it is now, and we were sure that the elephants we bought were genuine as we chose the tusks and watched a little man in Breadfruit Lane start carving.

We were often invited out for meals and found Ikeja and Ikoyi would have been like suburbia anywhere had it not been for the broad avenues lined with palm and flame of the forest trees, and the gardens with masses of purple bougainvillea, hibiscus and frangipani. The expatriates frequented the clubs in much the same way as they used local Pubs at home, meeting there for drinks and meals, watching films, or playing Bridge or Bingo. Despite the heat the more energetic found escape in sports like tennis or golf, and cooler forms of recreation in the yacht and motor boat clubs.

At weekends Palm Oil Chop parties were often held – usually chicken cooked in palm oil with lots of accompanying dishes – coconut, peppers, pineapples etc. Victoria Beach had glorious golden sand, with a dangerous swift running tide but Tarkwa was a safer spot for weekend relaxation. My friends the Townsends had the yearly lease of a hut up one of the Creeks and frequently went across the lagoon in their boat to swim and relax under the palm trees.

They invited me there one Christmas. Other Christmas times mix together in my mind – the thrill of opening a lumpy stocking, the smell of oranges and log fires, a snowman in the garden, church bells, panic in the Hydro, when the Second Chef came on duty drunk, the swish of evening dresses in the ballroom, carol singers under a starry sky, excited children on the ship crowding round Santa. The one "up the Creek" was so different it was unforgettable. A little prickly pear tree decorated with paper stars and tinsel, standing rather crookedly outside the hut pretended it was a real Christmas tree with glass baubles and coloured lights. Denise had been delighted to get a turkey from the Kingsway cold store and served it up proudly. Somehow cold turkey and salad didn't taste the same as the hot traditional fare with brussel sprouts, stuffing and roast potatoes. With well iced glasses of gin and tonic we toasted absent friends and pretended that we were having a rip-roaring time.

Dusk came swiftly on the story book setting with palm trees swaying gently under the welcome breeze, sitting at the water's edge we sang carols under a bright silvery moon. "Surely," I thought, "that isn't the same moon as the one that Jack and I looked at in the early years of the War, or the one Douglas and I stood under in Singapore?" My thoughts twisted back to dear old Rothesay Bay where the moon would rise in a few hours behind the lighthouse at Toward.

On the ship Christmas Day was a working day like all the others. The presents for the children, purchased by the Liverpool office, were roughly marked "Boy aged 3 – 4" etc. We had a hectic time selecting the most suitable present for each child and labelling them all properly. It took ages to work it all out and ensure that no one was omitted.

One Christmas Eve, Ann and I filled stockings for fellow crew members. We even ventured up to the Captain's cabin while he was at dinner, and sneaked in when we saw his Tiger (Steward) go down below. At the end of his bed we hung an old sock containing an orange, an apple, a new penny and a clockwork mouse. I like to think it brightened his day, and that once his cabin door was firmly shut, he found time to race the little mouse over the deck and momentarily cast aside the responsibility and loneliness of his position. We never knew what his reaction had been or if he suspected us, but next day I glimpsed an extra twinkle in his eye!

Being the Master of a Passenger Ship isn't half as glamorous as is generally depicted. There is a popular myth about the Captain's table with flirtatious exchanges being served between the soup and fish courses – and it probably is so on liners like the Q.E.2. Elder Dempster usually had so many V.I.P's travelling that strict Protocol had to be observed and this was decided by Head Office. It was a nightmare with, say the Governor General of Sierra Leone, the King of the Ashanti Gold Coast and the American Ambassador to Nigeria all travelling on the same trip! The Captain wasn't free to select companions of his own choice, and since his table wasn't elastic, the Chief Engineer, the Doctor, Purser and Chief Officer had to help out too, and each had a selection of V.I.Ps at his table.

One particular Chief Officer with an eye for the ladies greatly deplored this part of the job. They also had to be acutely aware of the sensitive political situation in each country. A thoughtless remark could easily cause offence or resentment and set a couple of volatile types at each other's throats!

My favourite Captain came from Argyll. One morning at 2.00 a.m. he'd unexpectedly gone up on the Bridge and found the Cadet playing a tape of mine with songs from the televised version of Para Handy. The "Old Man" was intrigued and eventually got a copy of it himself. Not long after that passing me on the way up from the Dining Saloon he muttered "The Crinan Canal for me". Joyce overheard and queried "What does the Old Man mean? The Crinan Canal?" I replied "It is a canal in Scotland" "Oh yes," she said, "I remember, isn't that the one where the monster is supposed to be?" "No", I answered "That's the Caledonian Canal. This one is nearer home, much smaller and nicer."

I didn't think that anyone whose roots weren't in the Highlands or Islands would understand that the Captain wasn't really talking about the rough sea. We were both thinking nostalgically about that sleepy little waterway and all that we held dear in a faraway green world. Often scenes from Neil Munro's "Para Handy" flitted through my mind.

Although when a child I had read "Uncle Tom's Cabin" and was horrified at the treatment of the slaves, I blamed the rich cotton planters of America, and stupidly never stopped to wonder about the origin of these unfortunate people. Here I was in Africa and, like a splash of cold water came the realisation that most of the slaves had been taken from the Coast by ruthless traders who became immensely wealthy by providing labour for Brazil, Haiti, and the U.S.A. Some unscrupulous African Chiefs had even sold their black brothers into slavery. The full implication of the horrible injustice came rushing at me when I looked at the Portuguese-style of houses still standing in Lagos; relics of the past and reminder of Brazilian architecture.

I borrowed Ellen Thorp's book "Ladder of Bones" and learnt much of the country's dramatic history. Many things became clear – especially the huge part played by the Royal Navy's "Coffin Squadron" in blocking those engaged in the "Carrying Trade". With sharper eyes I recognised the tremendous engineering feats that had taken place, clearing all the obstacles at the Bar, opening up and dredging the harbour, and of course, the building of Apapa docks.

Before my eyes I saw many new buildings, new roads and especially in Apapa factories springing up like mushrooms. The main causeway between Apapa and Lagos was extended, and carried an enormous amount of traffic – private cars, mammy wagons and huge lorries. The lorries with names like God-go Fast, Mango-Man, or Gabriel's Train had dashboards decorated with garlands of paper flowers and pictures of film stars or pop idols.

For the most part, Lagos with its new hotels, busy bars, cinemas, race-courses and clubs had the outer trimmings of the Western world. The boundaries of Nigeria contained people with known histories stretching back over a thousand years. It couldn't have been easy for the various tribes to think of themselves as Nigerians rather than Housa, Yoruba, Ibo or Fulani but gradually they were beginning to work together towards self-government. When I first went out to Nigeria there was an air of excitement around. Most officials had a Nigerian counterpart shadowing their jobs, and hopes were high that the country would soon be self-governing. There was no colour bar in Nigeria. For example the exclusive Island Club was banned to white people, unless those specially invited by an African member. Only Nigerians could own land and certain schools did not admit white pupils. No one could blame them for trying to forget the past, and race towards Independence, especially since neighbouring Gold Coast (Ghana) had become independent in 1957. Some expatriates voiced doubts fearing that the Nigerians were trying to encompass in twenty or thirty years all that it had taken others centuries to achieve.

The Parliament Building in Lagos with the Federal House of Representatives was ready and waiting for the great day. At last the 1st October 1960 dawned – Independence Day had arrived! The Federal Palace Hotel specially built near Victoria Beach was the venue for the official receptions. Nigerian waiters splendid in tail-coats ran about with trays of drinks, desperately trying to give the same service as the waiters at the Ritz. A grand Ball was held and each lady tried to outdo her neighbour in the magnificence of her dress. African and Indian ladies outshone all the others with the vibrant colours they wore so well.

Recently sprung up nightclubs and Chinese restaurants were crowded, but doubtless the best parties were the impromptu ones started in the fishing villages up the Creek, or on nearby Victoria beach. In Yaba and in the little streets near the Mainland Hotel, shadowy figures could be seen dancing the High Life with gramophone music blaring out into the flag-decked streets. Everyone was celebrating. Although it was reported, by the media, most people in the U.K. didn't realise what a momentous thing had happened in Nigeria – a country several times larger than Great Britain. While I was on leave I was afraid of being deadly boring talking about things of which the islanders hadn't the least conception, so usually didn't mention it at all.

Micheline, my friend in the Gambia once said to me "You shouldn't go on like this – leading three contrasting lives. You are three different people – one who works dashed hard ten hours a day, one off duty enjoying the bright lights of night clubs or going out to dinner. The third one is the daughter at home in Scotland for a few days. Soon you won't know which person you really are". I knew she was right but went on playing the three different roles – happy and contented most of the time. Buried deep beneath all these people there still was the schoolgirl playing round Ardbeg shore, and a shy young Wren.

Faces blur with time, voices fade and grow indistinct yet those who occupied a corner of my heart will be there always. Normally I was too busy to get my home self confused with the working one but one night when I couldn't sleep I went out onto the deck and thought back to home. It was as if the real self had started pushing the other one, arguing a little and soliloquising a lot. During the day an African woman had asked "Couldn't you take Gloria home for me? I'd let you keep her". I was startled at such a preposterous suggestion. She waylaid me later outside my cabin and explained why she had made such a proposal. "I have three older boys at home and am going to study dentistry. I love Gloria but at two and a half she will be a handicap. She gets on so well with you I'm sure she'd soon forget us and get a good chance in life."

Gloria was a loveable little girl with the most disarming smile. I was shocked at the way her Mother spoke about it casually, hadn't thought of finding a foster home, but was quite prepared to give her away to a stranger. I explained that I had to work for my living, and my Mother certainly wasn't physically able to bring up a lively pre-school child. Gloria was a most affectionate little girl and I hoped that life would be kind to her but never heard what happened and if her Mother really did give her away.

Throughout the years I turned down similar requests from other worried African Mothers.

As I stood on the deck looking at the phosphorus on the water that night I suddenly felt incredibly sad and lonely. I worked hard every day keeping other people's children happy. For a few weeks I was an important item in their lives but I knew I'd soon be forgotten. It was entirely my own fault that I wasn't married with children of my own. I watched the sea slide by the ship in oily looking streaks and lightning flashing blue on the far horizon. For a fleeting moment I thought of the wonder and pride there must be watching one's own baby grow into a crawling, talking toddler. It wasn't cold on deck, but a little shiver ran through me. I banished these silly fancies and went back to the cabin, hoping to sleep and be ready for the seventy children waiting for me in the morning! Less than two hours later I was up again. Something prompted me to tear up most of the photographs I had, especially war-time ones. The pieces fluttered down to the sea far below and quickly vanished, it seemed a symbolic token of leaving the past behind.

At the end of a working day I was usually mentally and

physically tired but I followed a strict routine. First there was uniform washing, a quick shower, dinner, ironing and then a leisurely bath. It was marvellous to relax there and meditate over all that had occurred in the 1960s. That decade will be remembered for the first human heart transplant, astronauts walking on the moon, and on 22nd November 1963 the assassination of John F. Kennedy, the President of the U.S.A. Beatle mania spread as the Liverpool pop group gripped the attention of young folk all over the world. Gerry and the Pacemakers, the Shadows, Freddy and the Dreamers all kept the Mersey Sound in the forefront.

Teenagers who came up to the Nursery deck were eternally singing "Please, please me", "Eleanor Rigby", and "Mull of Kintyre" but without doubt the favourite was "Yellow Submarine" and the young ones begged to have a submarine in the play. I had to change the plot but a benevolent King working with the Fairy Godmother soon made it possible. It wasn't so easy to make a submarine and the empty cardboard boxes I purloined from the Bar ended up looking more like a space rocket than anything else, but the children didn't seem to mind. Imagination is a wonderful thing.

In December 1961 an insignificant paragraph in the newspaper reported that Indian troops had taken over the former Portuguese colony of Goa. Threads twisted back again to the Anchor Line stewards. I wondered how Quadros, De Costa, Del Melo and all the others would fare. These hard working, gentle, kindly men would be most unwilling to be classed as Indians, but at least there was a chance of being united with their families.

There were many changes on the African continent too and with the British Empire rapidly shrinking leaving few pink patches on the map. The Gold Coast (Ghana) was the first of the West African countries to become independent, then Nigeria, Sierra Leone and eventually the Gambia. There always had been friction between rival tribes but back in February 1961 there was a serious incident with far reaching consequences. Patric Lumumba, the first Prime Minister of Independent Congo was murdered and violent demonstrations broke out all over Africa.

Safely docked in Apapa we heard of trouble across in Lagos. A mob had broken the American Embassy's windows while a hysterical group shouted obscenities outside the British Embassy; Europeans held up in their cars on Carter Bridge were sitting targets and vulnerable, as sticks were brandished and stones thrown. Dave, the Chief Tug master (who came from Inverkip) had his windscreen smashed and a couple of stones glanced his cheek. He said it was alarming that a normally happy-go-lucky group had so quickly become an unruly screaming mob. It was most improbable that they all knew where the Congo lay or who Lumumba was.

It was our first taste of the trouble that lay ahead.

Chapter Fourteen

Trouble in Nigeria

The year 1966 is one that no Nigerian will easily forget. Rumblings of discontent had manifested in violent rioting on 9th January. Only two days later on the 11th January a British Delegation headed by the Prime Minister Harold Wilson, attended the opening of the Commonwealth Conference in Lagos. With so many V.I.Ps present security was tight, but B.B.C. reported everything had gone as planned.

While we were in Lagos for a few days we had to get the ship ready for the next batch of passengers but we were free to do so as we pleased at the weekend. On Saturday 15th January we had been invited to lunch by Cedric and Flora Davies. When I asked the Purser if he had any mail for posting in Lagos G.P.O. he said that the African messenger from the Apapa office had told him there had been "plenty trouble" in Lagos during the night. Apparently, the Army had taken over the Telephone Exchange. We pooh-poohed the idea of trouble and said we had heard there was rioting in a nearby village, but we didn't think Lagos would be affected. My immediate reaction to the story about the Telephone Exchange was "Perhaps the phones will work now".

Off Marie and I went ashore. We normally went across the lagoon in Elder Dempster's motor boat which came across every morning from Lagos. It didn't have a very reliable time-table, and could come over any time between 7.40 and 8.35 a.m. That particular morning we were on the quay just before 8.00 a.m. Even at that early hour it was almost too hot to wait in the glare of the sun, and although we stood in the shadow of one of the cranes it afforded meagre shelter. There seemed to be nothing moving in the lagoon and after waiting about ten minutes we decided to walk up to the dock gate in the hope of finding a taxi. Much to our surprise there were several taxis. Most unusually we were greeted with "This one, Missie, meter he work very good". We were astonished at this but there was very little traffic on the causeway and we were over in Lagos in record time.

As we were buying newspapers in Kingsway we met the Martins from Tobermory. They were anxious to know if we had any news as the electricity had been cut off in the night, and they had been told that one or two Army Officers had been involved in a shooting incident A Military Coup d'état is a common occurrence these days, but it was not so fifty years ago. None of us dreamt for a moment that anything serious had happened. People were walking about as usual. The shops all seemed to be open and even the Post Office was operating.

We bumped into the Passenger Manager who appeared rather agitated. He reported that the electricity had just been restored, but the telephone and radio systems were out of action. The Agent and several other Europeans had gone to Ikeja to see their children off on the London plane, as they were returning to boarding-school after the
Christmas holidays. He understood they were all marooned there as the air-port was closed and all the surrounding roads were barricaded.

We began to think that perhaps the Purser hadn't been scare mongering after all and that there might have been a military takeover of the Government. Everything seemed normal but when Cedric arrived to pick us up opposite the Kingsway we knew there must be trouble as he had shut all the car windows as a precaution against any anti-European incidents. To get to their house in Ikoyi we had to pass the Prime Minister's residence and saw for ourselves that there was a large crowd milling around and an unusual number of soldiers outside the barracks. Cedric drove quickly and no one tried to stop us.

Once at the house we listened to the radio. The local station was still silent but at 1.00 p.m. the B.B.C. World Service announced "It has been rumoured from neighbouring Dahomey that there has been a military takeover of the Nigerian Government. All communication with the country has ceased meantime. There are no reports of any British subjects being involved. A further announcement will be made as soon as more definite information has been received."

Shortly after that the Nigerian radio station resumed service. They played solemn music and interrupted from time to time with the instruction "Stand by for a special announcement". As soon as the telephone service was restored the Shell Manager phoned with the order "Fill up your cars with petrol, and your deep freeze with food if you can get it locally. Thereafter stay in your compound. Do not go to Lagos".

The Passenger Manager had told us that if we had any difficulty in getting back to the ship we could shelter in Elder Dempster's office. We were toying with that idea when John (a friend who'd been invited to dinner) came to say that he had just heard there was to be a strict curfew after 7.00 p.m. He thought it best not break the rules and would take a rain-check on the invitation. As he lived on Marine Drive in Apapa he volunteered to drive us back to the docks. Although it was just about 5.00 p.m. there were fewer people about than usual but several African women were actually still sitting hopefully at their stalls.

To our surprise and relief no one tried to stop us going over Carter Bridge or crossing over the causeway to Apapa. Back on the ship they still didn't realise properly what had happened, but those who had heard the news on the B.B.C. World Service were eager to hear a first hand account. I hope Mum away back in Rothesay wasn't worrying about my safety and remembered that I'd constantly said that the media exaggerated things.

We listened to the radio all evening and several times the dreary dirge-like music was interrupted by the words "Stand by for a special announcement". Eventually we heard the official news – General Ironsi (an Ibo) had led a group of Army officers and taken over the Government in an attempt to restore law and order. The people were asked to keep calm and obey any new instructions. Several days later the badly mutilated body of Sir Abubaker Tafawa Balewa was found in the Bush. He was a Hausa man, and had been Prime Minister since 1960. It was said he'd been at prayers when a group of soldiers broke into the house.

The coup had been well planned, so well that we began to wonder if it could have been masterminded. The Army loyal to Ironsi had seized, as we knew, the airport, the telephone exchange, the radio station and cut off the electricity. These things had been accomplished all at the exact same moment. The Prime Minister, the Minister of Finance and several other officials throughout the country had been murdered, any Army officers reluctant to take part had been shot. Simultaneously the Sardana of Sokoto's palace had been set on fire and he perished with all his family and staff. Sir Ahmadu Bello, the Sardana, was Premier of Northern Nigeria and a most important figure in the Muslim faith.

At that time Britain was not only refusing to recognise Ian Smith's unilateral Declaration of Independence in Rhodesia but had introduced economic sanctions against the country. Accordingly we were rather puzzled when the very next day Harold Wilson's Government announced that they accepted Ironsi as the rightful ruler of Nigeria. We were somewhat shocked at this as when the Prime Minister's body was found he had been castrated and his eyes gouged out. - Surely, surely such brutality couldn't be condoned? It didn't seem consistent that Britain recognised this violence as the legal way to change a Government. The peace-loving man who had been accepted as a genial host to Britain and the other Commonwealth Countries only a couple of days before had met with a savage end. How could the world recognise the perpetrators of such brutality? "Ah", said all the cynics, "Don't forget the oil. Britain has to keep on the right side of Nigeria, no matter who rules the country". We were greatly disillusioned.

General Ironsi was killed by non-Ibo soldiers on 29th July that year when there was a mutiny in the Army so his spell of glory was very brief. General Yakubu Gowon then took over as the Head of the new Federal Military Government. On the ship we were all surprised at Gowon's appointment. He had travelled back from England with us (he'd probably been on a course in Sandhurst!). As far as I can recall he was just a Captain when he disembarked, certainly not a General. On the ship he was remembered as a quiet man – a good table tennis player. It seemed incredible that almost before he had time to unpack he had become the Head of State. He had a fairly long spell in office and wasn't deposed until July 1975 while he was in Kampala and a bloodless coup took place. Endless coups followed.

Nigeria, however, wasn't the only African country with self-appointed Heads of State. Swiftly following the January coup in Nigeria, Dr. Kwame Nkrumah, the President of Ghana was deposed on 26th February 1966. He was out of the country and in the Far East, thus avoided an unpleasant death. In Sierra Leone the Army seized power on 22nd March 1967. After independence Sir Francis Lightfoot-Boston had been appointed Governor General. He had travelled out to Freetown on the Aureol and, as befitting his position the ship was dressed overall and he was given V.I.P. treatment. There have been so many coups in these countries I've stopped trying to remember who took over from whom – and when, but I certainly remember that first coup in Sierra Leone.

A young Army Officer – Jeffrey Juxon Smith was appointed Head of State. We all felt he had been used as a puppet by other more powerful men. He had been recalled from London and flew back to Freetown. His wife and baby son followed on the Aureol. She was a quiet girl (a nurse) and stayed most of the time in her cabin. She told Marie that when she was listening to her transistor radio in her kitchen at home in London and heard her husband's name she was utterly amazed. According to her, he had absolutely no political ambitions or experience. When we arrived in Freetown she was even more bewildered. Her husband came strutting along the quay leading a company of soldiers. He paid little attention to his wife, brushed aside her eager welcoming kiss and ignored her anxious questions about her parents. He proudly held his baby son up to the assembled crowd, and let his wife go off down the gangway alone. It certainly wasn't the happy homecoming she had dreamt about.

On the southbound journey Juxon-Smith with a military support group was on the quay again. This time they were escorting Sir Francis Lightfoot-Boston out of the country. He seemed a disillusioned old man, frail in a long winter coat. In total contrast to his voyage out he travelled almost incognito and seldom left his cabin. We never heard any mention on the radio or saw the press report of his arrival back in Britain but there could have been a couple of lines somewhere, playing the whole affair down. We began to realise that news items omitted are often more important than ones embroidered and padded out for sensationalism. From then on I've been a bit sceptical about reports in the media. I prefer to believe the evidence of my own eyes. Juxon-Smith's term of office was short – he was killed quite soon after the takeover.

When President Tubman of Liberia travelled on the Aureol from Montavia to Ghana for the African Leaders' Summit Conference, he had the right idea. Taking great precaution to avoid anyone seizing power while he was out of the country, he had a tremendous entourage. The Commander of the Armed Forces, the Admiral in charge of the Navy, several Cabinet Ministers and even the Post Master General all sailed with him. There were four tough looking bodyguards, and, much to the Chef's indignation, an official food taster completed the group. A terrific reception party lined Tema Harbour as the ship drew alongside. It could almost have been on Horse Guards Parade as in the sweltering heat some unfortunate Ghanaian soldiers were dressed up in thick red uniforms and busbies.

In recognition of all the effort that had been made to ensure the President's comfort and safety he awarded several medals – (the Star of Liberia or something like that) to the Captain, Purser, Chief Steward etc. Alas, democratic rule gave way to military rule and in time that yielded to terrorism, as has sadly happened in so many Third World countries. Back home again for a few days I only mentioned little things like the Chef's anger at the food-taster.

At that time I used to go back to Liverpool by the overnight train. With no trains on the island the high arched geranium-filled Weymss Bay station was the way to the city – busy streets, crowded shops, high buildings – to another life style. In summer we used to pass family groups clattering down the wooden walk-way from the train to the pier. For them it was an exciting stepping off point leading to a seaside holiday. Laughing children with bucket and spade in hand, and swimsuits squeezed into the hamper, hardly noticed Weymss Bay station in their eagerness to reach the steamer taking them to Rothesay.

Crewe station, to many a busy bustling junction, remains in my mind as a gloomy dismal place. The service between Glasgow and Liverpool had been drastically cut with only one direct train daily. Returning from leave travelling overnight gave me more time at home. It proved better to ignore the stop at Preston and stay in the sleeper until Crewe. Most of the journeys are long forgotten but one particular one in May 1966 stands out from all the rest, not because anything unusual happened on the way to Liverpool, but because of what lay ahead at the Dock Gate. Arriving at Crewe around 6.00 a.m. there was little comfort in the waiting room and the minutes dragged slowly along. Only a handful of passengers boarded the local Liverpool train. It crawled along sometimes squealing to a halt for no obvious reason. Weaving stories about the pale faced girl opposite (perhaps going to work in a baker's shop?) and the man in the corner (a shifty looking fellow with a hammer sticking out of his pocket! – surely a burglar?). I didn't think they'd suspect that I was off to join my ship – that phrase still thrilled me!

From Lime Street station I always took a taxi down to Canada Dock – I'd heard vague rumours of a seaman's strike pending, but nevertheless I wasn't expecting to be confronted by a handful of men at the gate. "A picket!" I thought, "What next?" The group, more sullen than menacing, pressed forward when the driver slowed down. To my surprise and relief a policeman came into the taxi and saw me safely through to the foot of the Aureol's gangway. Later in the morning most of the crew came through the gate in a bus hired by the shipping company.

With the memory of their own abortive strike still raw, there was no chance of any of the Africans supporting the British seamen. In any case the derogatory cry of "black legs" wouldn't have offended them! Only a few of the Aureol crew joined in the protest and the ship sailed on time, with the safety and comfort of the passengers unaffected.

The early grumbling of the seamen developed into a roar of discontent causing the strike to become official and national. When we returned to the U.K. shipping was at a standstill with all British ports virtually paralysed. The strike, the only one of its kind since 1911, dragged on until 1st July. For the first time Elder Dempster's three mail boats – Apapa, Accra and Aureol, were all in port together. After the strike was over the Aureol had to wait in the U.K. for six weeks so that each ship's sailing date went back into the correct schedule.

This meant an unpaid holiday for me. The Union gave a token payment of a few pounds weekly to those who reported personally at the Liverpool office, but I headed for Bute as fast as I could. Apart from the few free days between voyages (and they were really compensation for Sundays worked at sea) we had no annual leave at that time. Working as hard as we did and for such long hours it was difficult to carry on without a good break from all the noise, tension, and the taxing climate. Most of us requested a voyage off or at least once every twelve or eighteen months. This was, of course, without pay.

There was always a strong thread pulling me back to the island. The sight of the steamer at Weymss Bay and the outline of the island with the peaks of Arran towering above on the far horizon sent a little quiver of excitement through me. I stood out on deck as we passed Toward Lighthouse, and when the hills proudly guarding Loch Striven came into view, I thought, "home – home at last!"

While in Rothesay, Africa seemed remote and almost as if I had imagined it all. It was good to be in a place where almost no-one had heard of Yorubas or Ibos, and where few knew and no-one cared where Ilorin, Ibadan or Onitsha were. I usually changed the subject if anyone tried to coax me to talk about my experiences. Incredibly few people imagined that the political situation in the West African countries would in any way affect me. Even now, so many years later there is much that I haven't mentioned. Many things saddened and angered me. I've always felt that Britain's reprehensible attitude towards early events has caused much of the trouble in West Africa today, especially in Nigeria.

When I had a voyage off I was usually content to stay at home, but a couple of times Mum and I flew to Belfast where Grizel, now married to an Irish lawyer, lived. One October we stayed with my Aunt in London and "did" the sights. We enjoyed it all but were glad to be home on beautiful Bute. Another time I went on a busman's holiday and crossed over from Mallaig, to the Hebridean islands – Rhum, Eigg, Muck and Canna. In glorious weather the Cuillins of Skye stood up dramatically against the blue sky. Many beautiful gold and blue threads twisted together to make a huge patch in the corner of that quilt of lifetime memories, alongside the grey and black ones caused by the sight of incredible poverty, misery and violence.

While I was at home I was never quite sure which of the three people that Micheline spoke about I really was. I ignored the one who coped daily with many, many more children than the Old Woman in the shoe ever had, and who acted as referee at arguments over whose turn it was to go on the swing or the rocking horse, be the teacher, the shop-keeper, the captain of the yellow submarine or the fairy godmother. I was only very briefly the person who lounged on the sand "up the creek" danced in the Bagatelle or dined in the Federal Palace Hotel. Very different was the real one – the one who had been so lucky to have such a super mother for a friend, the one who delighted in Scotland's peace and beauty, who loved to wander on the seashore, or stroll in the woods kicking through piles of fallen leaves, the one who enjoyed listening to music, reading poetry and browsing through bookshops. The real one had a marvellously relaxing time during the six weeks, chiefly just pottering about, chatting to Mum, visiting friends. At last I thought, I'm "ME"! All too soon it was time to pack my bags and set off for the ship with that tedious wait in Crewe station once again. When we arrived back in Nigeria it was obvious that discontent was growing throughout the country.

In May 1966 (just about the same time as the British Seamen's strike started) there had been mass demonstrations in Northern Nigeria. Many Eastern residents (Ibos) working in the North were killed in the riots and thousands fled back to the East. The total death roll of civilians in Eastern Nigeria in 1966 was estimated as at least thirty thousand Little mention was made in the British Press of these grim figures. It had been hoped that Independent Nigeria would be the showcase of Western democracy in Africa, but sadly all the carefully prepared plans had gone wrong, and dreams of a united Nigeria had been shattered.

Most of our stewards were Ibos and excellent workers. They daily grew more and more worried about the situation and had sent their families away from Lagos, back home to the river states in Eastern Nigeria. Ironsi had appointed Colonel Ojukwu (soon to be a General) as Military Governor in the East. There were signs that the trouble in the North was escalating and many expatriates, especially those in Sokoto, Kano or Maduguri sent their wives and children home. Several families came down from the North in a convoy of cars, staying at Rest Houses overnight and feeling safer while grouped together. Although there hadn't been many incidents involving Europeans, no one knew where next the ugly violence would flare.

We had an ever increasing number of children in the nursery, but only once did I hear a child talk about the trouble. Five year old Jim had a horrific experience on the way down from Kaduna. His father had to slow the car down to a snail's place as a jeering mob blocked the road. They edged slowly through the crowd and saw heaps of inflammable material being piled onto an old car with four African men trapped inside. Like flaming torches they were being burnt to death. What really upset Jim was that his Daddy didn't stop and help the screaming men. It was hard to explain that his father daren't interfere, or they too might have suffered a similar ghastly fate. His Dad told me he was thankful his tour of duty was over and he was able to accompany his family back to Britain. It would be a long time before that gruesome memory fled from Jim's mind, but for the adults who witnessed this atrocity it had more serious implications.

Before the Second World War the Muslim North had practically no schools and with the majority being educationally dis-advantaged many jobs were filled by Ibos from densely populated Eastern Nigeria. Once the massacres started there was turmoil everywhere. By the autumn of 1966 when we went ashore in Lagos change had come to the ordinary people and their once smiling carefree faces seemed restless and uneasy. It was very sad that the hopes and ambitions they had at Independence were failing to materialise. The joyful celebrations, the dances, dinners, fireworks and bonfires of the previous years had turned to blood and ashes.

On 30th May 1967 General Ojukwu announced the cessation of the Eastern Region (called Biafra) from Nigeria. Biafra's Rivers State produced a large percentage of the country's oil and Port Harcourt was, after Lagos, the biggest port in the country. On 6th July 1967 Nigeria attacked Biafra and captured the town of Bonny. The most b itter, savage Civil War broke out with brother fighting brother. The Nigerian army were ordered to "Capture Ojukwa and his rebel gang". Stories of recent atrocities filtered back to the ship and our stewards were petrified to go ashore in Nigeria. I can't with certainty recall the exact date that they approached the Captain as soon as we left Monrovia southbound, begging permission to leave the ship at Tema. They wanted to stay in Ghana, at their own expense, until the Aureol came back on her north bound trip. Although sympathetic the Captain wouldn't agree to this unusual request, telling the worried men that the ship was part of Britain and as long as they stayed on board in Apapa no harm could befall them. They weren't fully reassured that they could be absolutely protected. In a way their intuition was right.

As soon as the ship tied up, and before passenger disembarkation started, several officials from Customs and Immigration appeared with a typed list of Ibo men who were wanted ashore for interrogation. The Captain decreed that they could only be interviewed on the ship and insisted that, with the Chief Officer, he was present all the time. Fortunately there was absolutely no excuse for the Ibos to be taken ashore. Their papers were all in order and the Customs rummagers failed to unearth even one extra cigarette.

The grim faced officials were forced to leave the ship but the men felt that it was only an ordeal postponed. Fearfully counting the slow passing of the hours and dragging of the days they stayed below while the ship was in Apapa. Instead of the normal African spare crew the Captain ordered European quarter-masters to man the gangway. It was to be kept inboard, and only used by crew members or any office staff with the necessary identification pass.

On sailing day the main covered-in-gangway was fixed across from the Immigration shed so that passengers could walk straight over onto the ship. This also made it easier for the Baggage Handlers, Police, Customs, Immigration – and the Army (!) to come onboard. When I went up to the Nursery at 7.00 a.m. the door was locked and a chair jammed under the inside handle. In response to my insistent knocking and calling, James the steward who cleaned and did odd jobs for me, appeared. Grey with fear he begged me to let him hide in one of the children's toilets. Mindful of Cyclops days when I locked myself into one of the Heads during Captain's Rounds and was betrayed by my black legs, I told him that it wasn't a good idea.

The Purser phoned to say that if perchance any of the Ibos were called for, the Captain did not expect any of them to appear. I realised then that James had cause to be afraid, and decided that the best hiding place would be in the cupboard which housed the air-conditioning unit. It was a small cupboard but when Daniel, the suite room steward appeared and implored me to help him too I managed to squeeze them both inside. They were panic-stricken and I tried to reassure them that even a regiment of soldiers would not be allowed to search every part of the ship. Locking the door and popping the key down the front of my uniform dress I decided not to tell anyone else.

For a fleeting moment I remembered when, as a young Wren, I hoped I was going to work on some kind of espionage, and here I was more than twenty years later playing a small part in the harsh reality of a terrible Civil War. I was uneasy in case the children would be involved as many of them had already witnessed unpleasant and violent incidents.

Away up on the Nursery Deck we couldn't see what was happening in the main part of the ship. I suppressed my anxiety and gave no hint to the others that anything untoward had happened, but as soon as the children who had just embarked found their way up to the Nursery, I started a noisy game. Later I discovered that, as anticipated, a company of soldiers had marched onto the Main Square immediately the gangway was in position. With the same printed list as the Customs had had on Docking Day they again demanded that these men be taken ashore for questioning. Pandemonium must have reigned in the Square outside the Purser's Office with passengers, hand baggage being carried on board and the impatient Army personnel almost blocking the gangway. I didn't hear the first broadcast clearly but believe it was on these lines, "Attention please, attention. Here is a special announcement. If any of the following men are on board they are ordered to report to the First Class Purser's Office immediately". Then the full names and article numbers of the wanted men was read out. Everyone waited, but not one person answered the summons. The Army Captain was informed that it appeared that these men were not among the crew due to sail with the ship.

In the Nursery I had started the game of "Follow my leader". We were outside balancing on the edge of the paddling pool, when I heard the announcement relayed from the office. I wondered if James and Daniel had heard it. They would certainly be rather squashed and very hot, but thankfully there were ventilation holes at the top of the cupboard. It would have been ironic if they had been suffocated.

Apparently two diplomats arrived from the British Embassy and tried to help smooth things over. On the Promenade Deck the passengers waiting for a final glimpse of Lagos watched for any developments, realising the grim significance of the tannoyed request. With no sign of the Ibo crew anywhere, the disgruntled Army group left the ship, warning that the matter wasn't over.

Down on the quay the N.P.A. (Nigerian Port Authority) men were afraid to cast the ship off and disappeared as if under Army orders. The ship's departure was delayed a little, but after the soldiers went ashore the ship's European crew let go the hawsers securing the ship. Off we went! It was tragic that James and Daniel and the others in hiding throughout the ship hadn't been able to go ashore in their own country, and didn't even have a last glimpse of it as the coast grew fainter as the ship made for sea. We all gave a great sigh of relief.

A touch of normality came with the announcement "Children's lunch is now being served". I doubled back from the Dining Saloon to tell James and Daniel that the soldiers were no longer on the ship. We had sailed and were out beyond the breakwater. "It isn't safe yet, Pilot is still on the ship and he's an African man. We don't trust him" said Daniel. They refused to come out until the Pilot had gone ashore, and we were safely out of Nigerian waters.

Service in the Dining Saloon was slow with so many stewards

missing. Surmising what had happened none of the accompanying adults complained about the delay. Some of the stewards had been lying under piles of dirty table linen in the store behind the Dining Saloon and several had been hidden at the back of officers' wardrobes. By the time the adults' meals was due, all the stewards had reappeared and on the surface all seemed normal.

When we reached the U.K. these men were given political asylum. It was not reported by the media and kept very low key possibly to avoid reprisals against the families they left behind, or even against them. I've often wondered if they were ever reunited with their families but so many civilians in the East died of starvation, if not violence, the odds were heavily stacked against them.

Chapter Fifteen

At home – mother's terminal illness

Considering all that had happened in the course of that last voyage my frustration almost became irritation when once again Rothesay people greeted me with "That's some job you have sailing into the sunshine. You always seem to be on holiday". Sometimes I retorted "Yes, I'm home for four or five days but I'm sure you've been off every weekend while I've been away". Often I didn't bother to answer, but if the next remark was "Was it stormy? I'm afraid I'd be seasick". I'd be unable to resist saying "If you were prone to seasickness you wouldn't be do more than one voyage". Then smiling feebly I'd change the subject. Stormy? Most of the time we were totally oblivious of the fact that we were at sea! Mum complained that there hadn't been much news about Nigeria in the media. I told her all the funny things the children said and did, and enough about the War to interest her, but nothing unduly worrying. "Remember", I said, "The media usually exaggerate the slightest trouble".

It was unbelievable that Britain actually condoned genocide and refused to deal with Ojukwu in East Nigeria. There were around twelve thousand British people in the country then and many British business investments in Nigeria. Above all the crux of the matter was the rich oil in Biafra. The British Government's attitude towards Nigeria taken over by violent force wasn't consistent with its persistent refusal to recognise the Smith regime in Rhodesia (now Zimbabwe).

Today television brings right into our sitting-rooms scenes of rioting, of thousands of refugees, and of starving children in Ethiopia, Burundi, Rwanda and many other Third World Countries. I'm sure most British people are moved momentarily but then switch off or turn to the sports news, or a T.V. soap. Beyond perhaps dropping a coin into a collector's tin or handing unwanted blankets or clothing to a charity shop, the British public is mostly indifferent. I gradually realised that War in a far away country involving people with unpronounceable names wasn't something that gripped the average person's attention.

When the Biafran War started it was a barbaric one as most civil wars are. The President of the Red-Cross condemned all the countries supplying arms to Nigeria saying:-
"All the oil in Nigeria could not provide detergent enough to wash the blood from their hands".

The War dragged on month after month. The Federal Government announced that they and they alone would distribute relief. All planes alleged to be carrying food and medical supplies were to be inspected on Federal Territory. The starvation of the Biafran people reached catastrophic numbers. Although the Red Cross and Oxfam do marvellous work throughout the world, sadly much of the relief is misappropriated. I was further disillusioned having seen the packages of clothing and medical supplies, generously given to Biafra by the British public, unloaded at Apapa and taken away by the Army.

There were over a million and a half civilian deaths in Biafra, mostly children, and at least two million refugees. The figures quoted are from the book – "Biafra, Britain's Shame" written by Auberon Waugh and Suzanne Cronje. They lay the blame squarely on the shoulders of Harold Wilson and the Foreign Secretary, Mr Michael Stewart, with a contributory fact being that Shell B.P. negotiated only with Lagos, and not Biafra where the oil fields were.

On a lighter side there were incidents that made us smile. In the G.P.O. in Lagos, and a few other prominent places there were huge posters with instructions for procedure in the event of an air raid. One rule was something like "Don't look up in the sky, or you might get a bit of a plane in your eye". - no mention of danger from a bomb falling! The next rule, advised that in an air raid one should "jump into the nearest drain". We looked down into the monsoon ditch that had a revolting resemblance to an open sewer, running along the gutters, and decided to ignore that advice! In fact neither side had enough planes or trained pilots for a full scale air raid.

Once as we were coming across the causeway in the McKay's car the air raid siren went off. There weren't any drains or ditches in sight but most of the African drivers leapt out of their vehicles and vanished! It caused a traffic jam that took hours to clear, and made me think back to the little policeman I saw in Bombay many years before. When the traffic became too chaotic with horns blaring and people shouting loudly, he stepped down from his box and vanished into a never ending line of cars, bullock carts, lorries and bicycles.

Blackout regulations of a kind were instituted. On Apapa quay the ships' masters saw that the orders were strictly obeyed. Unlike Britain during the War when the Air Raid Wardens went round inspecting and shouting "Put out that light" at the sight of the merest chink of light escaping, most civilians only made feeble attempts to cover their windows. For some unfathomable reason the G.P.O. on Lagos Marina was quite brightly lit and even on Carter Bridge a few lights were showing!

One evening as we were coming back by taxi from a Chinese meal in Lagos, an Army patrol stopped us and demanded to see our identification. It was quite difficult to keep our boys from exploding as we were told – "Get out you white scum." Having visions of spending the next year rotting away in an African cell, and becoming a diplomatic incident, we implored the boys not to retaliate and hissed "Shut up and get out at once." After brief questioning they let us get back into the taxi and we arrived at the dock area without further incident. That was the only time I personally experienced the Nigerians being contemptuous of white people.

As the ferocity of the War became evident the stories of brutality increased. Embassies instructed all their nationals to leave Biafra. The last group of expatriates were brought out of Biafra on an Italian ship. One or two escaped in tankers and most of them had harrowing stories to tell. On May 19th 1968 Port Harcourt fell, this was a frightful blow for the Biafrans. Several British men stayed on until the very last dangerous moment. We heard of one who locked up the office in Port Harcourt, gave the keys to the African Manager, drove as far as he could, left the car, then walked out into the Bush. He had a hazardous journey but managed to bribe the owner of a canoe to take him across the river and into Nigeria. His wife was relieved to hear that he was safe, but when he finally reached the U.K. she was most indignant to discover that he'd brought his golf clubs but not their wedding photographs!

In September 1968 I was greatly upset when I arrived home and discovered that Mum had been in hospital for a few days. She had had a dizzy spell, cutting her eyelid as she fell and required to have umpteen stitches. Although she had written faithfully to me at every port she didn't give hint of any trouble. I wanted to go straight back to shipping office in Liverpool, explain the circumstances and ask for at least one voyage off. Mum wouldn't hear of this and was quite agitated when I put the suggestion to her. When I went to see the Doctor he strongly advised me to go back to sea. Mum had already spoken to him about her dread of "being a burden." In his opinion it would do more harm than good if I stayed at home and he felt Mum's fall had been an isolated incident.

At that time there was very little help or "care in the community." Now we are fortunate in Rothesay and have an excellent scheme with the Daughter Service, Meals on Wheels, Home Helps and the Day Care Hospital. Luckily a nearby neighbour looking for a job was happy to come in daily from 8.00 a.m. for two or three hours. Ann would light the coal fire, make breakfast, and start preparing lunch. I organised cover for Saturday and Sunday too. An extension phone on her bedside table made Mum feel help was always at hand, and several friends would pop in as usual during the day. The local grocer's shop delivered a weekly order and the butcher, fish and baker's van men would call.

I went back to the ship assured that that was what Mum wanted. I felt more tolerant towards the "Was-it-stormy-brigade?" as while I was at home I realised that the daily headlines in the news were usually something sensational like a train crash – a member of the Government involved in an embezzlement case, or a sex scandal. A single gory murder would be front page news while an ongoing War only merited a sentence or two.

Although I'd made as many arrangements as possible and didn't see any loopholes I still felt a trifle uneasy about the situation at home. I had extracted a promise from Mum that she would be honest and tell me immediately there were any more difficulties. Homeward bound when we took the Pilot on board at Holyhead, as usual he brought the mail out with him. Amongst my pile of letters was one bearing the news that Mum had been back in hospital. This time I didn't hesitate and explained to the office that I wanted to leave immediately. I was told that they would use temporary staff for a couple of voyages in the hope that I would be able to return but feeling the future was very uncertain I insisted that it would be better to consider that I had left altogether.

It was more serious this time. Early one morning Mum had been unable to see properly and had a thumping headache. Her immediate fear had been that she had had a stroke, but was enormously relieved to find that her speech wasn't affected and none of her limbs were paralysed. Keeping still and quiet all day it was early evening before she phoned the Doctor. The following morning she was taken to the Ophthalmic Clinic in Inverclyde Hospital, Greenock. A clot of blood had touched the retina in Mum's "good eye" and she had little sight left. The specialist explained that the clot had solidified and it was too late to do anything about it. There would have been a faint chance had they been contacted earlier. When I asked if there wasn't some way that the clot could have been dissolved, or moved they wanted to know "where would you like it to be moved to?" Your mother's lungs, brain or heart?" Any of these alternatives would have been even more serious.

It was difficult to reassure Mum that I would be happy to stay at home and look after her. I didn't consider it a duty – it seemed the natural thing to do. There was no way I could have happily sailed away to Africa and left her alone and almost blind. After a month things improved slightly and on the Doctor's advice I started looking for a job locally. He was convinced that it would be quite a boost to my mother's morale and recovery if I could find work and still be able to be at home with her overnight, for a month or so at least.

In those days there was no provision whatsoever for pre-school children on the island, and, only one residential home for the elderly. I was eager to start a nursery school, but on investigation found the red tape was enormous. I don't think there were any Government Grants then and the financial commitment required to fulfil all the necessary regulations was beyond my means. I hadn't realised that there ought to be a separate toilet for every five children, and, naturally, there were strict rules about fire exits etc. The idea was shelved.

Eventually I found a job as a telephone operator in the local G.P.O. Exchange. There was more to it than I first thought – other exchange codes had to be learned and tickets to be written etc. It was totally different from all my previous work experience and wasn't really my scene. I'd always dealt with people and not things. The other operators were a happy friendly bunch. Many of them had been there for years and weren't in the least frustrated, as I was, by not being able to use my own initiative. Many of the calls came from old ladies who seldom remembered any of the numbers. They'd say "Give me Muir, the baker, please". The operator's standard reply was "The number is nine-seven, please note it for future reference". They never did! I wondered how they'd cope when automation came in and there was no friendly operator at the end of the line.

There was some amusing incidents. Young children fascinated by the telephone often tried to contact Santa Claus or Uncle Jim in Saudi Arabia. A breathless, agitated lady complained one day "Operator, there's a cow in my garden. Do something quickly. It is trampling all over the rose beds". Another panicky voice demanded "Send help quickly, the bath has overflowed".

Public coin boxes held a special attraction for children. Hoping to be rewarded by a cascade of coins, a favourite game was pressing Button B and sometimes the emergency button. Immediately several operators on the switchboard plugged in. If the response to the query "Emergency, which service?" was nothing but a giggling voice or a cheeky remark the operator would say "Police? Yes, they'll be there immediately". At that threat the children would drop the phone and run off. Now and then there was a genuine call when ambulance, police or fire brigade had to rush to a real emergency.

Memories of that time only come in snatches, vignettes. I suppose I must have enjoyed all the benefits of being at home and in my leisure time went for long country walks, devoured books, listened to music, enjoyed meals and chats with friends but much has faded into obscurity. As well as failing sight, Mum had suffered for many years from neuritis – a particularly vicious painful type of arthritis affecting the nerve terminals. Sometimes it flared up in her arms and hands, and then it would move to her legs. The pain left her utterly exhausted.

Suddenly the flu bug hit me. My head seemed to be stuffed with cotton wool, my legs like lumps of lead. My nose dripped like a tap and my throat ached. Next I had a tight feeling in my chest and a pain when I breathed. The flu quickly developed into bronchitis. Fortunately I was at home when Mum collapsed one day. I had a terrific struggle trying to lift her up from the sitting room floor. As she fell she twisted round, hurt her back and banged her head against a bookcase. Wheezing and snorting, I phoned for the Doctor. He insisted that Mum went to hospital – up to the Annexe, which chiefly housed long term geriatric patients. I protested loudly and reminded him that it was with the specific hope of preventing anything like that that I had left the sea. There wasn't a vacant bed in the main hospital and he could see no alternative.

He was quite adamant about it and said that two or three weeks in the Annexe would make all the difference. Predicting that I was on the verge of developing pneumonia he warned us that if Mum wasn't hospitalised, he would send me there. It was blackmail as we all knew Mum couldn't manage at home on her own. Most reluctantly I agreed and the ambulance arrived within half an hour.

They were very kind in the Annexe and Mum tried bravely to convince me that she was reasonably happy. The pains in my chest subsided but the unseen ache in my heart grew worse. I felt that somehow I had failed Mum and trailed up the High Street to visit the hospital at every opportunity. All the hours alone in the house at night and worrying constantly about Mum – all that time is an unhappy haze. Soon I was just left with a wheezy cold. The two weeks the Doctor initially spoke of, developed into two months. Mum seemed to be growing frailer although her mind was still clear and alert.

My shrinking world revolved round my mother and the hospital routine, and, to a lesser extent, included the two ladies who shared a room with her. It was a pleasant little room facing the grassy slope behind the hospital, and from her bed Mum could see two lovely trees silhouetted against the skyline. She kept trying to reassure me that she was happy enough and grateful to be well cared for, and feverently hoped I wasn't worrying about her all the time.

The other visitors and I planned little surprises to brighten the days. A bunch of spring flowers, a tape of favourite music, some old photographs all helped a little. We racked our brains for snippets of local news to tell them – in preference to world news which was usually full of gloom and doom. Occasionally my mind flashes back across the years to the time I spent with the Third Submarine Flotilla when none of us dared to plan ahead or think of the future. In many ways, we, the visitors, were like that – standing on the sidelines – waiting, watching, wondering and hoping that we'd soon have our loved ones at home with us.

While I was away at sea, in her letters Mum frequently mentioned the sudden death of a friend or neighbour. She always commented "She was lucky, what a nice way to go. I hope that happens to me". Frequently she reiterated that she did not fear death and was much more afraid of living a restricted existence with a mind full of jumbled thoughts and little human dignity left. A great believer in euthanasia she declared vehemently that it was wrong to keep people alive in a vegetative state. She always felt that the person struggling for years and years to look after a stroke victim unable to speak or move, or who cared for a confused person deserved more sympathy than someone bereaved. In her mind a sudden death although a shock for relatives was a wonderful way to depart. She believed it was a move to the next adventure.

When I was only seventeen I witnessed a sudden death. One spring morning when the patches of daffodils smiled in the sun and all the trees were full of singing birds I had walked to the Hydro as usual, and was almost at the back gate when the farmer who had just collected the brock (pig food) passed me on his horse-drawn cart. He smiled and said "Lovely morning, good to be alive". Before I could reply, he gave a sudden lurch, toppled off the cart and fell to the ground. I'm sure he was dead before he reached the ground. It was incredible that he had died with a smile and words about life on his lips. Mum's ideas about death had rubbed off on me. I remember being more afraid of the horse than anything else. I tried to tie the reins to a bush and then ran up to the Hydro for help Nearly everyone thought it was bizarre for a young girl like me to say "What a great way to die and on such a beautiful morning too".

To get back to the Annexe, Mum preferred listening to the radio in her room to watching T.V. in the Day Room. The flickering light hurt her eyes, and she found radio programmes more stimulating. Zombie-like many of the patients sat for hours looking blankly at the T.V. screen without really seeing it or understanding what was happening. Sleep seemed to come easily to them and I hoped that they had momentarily escaped from the monotony of their narrow lives and were dreaming of happier times. The scene in the Day Room stayed with me as I walked home down the High Street. My thoughts were full of matters like physiotherapy, chiropody, and shortage of pillows. I spent no time thinking of the starving Biafrans!

I have no recollection of going off to work at the Telephone Exchange while Mum was in hospital. Although I had passed my driving test the previous year I hadn't yet achieved my ambition of buying a little second-hand car. As there wasn't a convenient bus when I went to visit Mum I walked up to the Annexe. All my thoughts were focused on the hospital with my greatest wish being to take my mother back home. At the beginning of March her general health had improved and the Doctor predicted that she would be discharged in a week or ten days. As there was no chance of her eyesight improving, he considered she should be registered blind. I was thankful that her mind, trapped in arthritic body, was still clear.

A friend helped me to repaper Mum's bedroom and with new curtains and a matching lampshade I was sure she'd be delighted with it all. I worked out how much extra help I'd have to arrange if I stayed on in my job. Just in case any setbacks occurred I didn't tell Mum that she could now start crossing off the days on the calendar until she came home.

Unfortunately she developed a bad cold. She had told me that when her hair was washed it wasn't quite dry when she went to bed; perhaps that wasn't a contributory factor at all but her cold seemed to get worse. She was rather breathless and Sister told me that her heart-beat was irregular but didn't give cause for alarm. The Doctor pronounced it was a viral infection, and fearing pneumonia, started a course of antibiotics.

Two days later she was moved to the bed at the door of the ward near the nurses' room. I felt that was an ominous sign indicative of how Matron and the Doctor viewed the seriousness of Mum's condition. It was providential that I had a few days off that week. On the Thursday I waited in hospital until midnight, and only went home when the Night Sister promised she'd telephone me immediately there was the slightest change. I couldn't sleep and walked all the way back at 6.00 a.m. and stayed in the hospital all day. No doubt I was given meals but have no memory of eating them although I know I drank several cups of tea. The Doctor came and voiced surprise at the rapid deterioration in Mum's condition. About 4.00 p.m. that Friday she whispered, "I'm tired, very very tired". She smiled and seconds later gave the merest of sighs and was gone, quietly and peacefully. Although I had known for a couple of days that the end was near, I sat for a moment in stunned disbelief. Mum looked so calm and serene that it was unbelievable that I'd never hear her speak again.

Gone? Where had she gone? The bright spark of light, her life, had been snuffed outlike a candle flame blown out by a draught of air, a dewdrop on a blade of grass vanishing in the sunlight, a shadow dancing on a wall, the last haunting note of a violin, a soft breeze gently kissing the leaves and then moving on, the blackbird's song lingering in the air for a second, and a rainbow fading from the sky. All gone irretrievably. Where do they all go? Awesome, unanswerable thought.

I kissed her dear, dead face and then went to tell the nurse that it was all over. I was so glad that I'd been able to be there, sitting holding Mum's hand and talking to her when she died, and glad too that she had got her wish and never became in the least confused. It was a great comfort to me that we had always been close and talked over things together. I knew there would be a tremendous gap in my life but it would have been selfish of me to have wanted her to go on living almost blind, breathless and only able to walk a few steps.

My good friend Shona collected me from the hospital and I went home – home to an empty house. Somehow I found the strength to make the necessary phone calls notifying people and arranging the funeral. In a strange way I felt I was watching it happening to someone else. My cousin travelled overnight from London, and was with me in the morning. Grizel and her daughter Chris came too.

Everyone was extremely kind and many good friends rallied round. I was overwhelmed by the letters and flowers to me personally. Two incidents stand out from the others. I greatly appreciated it when a rather deaf and very lame old lady whom I hardly knew called. Bringing me a bunch of violets and a pot of raspberry jam, she told me how much she'd valued Mum's visits and phone calls in the past few years. I was much moved by her kind action, and the nice things she sincerely meant.

Another friend baked two large sultana cakes and brought them "In case you have a lot of visitors" and left me these comforting words. * "Death is nothing at all. I have only slipped away in to the next room. Why should I be out of mind because I am out of sight? I am waiting for you, for an interval, somewhere very near, just around the corner. All is well".

The day of the funeral was an ordeal, but I was actually quite dopey after swallowing several pheno-barbitone. I hoped that I gave the impression of being calm and composed and not unfeeling and cold! It all blurred into a nightmare haze with a tremendous crowd of people coming to the house to pay their last respects, and bringing an amazing number of wreaths and sprays of flowers. Deep pools of tears welled up inside but did not flow until I was on my own at night. I was told all manner of things that I hadn't realised about Mum – how she had helped many people in various little ways, and how they would all miss her lovely smile.

189

One gruff farmer grabbed my hand and said, "I hope you realise what a wonderful woman your Mother was and how she will be missed. You must be very proud of her, make her proud of you today and every day" – That was an unusually lengthy speech from a Bute farmer, and I knew it came from the bottom of his heart. I became aware that not only had I lost a dear Mother, but many others had lost a good friend too. My comfort lay in all marvellous memories I had of shared happy times. It was gratifying to know that she had genuinely been held in such high regard.

The ache inside me was like a lump of ice that would not melt. For quite a while I had to stop myself calling "Hello I'm home" as I opened the front door; it was hard to remember there was no one there to reply. Nor was there anyone close for discussion on important matters. I tried to mask my true feelings with a brave smile. I went backwards and forwards to work at the Telephone Exchange and tried to do my best, but my heart wasn't in it and I had little enthusiasm for anything.

(Henry Scott Holland 1847 – 1918 Canon of St. Paul's Cathedral.)

Chapter Sixteen

Off to Paris

S omewhere I'd read the description of a "middle-aged orphan". At first it struck me as more comical than sad. Yet it was true, very true and exactly what I had become – a middle-aged orphan and now one of the older generation. Mum and I had often spoken about death and I knew how she would have wanted me to act. In quiet moments I could hear her voice telling me "Snap out of it, don't keep on being sorry for yourself". My friend Nan pointed out the advantage of my position with the familiar "Every day is the first day of the rest of your life. Now is the time to do exactly what you want" she said. If you have concealed a mad longing to abseil down a rocky cliff or want to study Arabic or Japanese, do it. There's only yourself to consider. Get out of that rut". None of Nan's suggestion appealed, but working as a G.P.O. telephone operator was merely a stop-gap and I didn't want to end my working life there. I felt I was drifting in an aimless way.

One May evening I made a determined effort and tackled the pile of unanswered letters lying beside the telephone. One was from Micheline who had left Cliff in the Gambia and was living in Paris where Michel attended a Lycée. I wondered how Michel would adjust to his new life at a big busy school in a world of noisy traffic and high buildings almost obliterating the sky. It was a great contrast to life in Bathurst where the little school stood on the hot white sand, with the sea lapping at the door. Michel was very devoted to his mother and hopefully he'd find being with her compensation enough for the things he'd left behind. It was planned that he'd fly out to Africa, and spend all the holidays with his father.

I explained to Micheline about Mum's illness and death and that I'd been in such an unhappy haze at Christmas I hadn't written to anyone. I told her that apart from a short holiday in June with my relations in London I had made no other plans, although if a vacancy cropped up on the ship I'd be off to sea again. By a change quirk of fate, realising that she had had no news of me for ages, she had decided to write to me. We posted the letters at the same time on the same day and when she noticed this she telephoned me.

She was working at the Centre d'Études et de Promotion du Tourisme in Paris, as "adjoint to Madame Janine Berthet, the Directrice Administrative". For all her diminutive size Micheline was well equipped for this position as she was extremely efficient, and her fluent English was a tremendous asset. I'd seen her so often – small, blonde and chic, boarding the "Apapa" in Bathurst. Immaculate in trim white shorts she stood out from the other expatriate wives. She was too ambitious, too strong a character to live a restricted life in a small community. Idling on the beach for hours, attending cocktail parties or playing Bridge weren't pursuits that attracted her. I admired her positive attitude and how she knew exactly what she wanted to get out of life.

The C.E.P.T. (as it was always called) was a Government supported organisation set up for training young people in all aspects of tourism. The stagiaries (students) hoped to become qualified as Travel Agents, to work as Tour Operators or Guides with Air France or in Hotel Management. It all sounded very interesting and a better system than in Britain where anyone untrained can run a Travel Agency.

Micheline dropped a bombshell suggesting that while I was in London, I went across to Paris for the weekend and sat on the jury panel for the stagiaries' English Exam. My immediate response was "That sounds wonderful but I would find it too expensive after being in London, to come over to Parish just for a weekend. Beside I've forgotten most of my school French".

This wasn't strictly true. The Townsends (another English/French bilingual couple) in Apapa frequently gave hospitality to French people. When they asked me to their house in Marine Drive for dinner, I used to secretly hope that they hadn't any French guests staying with them as it made my head ache trying to follow the conversation. Micheline explained that I would only be required to speak English and furthermore would be paid for the afternoon's work. It was so unexpected it took my breath away and I hesitated a little. Micheline soon talked me round and persuaded me that I could cope.

One hot June Friday afternoon I went by train from London Victoria to Folkestone caught the hovercraft to Boulogne and the train to Gare du Nord. Prices were very different then – my fare from London was £14 return and I was given the equivalent of £8 for a few hours work on the Saturday afternoon – in fact for £6 had a weekend in Paris!

The C.E.P.T. was in an old building at Soixante-huit (68) Rue de la Chaussée d'Antin – a busy street off Boulevard Haussman and fairly near l'Opera. The exam wasn't nearly as much of an ordeal as I had first feared. The Press Officer was on the jury panel with me, "C'est du gâteau" he declared. I wouldn't have called it a piece of cake, but he certainly tried to make things easier for me.

Before they were admitted to any of the courses the stagiaires, mostly between 19 and 25 years old, had all passed their Baccalauréat in English. My heart sank when I saw them assembled in an outer room. Twisting threads led me back to the Aureol, and I wished they were all a group of five year olds whom I knew I could control. Their names were unfamiliar, and in my nervous state I mumbled to the first one "Bonjour Monsieur Delfarge" instead of bidding him "Good afternoon". The Press Officer had warned me that their English was for the most part grammatically correct but was too stilted.

How right he was! We started with role play, and I said to Philippe Delafarge "Pretend that I am an American Tourist with just 24 hours to spend in Paris, and, as a Travel Agent, tell me what you would recommend I should visit. Where should I start?" He answered "Good afternoon Madam. I thank you for your enquiry and trust you will be able to avail yourself of my vast knowledge of Paris (pronounced as the French do – Paree). This undoubtedly is the most beautiful, most renowned city on the entire continent of Europe. Firstly may I suggest you commence your tour at thethe Arc de Triomphe. This magnificent arch, above all is a monument to Napoleon whose hearse passed underneath on his return from Elba in 1840. The panels depict the battles of the glorious French Army" – and on and on he droned. He took so long going into all the details that I'm sure the tourist would have felt obliged to spend several hours out of his precious twenty-four there, and would see little else.

Another suggestion was that a view from the river was the best way to "capture the spirit of this enchanting city" and the tourist was advised "If you take a Bateau Mouche (named after the original owner Monsieur Mouche) from the Pont de l'Alma or various other departure points you will have the opportunity of glimpsing all aspects of Parisian life from the River Seine which winds through

Paris like a silver ribbon passing under the famous pont de Paris."
I smiled at the fanciful description, but there was more to come –
on she went elaborating about the ornate Pont Alexandre III and the
French/Russian friendship. It was more of a history lesson than an
answer to a tourist's query!

It was an eye-opener hearing the variety of ideas they had
and how they perceived an American Tourist. One suggested Pigalle
(the Red Light Area) another the amazing Louvre Museum. One or
two suggested the American had a meal in Maxim's and then took
her along Rue de Faubourg St Honoré to Hermes, Pierre Cardin and
other fashion houses. Henri Rederau spoke of Boulevard St Michel
as a street pulsating with life and vibrant with the enthusiasm of
the students.

They all made the mistake of going into long boring descriptions
which I suspected were repeated parrot fashion from guide books. Their
English vocabulary was good, with no glaring grammatical errors,
but it was pedantic. Although passionately proud of their city and its
historical background, none of them thought of telling the American
tourist that a Tabac was a kind of corner cafe with a special counter
where horse racing bets could be placed and maps, postcards and
stamps bought. None of them told the tourist about the Métro system
and how it would be prudent to buy a carnet of ten tickets instead
of a single ticket.

In the second part when they were asked questions about the
best routes across the Channel and the various types of accommodation
throughout France, they answered in a more relaxed manner. I felt that
on the whole they were more proficient in English than a similar group
of British students would have been in a foreign language.

Following on from the exam it was decided that someone whose
native tongue was English, and who had experience of travelling to other
countries, should be employed by the C.E.P.T. A travel agent wouldn't
likely have a good enough command of English, and for the opposite
reason a teacher who spoke too formally wouldn't be suitable. The
ideal person would get the stagiaries to forget some of the old fashioned
phrases learnt at school and use more colloquialisms.

I had Micheline to thank for suggesting me in the first place but
I was quite startled when I opened a letter at home a couple of days
later from the Director General of the C.E.P.T. offering me the position,
I was panic stricken! Paris! I was thrilled to bits at the idea, but very

apprehensive about my ability to cope. My immediate reaction was to phone Micheline and say "Thanks a million, but I'm sorry – I'm very doubtful if I really qualify for the job. My French isn't good enough." That objection was squashed and I was told that they wanted someone who wouldn't speak a word of French (pas un mot de Français).

Phone calls to Grizel, Irene and Margaret brought the same response "Of course you must go – lucky thing! – Why not?" Far into the night I thought about it. Still awake at 4.00 a.m. I got up, found a large sheet of paper and wrote down all the advantages of accepting such a challenge, and all the reasons against it. The positive aspects outweighed the negative ones. I had no one else to consider. It was all very unreal – almost like Captain Clark setting me off on my wanderings by saying "It is ONLY to Singapore". I told the Supervisor at the Telephone Exchange that I was leaving work at the beginning of October, and wrote and accepted the post of "professeur d' Anglais." Once again the pattern of my life was changing.

I had a few months to put my affairs in order. Mum and I had lived in a rented house on the seafront in Ardbeg Road for about thirty-five years. When she died the tenancy automatically passed to me as it was my only home. Throughout the years I had spent a lot of money modernising it. I had had a new bathroom suite and kitchen units fitted, also new windows. I paid for all sorts of repairs that were really the landlord's responsibility, but the rent wasn't high and I had been glad to be able to afford things that made Mum's life a little more pleasant.

The landlord in fact was rather a ferocious female who had inherited a lot of property. She wanted to sell the house at a ridiculously high figure. I was about to get a mortgage and buy it, when she suddenly announced that she wasn't going to sell it after all. Raising the rent to the highest rate allowed by law, she proceeded to intimidate me. Telephone calls at two or three a.m. threatened that if I didn't leave I'd suffer the consequences. Anonymous letters were pushed under the door and sometimes she'd stand on the road outside for about an hour staring into the garden. It was as if she was "casting an evil eye" on me! Foolishly I didn't go to the Police. In a small town I was reluctant to let everyone know my private affairs. I knew I wouldn't be happy going off to France and leaving the house unoccupied and started looking for a small house or flat which I'd be able to buy.

Just two weeks before I was due to leave for France I had the exciting news that I had been successful in buying a little attic flat. It was on Ardbeg Road but not on the seafront. There was, however, a view of the bay and the pier from one of the sitting room windows and even a glimpse of the sea from the kitchen.

All the legal formalities were completed but the entry date was Martinmas – the 11th of November. As I'd be in France then, I left instructions with various friends – who were going to collect the key and let the electrician in to rewire the flat, and have it painted white throughout. In the end I had a tremendous rush to get everything organised. I packed china, ornaments and pictures and took boxes and queer shaped bundles off to be stored by friends. I gave away some furniture, and put the rest in storage. Grizel came and took loads of books away in the boot of her car. There was no time to revel in the fact that I was now a house-owner.

I stayed with Kate, an old friend of Mum's for the last couple of days, and went along to the house daily. After I mowed the grass and tidied up the garden, I gave away the mower and the garden tools to a young couple who had recently moved into the district. The little attic flat didn't have a garden but I planned ultimately to have window boxes. The usual junk one collects after thirty-years – things one might use "some day" were all cleared out. I lit a bonfire at the top of the garden and kept the flames dancing higher and higher as if it was the symbolic destruction of the past.

After all the furniture had gone, I scrubbed and cleared every corner of the house with demonic energy. When all was finished I walked from room to room – feet echoing on the wooden floors and memories crowding in. I tried to convince myself that there was no cloud of sadness hanging around, but a contented air reminiscent of many happy years. When the house was sold, as surely it would be, I hoped children would come and fill it with carefree laughter and chatter.

I locked the door and walked down the path without a backward glance, knowing that if I allowed one tiny tear to escape it would start a flood. Nonchalantly handing the keys to the lawyer I pretended I hadn't a lump at the back of my throat. A curtain seemed to be being gently pulled over the past, and another one slowly opening onto an unknown future. I set off for France wondering if the twisting threads leading from Bathurst to Paris and Rothesay would form another bright corner in the patchwork of my life.

Chapter Seventeen

Salt in my veins

With mixed feelings I boarded the steamer at Rothesay Pier on the first stage of my journey to France. Part of me was thrilled at the thought of going to work in Paris, but the other, more cautious part, kept thinking of all the difficulties ahead. I stood on deck taking a last look at the beautiful hills that made a splendid blue-green back-drop for the wide curve of the bay. No photograph to remind me of it all was necessary – the picture was imprinted on my heart.

I spent a couple of days in London with my cousins who were all envious of my wonderful opportunity. Gradually I became infected by their enthusiasm and pushed the nagging doubts to the back of my mind. Although it had been made clear to me that I was not expected to speak French in the C.E.P.T. I knew I'd need to use it in my daily life. I hoped that half forgotten German, Spanish or even Hindi words wouldn't pop back into my mind and cause confusion!

Fortunately I had had lots of practice – first in the Hydro, and then on the ship, of quickly matching names and faces and was soon able to distinguish Lebrun from Légard and Dupont from Delfarge. It was fairly easy with the girls. Each one had an individual style of dressing. Claire always added a little unusual touch like a tiny extra buckle on the back of her gloves or white laces in her long black boots, while Claudine twisted her scarf in a subtle sophisticated way. There was an aura of "je-ne-sais-quoi" about them emitting an air redolent of glamour. Mini-skirts were at their shortest in the U.K but the French girls favoured a much longer length and seldom wore trousers or jeans. The majority of students came from Paris but Jean-Paul's home town was Marseille, Henri came from Lyon and Jacques from the island of Comoro.

I was allowed to organise the timetable for the English classes myself and carefully thought out schemes to prevent the classes becoming yawningly boring. After two weeks Helene and Marie-Rose waylaid me in the corridor and told me that they found the classes "jolly ripping." They wanted to know if they had used the correct expression or if they should have said "spiffing" "topping" or "ace." I realised that I'd have to enlist the help of young friends at home to keep me up to date with all the in-vogue phrases. I knew of "bloody good" or "bloody marvellous", and then there was "jolly D." etc.

French business letters were still formal and stilted, so I devoted an early lesson to explaining the more relaxed British style. I organised a quiz on the capitals and currencies of other countries and was agreeably surprised at the good response. Most of them were able to carry on a conversation about travelling on the Métro or motoring on the Périphérique. When "Top of the Pops" was mentioned I trod warily as I often found difficulty trying to make sense out of them and circumvented that problem by asking the class to give their interpretation.

It wasn't just a one-side affair – the stagiaires learned a lot from me and in turn I learned a great deal about Paris from them. Lots of handy snippets of information came my way, for example, I knew the best entrance to use at the Louvre if I wanted to show friends the Venus de Milo and the Mona Lisa and not become side-tracked into other galleries. Another invaluable tip was that if one took the Métro to Trocadero and stood on the terrace between Musée de l'Homme and Musée de la Grande Armée – just at lighting up time, everything would suddenly magically change from the darkness of dusk to amazing dancing light. It proved well worth the effort to get to the right spot at exactly the right time. To see the Eiffel Tower and the Académie Militaire brightly silhouetted beyond the vivid green of the Champs de Mars is truly memorable.

I often boasted about Bute and the breath taking beauty of the West of Scotland. They all thought living on an island romantic. The girls especially enjoyed role play and had a hilarious time pretending to be a coach load of awkward passengers grumbling about the speed at which the driver negotiated dangerous bends, the inadequate air conditioning and the insufficient time allowed at stops. Travel films were very popular and most of the embassies were quite happy to lend their films, or give out brochures in English. Often the commentary was delivered in strongly Americanised English, difficult even for me to understand Many of the stagiaires had had American teachers, and I had to agree to the spelling of color, and favor, but words like gotten were hard to accept!

Following the film there would be discussions but often, before I had the chance to ask questions they'd be fired at me! I strongly suspected that they were hoping to catch me unawares. In particular I remember Henri Drefus (a red-haired lad whose English was quite fluent) asking "How many tourists would there be in Katmandu on an average March weekend?" In response I bluffed my way through, concentrating more on the Indian frontier and the wonderful palaces and temples in Nepal.

They all loved idioms and clichés and applied "chips with everything" to what they considered were hopelessly insular British tourists. Some rattled off phrases like "What is a nice girl like you doing in a place like this?" "On your bike" and "Get up them stairs". I warned them against overuse of clichés as on lots of occasions casual expressions aren't really appropriate. For example a tourist whose travel arrangements had gone hopelessly wrong wouldn't appreciate being told "Getting there is half the fun" if it was delivered in a flippant voice.

Someone brought up the problem of words spelt the same but with a totally different meaning. The obvious one was to book a room or to read a book. We had a competition and came up with things like record and row – each word with several meanings. The more I thought about it, the English language was very confusing at times. There was nothing for it – all these things had just to be learned by heart.

I had a couple of private pupils, Simone Fournier worked for the Olympic Games Committee and I went to her office at lunchtime. Her mother had survived the horrendous years in Buchenwald, the notorious German concentration camp. She had a number tattooed on her shoulder and a permanent haunted look as if still living in a dreadful nightmare. Her husband had been spared the torture and degradation of a camp, as he had been shot trying to escape from his office. She had remarried in 1950, had a kindly understanding husband and lived in a luxurious flat in Rue Fabourg St Honoré, but material things did not recompense for lost unhappy years. Simone confided in me that she had met a nice Austrian boy at college, but was afraid to mention him at home knowing her mother would associate him with all the sins of the Nazis. Poor Madame Fournier had lost faith in human nature and although Claud wasn't even born when the atrocities occurred she was unlikely to agree to meet him. It was a real problem for Simone, especially as the next Olympic Games were due to be held in Munich. I often wondered how that story ended.

Jeanne, the other pupil, worked as a chambermaid in the prestigious George V hotel. Her ambition was to work in an office, and she was desperately keen to improve her basic English. She usually came to my studio on a Saturday morning and after a few weeks made considerable progress. On Saturday afternoons I often went to the British Council Library in Rue des Écoles near the Sorbonne. It gave me a chance to find books written in English and an excuse to wander through the Quartier Latin where the little streets had intriguing names like Le Chat qui peche.

When I went to Paris at first I stayed with Micheline but I was soon able to find accommodation in a French girl's flat. It was recommended by the ubiquitous friend-of-a-friend, reasonably priced and within walking distance of the office. It didn't turn out as ideal as it first appeared. The great drawback was that I shared the kitchen and bathroom with tall, blonde, good-natured but incredibly untidy Ginny. The kitchen sink was usually full of saucepans and dishes often still containing scraps of food, and she used the bath as a depository for dirty clothes.

I would have left after the first couple of weeks had her ex-husband not appeared on the scene. He was a nice man full of Gallic charm, but unfortunately, an alcoholic. When he was desperate for extra cash he came round to the flat. Poor man with little self-respect left he acted like an homme de ménage. Ordered by Ginny as she lay in bed he did all the domestic chores, cleaning the kitchen and restoring order in the bathroom. After a while I could stand her slovenly ways no longer and looked for somewhere else. I puzzled over the abbreviations in Le Figaro's advertisements, and worked out that "Studio a louer 2 belles p. meublees c.c. s. de.b. gds cft, Métro Madeline" meant that there was a two roomed comfortable furnished flat with bathroom, central heating near Métro Madeline to let.

Eventually, I went to a housing agency and decided to take a studio in Rue Légendre. (Métro Guy Moquet). It was really a bed sitting room with a corner kitchen and a small bathroom next door. There's quite a snobbish streak amongst the French and almost immediately on introduction they enquire "Quel arrondissement?" (What district?) Now that I was able to say dix-septieme (17th) my status rose greatly as Ginny's flat in the neuvieme (9th) was in rather a more commercial area.

Quite a few differences in etiquette soon emerged. I was told that it showed a lack of respect when I went into the office and said "Bonjour Monsieur Guillet". As a subordinate I should just have said "Bonjour Monsieur". On the same subject a memo went round all Departments drawing attention to the fact that someone had been overheard talking about Monsieur Fety and actually using his name instead of his title Monsieur le President. At all times even in casual conversation everyone's proper title would be used. I suspected I might have been the guilty one! In the same way I was always addressed as Madame in deference to my position and age, although they all knew that le professeur d'anglais was a plain Mademoiselle.

The market outside Guy Moquet Métro station lured me in most evenings – if not to buy something at least to admire the wonderful coloured piles of fruit. In particular the fish stalls fascinated me with queer unknown fish and great fat sardines 3 or 4 times larger than the tinned variety. Having grown to love moules marinières and soupe de poisson I often bought mussels from the jolly fat stall holder. Like everyone else I bought bread daily. The rosy cheeked girl in the boulangerie greeted me with a smile and said "Bonjour, Madame, Ça va? Voici votre demie baguette" as she handed over my half stick of bread. In the charcuterie in Rue Légendre there was a very helpful assistant whom I found out wasn't French but Hungarian.

At first if I felt tired I used to go to the supermarket imagining I'd avoid the effort of thinking and speaking in French. Even there, if I'd handed over a large note, the girl in the checkout would say "Vous n'avez pas de monnaie?" It didn't take me long to realise that she wanted to know if I had any change. After a while it became almost second nature to speak and think in French. I was, however, conscious of the fact that I wasn't able to remember all the grammar off hand especially the subjective which was never my strong point.

I shudder if I hear someone saying in English "I seen two boys" or "I didn't ought to have went", and hated to think I was probably committing worse offences. The French are usually pleased if foreigners try to speak their language and yet are often critical of any mistake. A joke typifying their attitude is the one about an English tourist looking for the station and stopping a policeman. In response to his query "Où est le gare?" the policeman shrieked "La gare" and stamped off offended. Whereas a policeman in Britain would never dream of correcting anyone's grammar, or for that matter care about such things. I'd forgotten a lot of French but had never ever known practical things like "The lights have fused" or "There is a leak under the sink" – I very quickly had to find out both these phrases.

I was told that I couldn't do better than attend classes at Alliance Française, so taking the Métro to Notre Dame des Champs in Boulevard Raspail, I enrolled there. It was an amazing place with adult students from almost every imaginable country. The way they managed to assess one's capability, after the completion of a short written test was impressive. The class that I joined was at a lesson which I understood, but the next one was fairly new ground. Inside the college not a word was spoken except in French, – it being the common language that we all shared. In a surprisingly short time we actually began to think in French. We had a lot of homework and between that and preparing the lessons for the C.E.P.T. I had little spare time.

The concierge at Rue Légendre was a plump Breton lady. Obviously dyed black hair, thinning and greying on the crown, hung in unruly curls round her face. Her untidy room by the front door was dimly lit and huge pots of geraniums in the window obliterated the daylight. An amazing clutter of magazines, newspapers and empty Gauloise packets spilled over from table to floor. Three well fed cats usually slept amongst the gaudy cushions on the settee, quite oblivious of the two budgerigars chirping from a nearby cage.

I called there every evening hoping that there would be some mail for me. When the long awaited letter arrived from the Rothesay lawyer I rushed up to my room expecting to read that all was well with the flat and that my friends were tracking down the elusive Rothesay tradesmen. To my dismay I learned there had been a hitch and the keys had not been handed over. Since all the legal formalities had been finalised before I left home I hadn't suspected that anything could go wrong.

The flat was owned by someone in Australia and its sale would mean the closing of a Trust. When I phoned next morning the lawyer explained that it had been tenanted for a number of years by an elderly Glasgow lady who only occupied it in the summer months. She had died and a nephew was trying to claim tenants rights. He owned his own house, didn't make his home with his

Aunt and none of the neighbours had ever seen him even visiting far less staying in the flat.

Hearing it was for sale he had tried to bribe Mr Cullen to let him buy it. He made a mistake there. His suggestion "Name the price and I'll give you a couple of hundred pounds under the counter just between us" infuriated Mr Cullen who told him to put in a bid on the open market as one does in Scotland. He assured me that the flat was legally mine and if necessary he'd pursue it through the Sheriff Court. It was a worrying time for me, with phone calls and letters going between us. The day before the Court Hearing was due to be held in June the keys were sent in to the office – to my great relief.

On my return to Rothesay at the end of term I had a nasty shock when I saw the state of the flat. Every window cord in the house had been slashed, and a pane of glass in the sitting room window badly cracked. It looked as if the kitchen sink had been attacked by someone brandishing an axe, and hundreds of nails had been hammered into the floor. Most of the electric fittings had been damaged and bare wires left dangerously exposed. The most spiteful act of all was that the letter-box had been cut out and a great gaping hole left in the door. I felt like sitting down and weeping, but with hindsight I suppose should have guessed that he would try to cause as much damage as he could. It was surprising he didn't put a brick through Mr Cullen's office window!

The nephew's name escapes me. As one does with unpleasant things and nasty people it seemed to be easily blotted from my mind, so I'll continue calling him "the nephew". I was told that I could charge him with causing malicious damage, but I didn't want any contact with such a vindictive person. No matter what the outcome would be it wouldn't compensate for all the worry I had had. A cloud of vengeful thoughts hung over the place, even after it was repaired and redecorated. If I heard a faint rustling noise in the night I imagined someone trying to push a lit paper through the letter box, or that something unpleasant like a dead rat would arrive on the hall floor. As I felt the flat had been grudged to me I never settled properly there. I was delighted when a few years later I was able to move to a bigger, better flat with a wonderful panoramic view.

As the English classes at the C.E.P.T. didn't start until late October I had to look for a temporary job. There wasn't much choice. With a heavier volume of calls in the telephone exchange during the summer months, temporary staff were required and I, somewhat reluctantly, went back there. The girls were eager to hear all about Paris. It is a city of many moods, many faces showing different things to different people, and I wondered which one they wanted to hear about. The city of history – The Revolution, glories of Napoleon, of bravery and treachery too during the German occupation, or would they rather hear of the city of luxury with fashion houses like Chanel, Balmain and Pierre Cardin? Or were they thinking of the frivolous city with fabulous shows like Moulin Rouge, the Bluebell Girls and Crazy Horse? Perhaps they wanted to hear about the city of culture – the Impressionist Painters and all the famous writers, or the wicked city with Pigalle's risqué nightclubs and sleazy sex shops?

I tried to explain about the cafés like Coupole, Dôme or Deux Magots where I sometimes sat dreaming of the past, with the ghosts of Hemingway, Scott Fitzgerald and Jean Paul Sartre as companions. Nearer home the narrow cobbled streets of Montmartre were peopled with stories of Picasso and Toulouse-Lautrec. Van Gogh had lived at 54 Rue Lépic and I thought of him every time I passed on my way uphill to Place du Terte.

I reminded the girls that I wasn't a holiday maker and hadn't seen any shows like the Folies which were incredibly expensive – I had, however, been to the Opera House several times, and had seen quite a few French films, but most evenings were spent working on preparation of lessons for the C.E.P.T. As for the weather - many days were cold and rainy just as they were in Bute. The girls still thought I had a very exciting life.

When I went back to the C.E.P.T. in October I found that a language laboratory had been installed. The control console was fairly easy to operate but I felt somewhat distanced from the stagiaires. Sometimes I'd catch one of them playing a cassette of his own, so I'd interrupt with "Ah Henri I hear that Joan Baez is a great favourite of yours. I suggest you share it with us. I'll switch the lesson off and we'll all listen to Henri giving us his interpretation of it."

On 19th January 1971 there was a general strike of all the Post Office employees in Britain. Not only were there no letters, but only a fraction of the overseas telephone calls were handled. Now that Mum was dead and my friends were increasingly important to me, I felt really cut off and isolated. Nightly the concierge would say "Ah, M'mslle, pas de courrir pour vous. Dommage!" I spent many hours trying vainly to get through on the telephone and eternally twiddling with the knobs on my little radio hoping to raise Radio Scotland. Even weather reports and traffic jams interested me! Eventually the strike was settled, although it took many weeks for the backlog of mail to be sorted.

When I first went to Paris I had only been at the C.E.P.T. for a month when I heard there was a vacancy on the ship, but I had to let the office know I wasn't available.

Since then I had heard nothing official, but letters from the girls posted in Nigeria that time in 1971 cheered me up enormously – doubly so when there was no possibility of mail from home while the strike dragged on.

At that time the rate of exchange was against anyone like me working there – (13 francs to the pound) but I still got an enormous thrill from being in Paris. Having the opportunity to explore it all properly was great but I missed being able to see the sea tremendously. Looking at the Seine and watching the crowded Bateaux Mouches sailing under the famous Ponts de Paris only increased my nostalgia. It was interesting to stroll along the river banks and browse among the books and old prints at the bouquinistes but in no way did it compare with wandering along the promenade at home. I missed the sound of the waves lapping gently onto the shore or crashing wildly against the rocks.

The sea has always been a part of my life. John Masefield's words "I must go down to the sea again, to the lonely sea and the sky" kept hammering through my mind. Even the sky didn't compare favourably with the skies at home. The little scraps of grey and yellow above the Paris rooftops and endless chimneys were surely made of different stuff from the wispy clouds that drifted high in the blue skies at home. It grew to become an obsession with me and at weekends I spent my hard-earned cash searching for the sea, and escaping from the bustle of the city.

At Gare St Lazare and Gare du Nord I'd study the Departure Board or go off to find the price of a return ticket at Le bureau de renseignements (enquiry office). I went by train to Dinard, Boulogne, Le Touquet and Le Havre, but I still wasn't satisfied. None of these places seemed to have a proper sea full of white horses. (The French say la mer moutonnée) (white sheep). In Bute there would be seagulls screeching overhead, eider ducks cooing as they bobbed up and down on the crest of the waves, oyster catchers wading in the pools, and of course the hills in the background looking down on it all. Was it the hills I missed too? I spoke to a couple of fat seagulls walking along the dockside at Le Havre. Perhaps they didn't understand my accent, or were disappointed I hadn't a piece of baguette to offer them, but I thought they looked very supercilious. An attribute I have never assigned to a Scottish seagull!

The problems with my flat had made me feel insecure and certainly made me realise what a ghastly predicament it would be to be truly homeless. Amy, a young girl from Bute, married to a Frenchman, came to Paris almost as the same time as I did. They weren't homeless but had housing problems. The first rented flat that they had was rather ambitious, and to avoid huge debt they moved to a really miserable room in a crummy place that called itself a hotel. The other tenants, mostly Algerian or Moroccan were frequently standing in the doorway or shuffling down the dimly lit stone corridors. Fearing that her parents might find out her straitened circumstances she found endless excuses to prevent them visiting. Things improved after a while and they were able to get better rooms not too far from mine. I first met her while I was at the telephone exchange during the time of Mum's illness. These invisible threads linking the pattern of my life twisted back again.

We used to reminisce together about mutual friends in Bute. Unlike me she had no strong feelings about the sea, but confessed she'd sometimes scan the crowd in the Métro, hoping for the glimpse of a familiar face. We agreed that if we fell unconscious in the street people would step over us, neither knowing or caring who we were. At home, in contrast, everyone would rush to help and in a flash we would be in hospital and our relatives notified. Although living at a slower pace, insular in outlook, and blinkered to most of the problems beyond their shores, the Brandanes were a caring community.

We looked longingly at the chic clothes beyond our price range. A great coup, however, was when I bought a fabulous pair of long black boots that buckled over my knees. They made me feel like a million dollars. When I went back to Bute I was the envy of all the youngsters. Alas, they were just fashion boots and didn't withstand the frequent changes of the British climate.

I went back to Alliance Française to practice conversation. There I met Helena travelling on the same Métro line. She introduced herself saying "Je suis Juif". When I got to know her properly I asked why she had immediately told me she was Jewish. She explained that having red hair and a little button nose her origin wasn't obvious but she always made sure people knew right from the start in case they had strong feelings about Jews. "We are persecuted everywhere and my people wander the earth" she said. To her amazement I told her that I doubted if there was a Jewish family on the island, and even if there had been, they'd be treated like everyone else and wouldn't be discriminated against.

Helena was a Polish political refugee, deprived of her nationality. As a journalist she had dared to write an article against the communist regime. She was very lucky to have been able to escape from Poland with her ten year old daughter. Her husband, a University Lecturer, had had his plans to join her thwarted being unable to get a passport. Her two brothers had left Poland several years previously - Pieter was a dentist in Copenhagen, and Simon worked in the film industry in Paris. She made her home with Simon in a flat near Métro Jules Joffrin. It was within easy walking distance from Rue Légendre, where I lived.

Helena never ceased to long for her homeland, although she knew it was extremely unlikely that she'd ever be allowed to go back behind the Iron Curtain. Simon used to complain when she persisted in listening to the Polish radio. He kept telling her "All that is past. Try to forget. Concentrate in improving your French and you'll be able to take a job soon". Several other Polish refugees frequented the flat, and I met a Hungarian couple and a very old Russian man. It was a glimpse of another world. French was our common language and we chatted away freely, ignoring each other's grammatical errors.

I felt really guilty thinking of how I had agonised over a detail like no mail from home during the seven week long strike. It had clouded my life but was totally insignificant compared with the despair felt by all those refugees. I couldn't begin to imagine how I'd feel if I had been separated from family and friends, stripped of my nationality and forced to live in another country. I had great empathy with these unfortunate people.

The classes at C.E.P.T. finished in July. Again, there was a problem. Three months was too long to be out of work and I certainly couldn't have afforded to be idle for long. I had heard that as the tourist season at home was shortening dramatically it was unlikely that extra telephone operators would be required for more than four to six weeks. I toyed with the idea of looking for a job if not at the seaside, at least within easy reach of it. Somewhere if possible where I could use my French. Out of the blue a telegram arrived asking if perchance I was free to return to my job in the Aureol nursery. It couldn't have arrived at a more opportune moment.

I had to make an on the spot decision as I had to join the ship in Liverpool on Monday 25th July, and I was working at the C.E.P.T. until the afternoon of Friday 22nd July. My contract expired at the end of that summer term so I didn't have to give notice. Micheline persuaded them to give me holiday pay and I was grateful to her. I'll gladly shout about the rights of other people but I'm quite reticent about speaking up if it is something that only concerns me. My rent had been paid monthly in advance and I had to forfeit that when I left so suddenly, but had no alternative.

With all my belongings hastily packed I left early on the Saturday morning for an Air France direct flight to Glasgow. Exhausted but exhilarated on a sunny evening I eventually reached my little flat. It seemed quite welcoming. With just one full day at home I had barely time to unpack and get my uniform and everything organised. Sunday passed in a mad whirl – I made a few quick phone calls scribbled some notes to tell friends I was off to sea again. Off to West Africa.

Chapter Eighteen

Back on Aureol

A strong sense of déjà vu was with me as I crossed the Aureol's gangway. Everyone appeared pleased to see me, but no one seemed to care where I had been in the previous two years. The typical seaman will enquire about one's last ship, or happily discuss a rival shipping company, but has little interest in one's private life ashore. That suited me fine. I was pleased to be back in the Nursery, and my time in Paris soon faded into a hazy dream.

Glancing at the Passenger List I realised that unlike previous voyages, African passengers outnumbered Europeans by about three to one. The main reason for this was that expatriates' leave was now calculated as starting the moment they left Africa, whereas originally it didn't officially begin until they reached their own country. Naturally in order to have the maximum time at home, the majority now opted to travel by air. Many of the Nigerian passengers having spent several years in the U.K. were returning to use their professional skills to help their native land. Now that the Biafran war was over they were full of enthusiastic plans for the future. Their children, born in places like Bradford and Birmingham, unfortunately had little knowledge of African culture. They were English at heart, despite their black faces.

The toddlers kept repeating, "Soon we are going on a nice big ship to Africa. We'll all have a good time." I tried to explain "You are on the big ship now. Do you see all that water? That is the sea and we are on the ship going across the sea to Africa." They weren't convinced and I continued "Look out there. You can't see any houses, buses or streets can you?" On sailing day in the bewildering hustle and bustle they had come straight across a covered gangway from the emigration shed to A Deck Square which had all the appearance of a hotel entrance hall. To them alleyways resembled hotel corridors and the cabins were like bedrooms. I remember one nine-year old saying "I know we are on the ship, but the funny things is I never saw it. One minute we were in a kind of shed and then suddenly we seemed to be on the ship." New experiences crowding round them must have been very confusing.

A welcome break came one morning when bathed in sunshine, Las Palmas appeared on the horizon. Alongside the long quay a line of taxis and a few horse-drawn cabs awaited the passengers. After three hours ashore they returned laden with bottles of wine, flowers from the market, Sunday newspapers and cheap souvenirs. When four year old Olu came back to the nursery he spluttered excitedly," I'm on a big ship now. We saw it today and climbed up a funny wobbly kind of stair to get here." "Yes", retorted his sister, "We saw the ship today, and, the next stop is Africa. I can't wait to get there."

After climbing up the steep gangway from the quay and seeing the ship towering above them, there was no longer any doubt. We were all on a ship and all going to Africa. Alas, it was a different story when they came back from being ashore in Freetown. They weren't so sure it was going to be the wonderful place they'd heard about. Their comments ranged from amazement to disgust. I managed to capture a few on tape.

"It stinks. We saw lots of women's' bosoms when they were feeding their little babies."

"It was a rude place."

"Some of the children had no clothes and lots had no shoes."

"There was a smell of rotten fish or things dead."

"My Mum was angry when we saw some men piddling in the street and they didn't even turn away."

"Most of the men walked about in their pyjamas or long kind of skirts and lots of ladies were sitting on the ground."

"It is too hot, too dirty and too full of nasty smells."

"All the road sweepers must be on strike, there are so many old tins and bottles, and nasty things."

The older children asked anxiously "Accra won't be like that will it?" and "Anyway Lagos is far bigger and better."

Apprehension also grew amongst the adults, especially those who had spent years in the western world. "We've been away too long. It'll be alright once we settle down with our own people" they'd say. The first trippers, mostly young British couples, regarded it as a great adventure in the sunshine, but were quite clueless about what lay ahead. They voiced reassuring thoughts "We only saw the dock area and that's usually grim in any country."

There were new types of passengers "Round Trippers". That voyage there were six people travelling out to Lagos and back. They were cruise veterans and had been to the Mediterranean and the Caribbean, had sailed down the Nile and even up the Amazon. Although the Aureol wasn't exactly a cruise ship, the Public Rooms were well appointed and the first class cabins all had en suite facilities. The Pursers Department were on their toes organizing extra tournaments and entertainment.

Ship gossip spreads like wildfire and in no time everyone was discussing Mrs Birch, one of the Round Trippers. She was a very obviously dyed blonde with miniskirts more suitable for a teenager than for someone of her age (sixty was the age estimated by the more charitable ones). Before the pilot left the ship at Holyhead she knew the Christian names of all the Lounge and Smoke room Stewards, and before the ship was two days at sea she had made a conquest! A normally crusty old Coaster asked to be moved to her table in the Dining Saloon, and could be seen immediately after breakfast carrying her straw hat, her swimming gear, and even her handbag. It was so far removed from his normal behaviour that everyone waited with baited breath for developments.

No one could visualise her fitting into the old Coaster's life style in the Bush, or imagine him settling down in England with her. She came from Blackpool, and was alleged to be the owner of several candy floss stalls and ice-cream barrows. On the homeward voyage she spent several days in her cabin nursing a snuffly cold. When she emerged she appeared content to sit quietly beside the swimming pool chatting to those nearby. "She doesn't seem the same woman," said Peter one of the barmen. "Maybe she's pining for her old friend." He thought of taking on bets amongst the crew that she'd be back again in a couple of trips to settle in Africa. Interest in the matter quickly dwindled and we never saw her again.

On the next voyage, attracted by the sound of children laughing, another Round Tripper came up to the Nursery Deck. He wanted to sketch the children frolicking in the paddling pool but left after less than an hour saying the noise was driving him mad. He congratulated us on keeping our sanity after working there all day, and making the children so happy. He said, "It's a blooming nightmare of a job. You really should be on the Queen's Birthday Honours List."

We had heard that so often throughout the years it became a joke between us all, and we would often quip, "When I go to the Palace, I'll tell the Queen…"

The Head Office had another bright idea to boost the decline in passenger traffic and organised four day mini-cruises from Lagos. This proved tremendously popular with the expatriates who appreciated the opportunity to escape for a few days from the sticky humid heat ashore, relax with friends, patronise the duty-free shop and of course indulge in the duty-free drink. Deck sports were well supported as were the treasure hunt, cinema shows, concert, fancy dress parades and there was also all the fun of the Crossing the Line Ceremony. Needless to say, the Nursery was full, but most of the children already knew each other and had travelled out on the ship so these trips weren't difficult for us.

The stewardesses often said, "We see life in the raw". Mary was startled one day when she took morning tea into one of her ladies and found two heads on the pillow. The black balding one didn't move but the voice from the blonde lady said, "Goodness is that the time already? Please bring another cup for my friend!" By this time the friend was trying to pull the sheet up and hide but the lady passenger wasn't in the least embarrassed.

Working in the cabins the stewardesses made quite a lot of money in tips, but the passengers usually gave the nursery staff something like chocolates, perfume, or a silk scarf. African passengers travelling down the Coast sometimes would give a pineapple or a couple of coconuts. Difficult to open, and sickly sweet, coconuts weren't too welcome – I usually abandoned them in a corner of the Promenade Deck.

After fifteen years in London Dr Gloria Akabba travelled home to Liberia on the Aureol. As she packed feverishly she told Marie, her stewardess, "I'll never forget how well you looked after me when I was sick at the beginning of the voyage. I've decided to give you a very special present, I can't give it to you now but will come on board with it when the ship calls at Monrovia northbound." Marie having heard similar tales before didn't waste time speculating about the gift – thinking it would probably be an African picture, a thorn-wood carving or even a piece of ivory.

She was wrong – it turned out to be a hat! – a most unusual creation of rather gaudy petunia feathers. Glamorous enough to wear at Ladies' Day at Ascot it would have raised eyebrows if worn in Liverpool, or Rothesay! Dr Akabba had bought it from an exclusive Bond Street shop especially for her return home.

In contrast to Europeans sensibly clad in shirts and shorts the Africans usually disembarked in the most splendid expensive exotic garb, totally impractical for the shock wave of intense heat that hit them as soon as they landed. They seemed to be making a grand entrance into the country as a visual statement of success in stark contrast to the way they had left.

Then there was hair – nowhere on the ship was the difference in the two cultures more evident than in the hairdressing department. Europeans spent time having their hair cut, styled and made curly, whereas the Africans spent hours trying to have it straightened. Dorothy the hairdresser just hated setting expensive wigs and grumbled at the inanimate objects who couldn't indulge in conversation. She spent long boring evenings working with them. A small room fitted with washbasins, hand dryers and straightening combs had been allocated to the do-it-ourselves types. Some of the women spent hour after hour there endeavouring to get rid of their curls.

I was particularly sorry for the children who patiently endured having their hair treated. First it was covered with a greasy Vaseline-like substance, then divided into small twisty sections and screwed up tightly with coarse black thread in the feverent hope that when it was eventually back-combed most of the curl would be gone. They went ashore dressed up to the nines. Often the boys looked like pages at a wedding, while the girls were decked out magnificently in stiff satin or silk. I shuddered to think what they'd look like in these beautiful, but unsuitable dresses after an hour or so ashore.

But I digress – back to the hat. Although it was Dr. Akabba's treasured possession it was too garish for us. I remarked "It could really be quite fetching on a grand occasion." Marie said "That's it. People are always saying that you should have a medal for what you do. This is the very thing for going to the Palace." I laughed but she insisted I kept it. It languishes on a shelf in my wardrobe, but still no summons to the Palace has come my way! I really should give it away to a charity shop, and not keep it as a souvenir!

I can't remember exactly when Prince William of Gloucester travelled out to take up an appointment in the British Embassy in Lagos. Certain dates are fixed in my mind but others mix together in the misty memories of long ago. It was expected he'd travel out in one of the suite rooms, and Willie, the Steward was looking forward to caring for such a distinguished passenger. Willie, a lovely old man with a black smiling face and a heart of gold, had worked from boyhood for Elder Dempster's. He said to me, "When I tell the Prince how hard you work and how happy everyone is, he'll come and see the nursery. When he tells the Queen she'll give you a medal." I told him I didn't want a medal, but joked "It might be fun to go to the Palace for tea."

The Prince, however, said his position in the Embassy was too lowly to merit any favours and preferred to have an ordinary Deck cabin. He didn't want any publicity and insisted there was no fuss. It was a quiet voyage and he sat by the pool most of the day chatting to a District Officer and his wife. He never came up to the Nursery and Willie never had the chance to speak to him! When trouble brewed in the Biafran War I heard that the Prince had worked long hours up at Ikeja Airport helping British nationals to leave the country. Mavis, a missionary at a small home for deaf and dumb children told me that he had donated several large items of play equipment, and often worked there at weekends. Unfortunately, he caught hepatitis, was unable to complete the tour of duty and some time later was killed in an air crash.

Frequently African V.I.Ps travelled with us but unless they had accompanying children I never saw them. When the King of the Ashanti Gold Coast travelled out to Ghana an enormous crowd roared a welcome as the ship pulled into Tema Harbour. Normally we were far too busy to think of photography and the view from the Nursery was almost totally blocked by lifeboats. Many people had taken their children ashore to see what was happening on the quay. As it was fairly quiet I left Joyce to look after the handful of children left, and squeezed into a space beside a lifeboat with my camera at the ready.

There was a tremendous noise – drums banging, cheers and shouts from the excited crowd. A weird figure with his face and head hidden by straw danced and twisted in front of a splendid person in long gaudy robes who was walking away from the ship under a canopy of huge brightly coloured umbrellas. I didn't know if the whirling figure was a witch doctor or a wise man but he was certainly leaping madly in the air in honour of the King. I was pleased that for once I'd been able to take a photograph. When I mentioned it to Frank, the

Chief Electrician, (an excellent photographer) he said "Oh, I didn't bother at all when I saw him going ashore in a lounge suit and a bowler hat. It wasn't worth wasting a film." "Gracious" I said, "Who was that I snapped? He certainly got a great welcome." "Oh, probably some paramount chief," said Frank. I was really disappointed and didn't want to believe him!

One evening I was asked to look after two small boys who were travelling with their parents in one of the suite rooms. Their name has completely eluded me but their father was the first Nigerian Ambassador to the U.S.A. His wife hadn't been very well and had eaten most of her meals in the cabin. She had only been persuaded to go down with her husband to the Captain's Farewell Dinner, when assured that I had agreed to look after the boys. They came to the nursery every morning and played happily with the others. With strong American accents they used to say things like "Gee, this is wizard fun."

I told them a long rambling story about a sailor who found a mermaid's comb and searched for her, like the Prince who looked for the owner of the slipper until he found Cinderella. "Gosh", said the little one "You are just like Lucy."

"Yes", echoed his brother "You really are just like Lucy."

"Who", I asked "is Lucy?"

"She looked after us in Washington."

"Did she wear a white dress like mine?"

"No, but you are just like her, and she sometimes read us stories."

"Where is she now?" I queried.

Came the startling reply, "She has gone back home to Jamaica to be with her Mama, Papa and her little sisters."

I never knew if Lucy physically resembled me in any way, but it reinforced my theory that skin colour means nothing to children. It is something they don't usually notice. Sadly, somewhere through the years they lose their simple innocent outlook and develop adult's complexes and prejudices.

Chapter Nineteen

A not-so-diplomatic scuffle

When the Aureol left Southampton on May 23rd 1973 on the regular run to Lagos, she had several empty berths. Three quarters of the passengers were Nigerian, as was beginning to be normal. There were no more than ten white children amongst the fifty on board in first class but, as usual, they all played happily together.

It was a quiet uneventful voyage until Friday 1st June when an unpleasant incident took place. There was nothing to indicate that it was going to be such a memorable day. Memorable, alas, for the wrong reason. When I closed the Nursery at 5.30 p.m. I went straight down to the Dining Saloon, where we helped with the baby food etc. Eve slipped into her cabin, saying "I'll just have a quick wash" but I suspected it was for a quick smoke. The European Head Waiter and the Extra Second Steward should have been on duty, but were a few minutes late – normally that wouldn't have mattered a great deal, but, unfortunately , that was the very day it certainly did matter.

Parents and children were settling down to study the menu and the African stewards waited patiently for orders, when suddenly angry raised voices came from the corner of the room. I turned and saw that Mrs Sojami, a Nigerian lady travelling home to Lagos with her three children, was standing menacingly at the next table where Mrs Sandra Lee sat with Julia and Nicholas. Mr Lee was about to join them, and as he approached seemed to be saying something like "what on earth is going on here?" Everything happened so swiftly that it was difficult afterwards to recall authentically the sequence of events.

Several African passengers jumped up shouting in support of Mrs Sojami and advanced to the corner. The situation grew uglier every second, and as the shouts grew angrier and louder I instinctively moved to the Lees table, lifted up young Nicholas, took Julia by the hand, and rushed them up to B Deck. Fortunately Nora, the stewardess, was standing in the square. I gabbled something like "Quick there's terrible trouble brewing between the passengers. Keep Julia and Nicholas out of sight and 'phone for the Purser and the Captain to come at once." Luckily there was a vacant cabin nearby so she took the bemused children there.

When I got back a couple of minutes later Mrs Sojami, a tall well built woman, had pinned Mr Lee against the linen cupboard door, preventing his escape. Mrs Lee obviously terrified and more tearful than angry shrieked "David take me away from these horrible black people." This pejorative remark fuelled the trouble. Most of the male Nigerian passengers in the saloon were forming an ugly unruly screaming group mobbing round the Lees and preventing them moving out. All these years later I don't know whether to call it a scuffle, skirmish, melee, bedlam, or pandemonium – it certainly was a most disturbing situation. To avoid becoming involved the few European parents present wisely led their children out of the saloon.

One of the mothers told me that it all started when Mrs Lee accused the youngest Sojami boy of picking up and keeping Nicholas's dinky car. David Lee yelled that he had been bitten, and accused Mrs Sojami of lifting up his shirt and biting his stomach saying "I'll have teeth marks to prove it." She counter claimed that when he pushed her he knocked out one of her teeth. There were so many people milling around it wasn't easy to distinguish one voice from another. The air was thick with "bitch" and "bastard" and other choice words.

Accompanied by the Chief Officer and the Purser, the Captain appeared amazingly quickly. Bewildered by the scene, he asked "What caused all this?" I muttered a hasty explanation. One dinky car looks very like another and it was incredible that such a little thing could create such an uproar. The Captain sized up the situation at once and in the loud voice of authority commanded "All sit down immediately and get on with the meal." Most of them did. The doctor was sent for and took a hysterical crying Mrs Sojami to her cabin. The Lees were escorted away by the Purser. The Captain went off leaving the Chief Officer in the saloon to ensure that the uneasy calm was maintained during the meal. I admired the African stewards tremendously, as throughout all the commotion they had remained quite impartial. They must all have been as thunderstruck as I was at the sudden fracas and torn between loyalty to their employers, the shipping company, and joining in with fellow countrymen.

I sat down beside the Sojami children. Honey was about nine

at the time and somehow had managed to keep her little brothers at the table. They all looked numb and frozen in their seats. Suddenly Honey burst into tears. Between the loud sobs I was able to make out "Everyone hates us because we are black. You don't hate us, do you?" "Don't talk nonsense" I retorted "You know that I don't. She went on,

"It'll never get better. We'll never ever be white even when we keep out of the sun and grow very old. I'm glad we are going to Nigeria because you white people aren't the Boss there any more." I wasn't surprised at her remark about the sun as frequently coloured children going to Africa for the first time used to say "We are black, because our grandpa and grandma have always lived in a very hot place, and have been too long in the sun!"

I found it difficult to find words of comfort so concentrated on coaxing Honey to eat the fish fingers and chips set before her. It was sad that she had sensed that people from two different cultures often didn't respect or understand each other. She was beginning to glimpse racial discrimination and prejudice. When I took the Sojami children back to their cabins I found their mother lying on her bed, with three or four females fussing round her, all babbling excitedly.

As I was unlocking my own cabin door, one of the Assistant Pursers came to say that the Captain would understand if I was reluctant to be further involved, but he hoped I would be prepared to take the Lee children up to their parents, now moved to A suite, up near the Bridge. He suggested I went up, out of sight, through the midship deck pantries.

I readily agreed and they came willingly, thinking it was great fun going up this ladder-like stair. A European quarter master guarding the suite-room door took the children from me explaining that he had orders that on no account was I to speak to the Lees. It was then I appreciated how admirably Captain Campbell was dealing with things. He realised that it would be unwise for me to have any contact with the Lees as we later could have been accused of collaborating over our version of the trouble. He had had the foresight to consider the safety not only of the Lee family but of everyone on board. The Nigerians on the ship outnumbered the white passengers by more than three to one, and it was not beyond the range of possibility that they might even attempt to take over the ship. The incident had been blown out of all proportion and the Africans were, for the most part, working themselves up into a state of frenzy. It was quite incredible and alarming to see how quickly things had got out of hand.

A hysterical group shouting abuse and hammering at the door of what they believed to be the Lee cabin on B Deck made such a noise that a Ghanaian family in the next cabin went out into the alleyway complaining and arguing. Hasty words boiled over into heated discussions and mini-squabbles into fights throughout the ship. The most irate Nigerians were those who hadn't even been in the Dining Saloon. Loud in indignation, they blamed every white person they saw for all manner of totally unrelated incidents. Soon everyone in the ship had heard of the trouble, and few expatriates lingered in the Public Rooms, preferring the safety of their cabins.

I was told that the entrance to the Bridge, Radio Room and Engine Room were all guarded by European sailors. The situation was especially delicate as Mr Lee had been going out to take up an appointment as Assistant Information Officer in the British High Commission in Lagos.

After I left the Lee children I retraced my steps and went through all the midship pantries to the galley and our Mess for an early dinner. I was met by one of the African stewards, eyes rolling in his head as he told me "Plenty trouble still. No dinner tonight. Some men are blocking the room." Only half believing him I shot through the swing doors and, sure enough, half a dozen men were piling chairs on top of tables in an attempt to barricade the entrance. They had swept all the settings off the table and left the cutlery scattered around the deck among broken glass and china. I immediately retreated to the galley, phoned the Purser and told him of the latest trouble. Back came the Captain, Chief Officer and Purser. The Captain let out a roar and demanded that all the furniture was put back in order. After dinner he said he would be prepared to see a delegation of no more than three people in the effort to get to the bottom of all the trouble. One of the African Chiefs on board, I think he was a lawyer, had agreed to co-operate in the enquiry.

The Chief Steward sent word round to all the passengers that it was the Captain's express wish that they all went to dinner and acted normally. Some of the unaccompanied ladies were a little nervous but to their credit, wearing their prettiest dresses, an extra dash of lipstick and a brave smile all obeyed the summons of the gong. As the only white crew member who had been an eye witness at the start of the trouble I was sent for by the Captain and gave my version of the affair. The Chief asked a few pertinent questions but made no comment.

After dinner an uneasy feeling of apprehension pervaded in the smoke room and lounge bar. The barmen were mindful of the Chief Steward's warning "For God's sake, don't forget an order, spill a drop of drink or say anything controversial. We don't want to give anyone the chance of making another scene." Only half a dozen people joined in the Horse Racing and there wasn't a soul in the cinema.

In the meantime, Mrs Sojami had sent cables to her husband, to the Nigerian High Commission in London and also to General Gowon, the Head of State. The Captain had been in touch with the Foreign Office, the British High Commissioner in Lagos, Elder Dempster's Head Office in Liverpool, the Agent in Lagos and in Monrovia, and the British Ambassador there. The wires were burning red hot.

The Purser told me that it was all being viewed very seriously in London, as General Gowon was about to make his first official visit to the U.K. Britain dare not risk offending him – once again – because of the oil. The visit was reckoned vital to British economy and the General was to be a guest at Buckingham Palace. The Captain had been told that it was all to be handled most carefully and kept low key. Mrs Sojami was to be treated with great courtesy and tact, and the Lee family landed ashore in Monrovia. It proved difficult to carry out the latter instruction.

Early next morning we berthed in Monrovia. As the ship approached the quay a group of passengers hung banners over the side, proclaiming "Apartheid on Aureol."
"Hang Lee" and "Drown Campbell." The Monrovian police, white-helmeted and armed, looked up at the ship disinterestedly. They had been warned from the highest level that they were not to get involved in the trouble as "It is the ship's palaver, not yours." The banner holders must have been disappointed as there was virtually no reaction from the shore.

Passengers were granted shore leave, leaving their children with us in the nursery. It was related to me afterwards that almost every Nigerian passenger swarmed down the gangway and stood on guard round the foot of it. We hadn't a proper view from the nursery but now and again popped out between the lifeboats on the outer deck to view the drama on the quay below. Threads twisted back throughout the long years to Cyclops days when we could only vaguely hear what was happening up top – this was even more frustrating. Some of the Nigerians were armed with huge long sticks which proved to be pieces of wood broken off the bunk lee-boards. The banners too seemed to be made from torn sheets and the black paint used probably came from the ship's stores. They may have been helped by sympathetic crew members but the matter was never investigated.

A couple of tall Embassy Officials conspicuous in lounge suits parked their cars on the quay near the stern and pushed their way through the mob. They were jostled but not prevented from boarding the ship. Once again I was sent for and gave a statement.

The crowd on the quay waited and watched for any sign of the Lees being taken ashore. Obviously, it was useless for them to escape by the main gangway, so the decision was made to use the smaller crew gangway at the stern. Mrs Lee and Julia after being taken through the inside of the ship went down the other gangway while deck passengers were boarding. They were half way down when a cry got up "There goes that white woman" and there was a mad rush along the quay. The mob arrived just as Mrs Lee was getting into one of the Embassy cars. The driver tore off at breakneck speed. Several Nigerians jumped into a lorry waiting for cargo, threw the Liberian driver out of the cab, and set off in hot pursuit hoping to overtake the car with the C.D. Number Plates. Despite the decree that they were not to get involved, the enraged Liberian Police immediately gave chase. We never knew what took place when they caught up with the illegal Nigerian driver and his accomplices.

I heard that the Liberian lorry driver had been taken on board in order that the doctor could certify that there were no real injuries. He was more startled and indignant than hurt. The Captain wanted to make sure that there would be no complaints whatsoever against any of the ship's personnel.

We were all greatly relieved when the news came that Mrs Lee and Julia had arrived safely at the Embassy. The major problem remained of getting Mr Lee and Nicholas ashore now as obviously it would be impossible to use either gangway. Contingency plans were swiftly put into operation. The ship had to take on fuel and water, and a special door near the engine room was opened on the harbour-side of the ship. While refuelling was taking place great fat pipes led into the inner depths of the ship. It didn't seem possible for a man to squeeze out of that little space, but desperate circumstances need desperate measures, and that was the plan. The water boat lay a little distance offshore, while several other craft cruised about the harbour. It all looked very normal.

Those of us who for many years had travelled between the U.K. and Nigeria still found it hard to believe that a few ill-chosen words could possibly cause trouble that had rapidly escalated into an international incident. Suspicion arose that it was a mere excuse to stir up anti-British feeling. Stranger things have happened.

I thought back to 1961 when Patric Lumumba was murdered in the Congo. At that time we couldn't understand how the smiling Nigerians who had tried to sell us black boot polish and feather dusters, suddenly became part of a screaming mob hurling abuse and stones at every white face. None of us believed that the people shouting as they ran across Carter Bridge even knew the whereabouts of the Congo or the identity of Lumumba. It seemed that someone, somewhere, somehow had started sinister rumours that had been fuelled into a riot. The world's press minimised the whole situation and all this trouble on the Aureol would probably be condensed into an insignificant corner of the newspapers. Often we read of "civil unrest" and can only suspect what that phrase conceals.

I digress. Back up in the nursery deck that hot sticky day we went on playing games like the Hoki-Coki (usually a great favourite) but the children seemed only half interested. The older ones knew that something unusual if not unpleasant was being enacted on the dockside. Frustrated at not having a clear view of the quay, we resisted the impulse to phone the Purser's Office for the latest news.

On his way up from working on the swimming pool deck Adam popped in with a couple of snippets of information. As soon as the ship docked the agent had driven Mrs Sojami to the best dentist in Monrovia. "Felix, the steward has just told me that they are back on board now" said Adam. "It seems that the dentist couldn't find any trace of a tooth recently knocked out or broken. I bet she wasn't too pleased."

"I wonder if they will get a shore doctor to look at her teeth marks on David Lee's tummy?" I queried.

"I don't think they'll bother as long as they are able to get him off the ship, that's the main problem. Oh, another thing, those types who hi-jacked the lorry have just been brought back. I hope they had a rough time at the hands of the Police. They blooming well should all have been clapped in jail."

"No, they wouldn't do that. Things are bad enough without Liberia being dragged into it."

"That's all very well but I'm dammed sure if I pinched a lorry and clobbered the driver I'd have been left to rot in jail, and sent home D.B.S." (Displaced British Seaman). I agreed "Yes, they probably would leave you behind. You are unimportant ."

"It is all a lot of rubbish. Don't tell me there haven't been lots of bitches and bastards said before and there was none of this fuss. There's more behind this than meets the eye" he retorted and grumbling went on his way.

The relentless sun beat down on the crowd waiting and watching on the quay. The minutes ticked slowly by. A few excited Nigerians still brandishing sticks continued to group round both gangways. A couple of lookouts had been posted on the upper deck to watch the harbour, and another two were stationed on A deck square beside the pilot door. They were convinced that all possible escape routes had been covered.

The dockers as if sensing the tension around them, were working slower than usual. The normal ship's routine had to be carried out – the passengers' baggage having been landed, a start was made on unloading cargo. Suddenly there was a loud bang and a car crashed onto the quay. It could not have been properly secured in the sling taking it out from the hold, and the crane driver's attention had been diverted. It couldn't have happened at a better moment, even if it had been planned with careful precision.

All eyes swivelled to the scene on the quay.

The Lees were waiting impatiently and nervously inside the oil door. Immediately the diversion occurred on the dockside Mr Lee, carrying Nicholas, leapt on to a waiting boat. This boat had been cruising round the harbour and came alongside exactly when it was required. The look-outs suddenly realised what was happening. A loud cry went up "There goes that bastard Lee."

It was too late. They were powerless to prevent the boat speeding across the harbour to the safety of the Embassy. As we sailed in the late afternoon a wave of relief swept through the ship. Foolishly, we imagined we had left the trouble behind and the nerve-wracking experience was over. How wrong we were! The trouble wasn't over by a long way. Next morning as soon as we approached Tema harbour, several belligerent Nigerians on the Promenade Deck hung the banners over the side again. Their protest was short lived.

Fate intervened. Hidden in the bowels of the ship, a considerable amount of coinage from the Mint lay awaiting collection by the Ghanaians. An army contingent marched down to escort this valuable shipment to the Treasury. The protesters, convinced that the Captain had sent for the Army to deal with them, quickly hid the banners and then lounged nonchalantly at the deck rail.

By this time the British Press had picked up scrappy bits of information about the "not-so-diplomatic-scuffle-on-the-ship" (as the Daily Record put it.) The Cable Office was the prime suspect for the leakage. A couple of Reporters had been flown out from the U.K. in the hope of getting on the spot interviews. The shipping company's agent in Accra refused to grant them boarding passes so they had to be content with any information that they gleaned from disembarking passengers.

What intrigued the media more than anything was that the whole affair seemed shrouded in silence – "What was the mystery? What was being covered up? – by whom? and why?" We learned that the Foreign Office and Elder Dempster's Head Officer in Liverpool, had both issued discreet statements. They admitted that "Owing to a dispute amongst the passengers Mr David Lee and his family were asked to leave the ship Aureol at Monrovia, 1,000 miles short of their destination. The Captain of the Aureol and the British Ambassador in Liberia have made statements about the incident and until they are received no further comment can be made."

We sailed on to Lagos expecting a full scale demonstration there, but none occurred. For some time the African Port Authority had been using Police Dog Handlers to help with crowd control when the mail boat docked. They were certainly effective amongst the seething mass on the quay. As the tugs manoeuvred us into our berth in Apapa we were surprised not to hear voices raised in anti-Lee threats. Maybe the thrill of home-coming was paramount, and the grievance over the Lees had faded now they had left the ship or maybe the sight of the Alsatians straining eagerly at the leash had been a deterrent! - It could have been that because of the importance of Gowon's forthcoming visit to the U.K. the Nigerian authorities deciding to squash the disturbance had issued instructions to that effect.

Mrs Sojami and family were quickly whisked ashore and taken home in a Company car. The next morning the Nigerian papers had a scoop and devoted the front page to a personal interview with the aggrieved lady, who painted a lurid picture of the scuffle. Stupidly it never occurred to me to keep these newspapers. Living through moments of history like D.Day, VJ Day etc. I've always been too busily involved in the job on hand to think of collecting memorabilia!

General Gowon's State Visit to Britain started on Tuesday 5th June and did not escape the media's attention. Although we had picked up some information from the radio it wasn't until we managed to get a hold of a British newspaper that we fully appreciated how desperately the Government had been to ensure that nothing should interfere with all the arrangements. Princess Alexandra and her husband Mr Angus Ogilvie met the General and his wife at Gatwick. The Princess had represented the Queen at the Independence Celebrations on 1st October 1960, and there she was (thirteen years, two military coups and a Civil War later) receiving the Head of State. When the Gowons stepped from the royal train on to the red carpet at Victoria Station they were greeted by the Queen, Prince Philip and the newly engaged Princess Anne. The other members of the official welcoming party included the Duke and Duchess of Kent, the Duchess of Gloucester, Prince and Princess Richard of Gloucester, the Prime Minister, the Foreign Secretary and the Home Secretary. No one could have had a more spectacular welcome!

A couple of days later I was taken aback to hear that Gowon's fantastic reception was the subject of discussion at the Apapa Yacht Club. Angus Graham had just flown out from the U.K.

with all the latest newspapers which were seized eagerly by the rest of the members. Expatriates who had been in the country for many years were well aware that it was essential for survival to show respect for the African and important never to treat him as inferior. A few felt that this tremendous welcome accorded to Gowon was a little over-the-top, but all realised it was because of the importance of the Nigerian oil. The Glasgow Herald stated "Whatever may be the political implications behind the green and white Nigerian flags flying all over the city, and the full jangling of the Household Cavalry, and the Regiment of Guards, the General enjoyed it hugely."

General Gowon, one of the first people to learn of the

unfortunate incident on board would find it especially meaningful as he had returned to Nigeria on board the Aureol. Even the Queen would have heard about the Lees, but I imagined it would not be a subject brought up with her guests at dinner.

Chapter Twenty

Slinging my hammock – Kames Castle

Elder Dempster merged with Blue Funnel formed a new company called Ocean Fleets, but most of us and all the Coasters still thought of the owners as E.Ds. With the rapid decline in passenger traffic it was no surprise when the sister ships Apapa and Accra were withdrawn from service. It could only be a short time before the Aureol was up for sale. The container ships and cargo boats could easily cope with the trading business of Ocean Fleets. I began to wonder where I'd find another job – again cross roads loomed ahead.

One day at home between voyages, I was attracted by the wording of a vacancy in the Glasgow Herald for "someone experienced in child care, with the ability to exercise firm control, and yet have empathy and sympathetic understanding of the problems of children in care, to work in a West of Scotland Children's Home." I can't remember the exact wording but it seemed to have been written by a kindred spirit, someone who liked, really liked children. I sent in an application and by return of post had a reply arranging for an interview the next time I was at home. The Powers-that-be took up my references and after a couple of interviews I was offered the post of Deputy Officer in Charge at Kames Castle, in Port Bannatyne, a home for 32 children in care. I had never imagined I'd be able to get a permanent job on the island and was delighted to accept.

I gave in my notice, and with mixed feelings said goodbye to my friends in West Africa and on the ship. In June 1974 I started to work with the Project Team of the Social Work Department in Glasgow City Chambers. This team was chiefly concerned with admissions to care. I was flabbergasted at the stories I heard of neglect and abuse, poverty and ignorance. It was almost beyond belief that these atrocities were taking place in Scotland, and I was horrified. I wondered how anyone could gain the confidence of a five year old sexually abused by her grandfather, or help an eight year old boy whose mother had gone off to Blackpool leaving him with his five year brother – and six packets of crisps and a litre bottle of lemonade. He'd stayed off school and had been scrounging round dustbins for food. On the third day he was found collecting drops of whisky from a stack of bottles behind a Pub, and both children were taken into care.

After a short spell in Glasgow I went down to Bute and started in Kames Castle. None of the children were orphaned, but all had been neglected, abused or abandoned. The majority came from the Northern districts of Glasgow. The ten years I spent there could not be condensed into a few pages or even a few chapters and I make no apology for only very briefly mentioning them. The children, now adult, would not want to be identified so I've changed all their names and ages. A few of them, especially those from large families were with us for years. Some went home, some were successfully fostered or adopted. Unfortunately, others had had such bad experiences, and developed such poor self images that they were incapable of fitting into a normal family life.

There was no problem in feeding and clothing them but a great deal more was involved. They went to the local schools, joined the Girl Guides or the Boy Scouts, had camping holidays, visited the zoo, the art galleries, the Irvine Sports Centre and were generally accepted by the local community. Although we tried to give them as many experiences as possible we were acutely aware that they missed what we were unable to do for them – provide a one-to-one relationship.

I went on courses, and practically slept with Bowlby's "Child care and the Growth of Love" under my pillow! After a day's work I was often emotionally drained, frustrated by red tape, and the lack of resources or of ability to wave a magic wand and solve the parents' problems. This was the task of the field workers not those of us in residential care. There was a good system with constant reviews and case conferences where we often disagreed with the social workers. We felt their blinkered view was biased towards the parents, and the home circumstances whereas our priority was the children's future happiness. We felt most keenly that we had a much clearer picture of the child concerned than someone who only visited monthly.

An increase in confidence and improvement in behaviour

gladdened our hearts. We saw a Tony reluctant to have a nightly bath or shower, grumbling when he had to sit at a table at meal times, and who certainly didn't want to go to bed before midnight, change into an unrecognisable little boy accepting the rules because he realised that they were fair and applied to everyone. After a few weeks this child would be enthusiastic about the football team and the school concert, and be saving part of his pocket-money to buy a second hand bicycle. It was rewarding when these changes took place, although there was sometimes a fear that change was only on the surface and not really deep rooted.

When I went to sea at first I had had to learn a whole new set of words and here was another group. I was soon talking social work jargon and added to my vocabulary – school phobic, sibling rivalry, stable relationship, maternal deprivation, putative father, psychopathic parents, irreversible deprivation, affectionless maladjusted child with lack of emotional response and shallowness of feeling. It must have been bewildering for parents at a case conference to hear the remark "There is acute sibling rivalry between Peter and John" instead of "Peter is very jealous of his brother John." If parents had difficulty in expressing their opinions the Social Worker would note "while their comprehension is adequate, ability to verbalise is extremely poor."

The initial reaction of most children coming into care was surprising. They were seldom tearful, excited or over-awed but wore blank expressions almost of mistrust. Somehow they had the ability to pull a shutter down and hide their true feelings. For a long time they regarded all the staff with suspicion. Between themselves they probably spoke of us as Them – The Enemy.

An outburst from eight year old Tony expressed it all. When he came to the Castle he accepted with no word of thanks, or even a change of expression, new clothes for school and play, pyjamas, a comb, face flannel, toothbrush, toothpaste and two towels for his own use. Seeing the large bedroom he was to share with another three boys, he could contain himself no longer and exploded "Hey, where's the catch? What's your bloody game?" It was too much for him to realise that this was a special room for sleeping in – not for cooking, eating, or T.V. viewing, and he didn't need to share a bed!

After a while admission procedure changed and the Children's' Panel sent us troubled teenagers – persistent truants outwith parental control, and even glue sniffers. It was difficult to blend this new older group with the toddlers and primary school children. One of our priorities was to teach them self respect, as well as respect for other people and property. A special teenage unit was set up to teach them how to budget, shop, cook simple meals, undertake normal household tasks, fill up forms, and attend job interviews, in the hope that they'd be able to get jobs once they left care.

Recently I unearthed an old notebook containing a daily report of a super holiday I had with fifteen Castle children in August 1975. It was full of sayings and glimpses of the inner child relaxing and forgetting to hide his feelings. Two houseparent and Allan, the mini-bus driver completed the party. We had three small boys with us – Jim was five, Keith and Ross were just six. They each had at least one sister amongst the twelve girls. Apart from Stella who was fifteen, their ages ranged from four to twelve.

We stayed in the Youth Hostel at Garth in Perthshire for twelve days and I can truthfully say I never once heard a child saying "I'm bored." The children were so happy that they didn't ask for pocket money, or once enquire where they'd find a sweetshop. It was the first holiday some of them had ever had, and among the best that many of us had ever had.

We discovered a perfect spot halfway up Glen Lyon. Most days we went in our bus early in the forenoon and stayed there until five o'clock. We christened this large flat grassy area "Our Place." It was ideal – lots of room for playing games, parking the bus and having picnic meals. A little slope led down to a small sandy beach hollowed out of a bend in the river bank. The river gurgled quite slowly over the stones, but was divided by a small island. Opposite, and beyond the island it flowed deeper and faster as it hurried down the glen. The island was a magic spot with wild flowers strewn in the grass, and in the centre, knee high bracken and a rowan tree to keep the witches away.

For safety's sake we only allowed those who could swim to cross to the island. Non-swimmers were forbidden to even try to venture into the deeper part. As a group we crossed to the far bank by The Wobbly Bridge – a rickety wooden one. Jim saw a cow standing at the other end of the bridge. He stopped. Although he had daily seen cows at the Castle, this one wasn't safely behind a fence. It seemed larger and fiercer than any he'd ever seen. He shouted "Stop staring at me." "Go on Jim, you aren't afraid of a cow are you?" queried Keith a couple of steps safely behind him.

"No", said Jim, "Course not, but he has four legs and I've only got two." "That's a she, not a he, isn't she Miss?" "Yes", I explained, "You say she for a cow and he for a bull." "So what?" said Jim, not caring about gender but feeling braver now that everyone else had stopped. "If someone shows me first, it'll be alright I'm not afraid of it." "Ok", said Keith, glancing round to see that I was close by. "Anyway we've lots more brains than cows. Come on." Once safely on the other side we skirted the field where several cows were so intent on chewing that they didn't even notice us. The children climbed up the hill remarkably quickly and breathless we sat at the top amazed at how far we could see.

The first morning at the hostel Allan reported that Jim had cried bitterly at bedtime. He feared that we were so far away we'd never find the way back home to the Castle. The youngest of a family of five having been with us since he was two, he had no memory of living in Glasgow. His father was in jail and his mother had run off with a neighbour. I had him moved down beside his sister but on the second night he still couldn't get to sleep. He'd had a very exciting day for a five year-old – spending most of the morning helping Ross and Meg dig for hidden treasure, then he'd had the encounter with the cow and finally climbed a steep hill. As he was still lying wide awake, after a bed-time story I said "Jim shut your eyes or you'll never get to sleep." The reply made me smile "I'm far too tired to shut my eyes."

Catherine was a hyperactive child at the best of times. Her mother, a single parent, a member of Gamblers Anonymous seldom visited her. At six o'clock one morning she started banging a shoe on the floor, in an attempt to waken the others. "Shut up you", said Joan leaning over from the top bunk "Clumping sae early isna fair!" Even Keith who had come to us from Yorkhill Hospital a very quiet cowed little boy having been thrown out of a window by his mother's drunken cohabitee relaxed, laughed, shouted and played with the others with previously unseen enthusiasm. His broken bones healed long before his scarred little mind.

When little packets of tartare sauce appeared with the fried fish and chips one evening Betty said "Fancy giving us salad cream with chips. They can't know nothing here." Four year old Sadie sat on the grass beside Allan one day as he made her a jam sandwich. Suitably impressed she said "You are a good cook Allan, who learned you?" She wasn't so complimentary when she said to me "When I'm big I'm going to be a lady like you with nothing to do all day but play." I couldn't imagine how she'd got that idea!

They were all intrigued when they saw the mechanical counter moving at the Pitlochry fish ladder as the salmon went upstream. Jean wanted to know "How does the man who does all the counting get behind that little machine?" As we were going into Blair Atholl Castle Emma asked "What we were going to get?" Stella retorted "Greedy pig. We aren't going to get anything we are going to see things." Stella had gradually changed from a stubborn sulky teenager, to a happy helpful girl. Emma's comment was "If I was the Queen and had so many lovely beds I'd never get up."

The sun blazed down daily. We couldn't get any colour films as with all the glorious weather they were in great demand but that was only a minor inconvenience. One evening there was a brief thunderstorm. Meg said, "If that's supposed to be God clapping his hands that's silly as it is nothing to clap about." Ella said she had been told that it was the angels pulling out the bath plug that caused rain. The others scoffed at that idea. Washing and drying facilities at the hostel weren't adequate for a large family like ours. In an attempt to cut down on the washing we told the children that they didn't have to wear socks, and unless they had got really messy, clean tee shirts wouldn't be provided every time they went out. They were quite shocked! We hung their swimming gear and towels out to dry on a makeshift washing line strung between the bus and a tree.

We noted lots of "firsts" – first time they saw an eagle, a toad, a ladybird, a mole-hill, a weasel, a mountain rescue by helicopter and helmeted canoeists at Grandtully. It was also the first time they had met any foreigners. A group of Germans en route for Skye made a great fuss of them. One said to me "They can't be from a Home they are all too happy." – that made my day.

On the way home we went to the Safari Park, Blair Drummond.

With the windows tightly shut, we bravely drove in beside the lions. What a let down! They were all asleep under the shade of a tree and absolutely ignored us! Even they found the intense heat exhausting. As we neared Colintraive Ross said, "I'm ashamed to be going home." "Ashamed?" we queried. "I mean I'm sad and sorry to leave Garth but glad we are going back home to the Castle." As we reached the Castle gates Lena summed it up "Why does time go so fast when you are happy, and go so slowly when you are waiting and wishing for something?" -

If only we knew . . . .!

These children had had traumatic lives and witnessed incredible scenes. During the holiday they were able to push the past unhappy memories to the back of their minds, and let slip the mask of I-don't-care. Sadly there are many reports of badly-run homes or of ones controlled with Victorian-type discipline, but hopefully it is the minority who hit the headlines.

Just as the children came in all shapes and sizes, so did the staff - some young and "cool", a couple who could have been models, and two grandparents. Maysie, the Officer-in-Charge made a special effort to employ people with varying talents - a farmer's widow, a good cook and housekeeper, hairdresser, a dressmaker, a compulsive knitter, and a couple keen on painting and drawing. Amongst the men there was a good singer and entertainer, a keen hill-walker, an all round sportsman, an academic, keen to help with homework, a good swimmer and a guitar player.

Maysie, a qualified social worker had many useful contacts in head office. Although not able to be with the children, she had booked the Garth holiday and organised treats like visits to the Carnival at Kelvingrove in Glasgow. An excellent system of review was set up and every effort made to give each child the chance of an ordinary home life.

There must be several places like Kames with devoted staff struggling to bring security and happiness into the lives of their charges. We seldom hear from them, except those who have been successful in career or marriage. I hope they remember their stay in Bute with affection.

In the fantastic pattern of my life there are unfinished patches and several loose threads. Time has faded some of the patchwork colours and quietened old songs to a whisper The soft pink of rose petals from happy schooldays and magic hours of play on the seashore mix with the subtle shades of green from field and wood making a bright corner. In contrast the dark grey of shattered dreams is threaded through and through with sombre black threads symbolising the stupidity and tragedy of War and cruelty of genocide. Multi-coloured bizarre shaped designs have been formed by brightly-dressed crowds in far-flung foreign lands.

There's a quiet misty corner with a hint of silver brightening as the twinkling stars look down to the glittering path of moonlight across the Kyles. Bits of sea and happy laughing children of all nationalities, all shapes and sizes appear in every corner. The pattern ranges from clouds of spray and waves battering against the Rothesay Esplanade walls to the sleepy sea at Port Sudan with all the exotic colours of coral shining through and clouds of flying fish skimming over the waves of the Indian Ocean. At a patch in the centre splendid orange and scarlet tropical flowers stand tall beside the purples of rhododendrons and heather nestling near massed golden yellow gorse bushes at Scalpsie, the avenue of azaleas at Kames, and the wild poppies of France.

The threads twist and turn this way and that. They tangle together, and zigzag back to the beginning, winding and curving finally down to my little cottage by the sea.

The pattern of my life is almost complete.

Now I'm retired – what next? . . . .